Foundation Unit 3

LEDGER BALANCES AND INITIAL TRIAL BALANCE

For assessments in December 2003
and June 2004

Combined Text and Kit

In this May 2003 first edition

- For assessments under the new standards

- Layout designed to be easier on the eye – and easy to use

- Clear language and presentation

- Lots of diagrams and flowcharts

- Numerous **practice activities** throughout the text to reinforce learning

- The Specimen Exam Based Assessment to attempt as a 'mock' under 'exam conditions'

- Up to date for developments in the subject as at 1 April 2003

- This Text combines the old Interactive Text and Practice and Revision Kit for this Unit

FOR DECEMBER 2003 AND 2004 SKILLS BASED AND EXAM BASED ASSESSMENTS

PROFESSIONAL EDUCATION

First edition May 2003

ISBN 0 7517 1093 8

British Library Cataloguing-in-Publication Data
A catalogue record for this book
is available from the British Library

Published by

BPP Professional Education
Aldine House, Aldine Place
London W12 8AW

www.bpp.com

Printed in Great Britain by WM Print
Frederick Street
Walsall
West Midlands
WS2 9NE

We are grateful to the Lead Body for Accounting for
permission to reproduce extracts from the Standards
of Competence for Accounting, and to the AAT for
permission to reproduce extracts from the mapping
and Guidance Notes.

Contents

Order form

Review form & free prize draw

BPP
PROFESSIONAL EDUCATION

Introduction

How to use this Interactive Text

Aims of this Interactive Text

> To provide the knowledge and practice to help you succeed in the assessment for Foundation Unit 3 *Preparing Ledger Balances and an Initial Trial Balance.*

To complete the assessments successfully you need a thorough understanding in all areas covered by the standards of competence.

> To tie in with the other components of the BPP Effective Study Package to ensure you have the best possible chance of success.

Interactive Text

Parts A to D cover all you need to know for assessment for Unit 3 *Preparing Ledger Balances and an Initial Trial Balance.* Numerous activities throughout the text help you practise what you have just learnt.

When you have understood and practised the material in parts A to D and reviewed the answers to activities in Part E, you will have the knowledge and experience to tackle Parts F to J of this Interactive Text which include the following.

- Part F: Practice activities
- Part G: Full skills based assessments
- Part H: The AAT's Sample Simulation
- Part I: Full exam based assessment
- Part J: The AAT Specimen Exam

These parts of the text aim to get you through the assessments, whether in the form of the AAT simulation or in the workplace.

Passcards

These short memorable notes are focused on key topics for Unit 3, designed to remind you of what the Interactive Text has taught you.

Recommended approach to this Interactive Text

(a)   To achieve competence in Unit 3 (and all the other units), you need to be able to do **everything** specified by the standards. Study parts A to D very carefully and do not skip any of it.

(b)   Learning is an **active** process. Do **all** the activities as you work through parts A to D of the text so you can be sure you really understand what you have read.

(c)   Before you work through Parts F to J of this Interactive Text, check that you still remember the material using the following quick revision plan for each of the chapters in parts A to D.

    (i)   Read and learn the **key learning points**, which are a summary of the chapter.

    (ii)   Do the **quick quiz** again. If you know what you're doing, it shouldn't take long.

(d)   Once you have completed your quick revision plan for each chapter, you are ready to tackle parts F to J of the Interactive Text.

    (i)   Try the **Practice Activities**. These are short activities, linked into the Standards of Competence, to reinforce your learning and consolidate the practice that you have had doing the activities in parts A to D of this Interactive Text.

    (ii)   Then do the **Skills Based Assessments**. This are pitched at the level you can expect when you do a full skills based assessment, they do cover most of the performance criteria of the elements indicated.

    (iii)   Try the AAT's **Sample Simulation.** This specimen simulation gives you the clearest idea of what a full assessment will be like.

    (iv)   **Attempt the Exam Based Assessment**. This will help you develop techniques in approaching the assessments and allocating time correctly. For guidance on this, please see Exam Based Assessment Technique on page (xii).

    (vi)   **Try the AAT's Specimen Exam Based Assessment**. It is probably best to leave this until the last stages of your revision, and then attempt it as a 'mock' under 'exam conditions'.

(e)   Go through the **Passcards** as often as you can in the weeks leading up to your assessment.

This approach is only a suggestion. You or your college may well adapt it to suit your needs.

Remember this is a **practical** course.

(a)   Try to relate the material to your experience in the workplace or any other work experience you may have had.

(b)   Try to make as many links as you can to your study of the other Units at Foundation level.

(c)   Keep this Interactive Text – (hopefully) you will find it invaluable in your everyday work too!

Lecturers' Resource Pack activities

Part K of this Interactive Text includes a number of chapter-linked activities without answers. We have also included one skills based assessment and one exam based assessment, both without answers. The answers for this section are in the BPP Lecturers' Resource Pack for this Unit.

BPP)))
PROFESSIONAL EDUCATION

Foundation qualification structure

The competence-based Education and Training Scheme of the Association of Accounting Technicians is based on an analysis of the work of accounting staff in a wide range of industries and types of organisation. The Standards of Competence for Accounting which students are expected to meet are based on this analysis.

The AAT approved new standards of competence in 2002, which take effect from 1 July 2003. This Text reflects the **new standards.**

The Standards identify the key purpose of the accounting occupation, which is to operate, maintain and improve systems to record, plan, monitor and report on the financial activities of an organisation, and a number of key roles of the occupation. Each key role is subdivided into units of competence, which are further divided into elements of competences. By successfully completing assessments in specified units of competence, students can gain qualifications at NVQ/SVQ levels 2, 3 and 4, which correspond to the AAT Foundation, Intermediate and Technician stages of competence respectively.

Whether you are competent in a Unit is demonstrated by means of:

- *Either* an Exam Based Assessment (set and marked by AAT assessors)

- *Or* a Skills Based Assessment (where competence is judged by an Approved Assessment Centre to whom responsibility for this is devolved)

- Or *both* Exam *and* Skills Based Assessment

Below we set out the overall structure of the Foundation (NVQ/SVQ Level 2) stage, indicating how competence in each Unit is assessed.

All units are assessed by Skills Based Assessment, and Unit 3 is also assessed by Exam Based Assessment.

NVQ/SVQ Level 2

All units are mandatory.

| Unit 1 | Recording Income and Receipts | Element 1.1 | Process documents relating to goods and services supplied |
| | | Element 1.2 | Process receipts |

| Unit 2 | Making and Recording Payments | Element 2.1 | Process documents relating to goods and services received |
| | | Element 2.2 | Process payments |

Unit 3	Preparing Ledger Balances and an Initial Trial Balance	Element 3.1	Balance bank transactions
		Element 3.2	Prepare ledger balances and control accounts
		Element 3.3	Draft an initial trial balance

| Unit 4 | Supplying Information for Management Control | Element 4.1 | Code and extract information |
| | | Element 4.2 | Provide comparisons on costs and income |

| Unit 21 | Working with Computers | Element 21.1 | Use computer systems and software |
| | | Element 21.2 | Maintain the security of data |

| Unit 22 | Contribute to the Maintenance of a Healthy, Safe and Productive Working Environment | Element 22.1 | Monitor and maintain a safe, healthy and secure working environment |
| | | Element 22.2 | Monitor and maintain an effective and efficient working environment |

Unit 23	Achieving Personal Effectiveness	Element 23.1	Plan and organise your own work
		Element 23.2	Maintain good working relationships
		Element 23.3	Improve your own performance

Unit 3 Standards of competence

The structure of the Standards for Unit 3

The Unit commences with a statement of the **knowledge and understanding** which underpin competence in the Unit's elements.

The Unit of Competence is then divided into **elements of competence** describing activities which the individual should be able to perform.

Each element includes:

(a) A set of **performance criteria.** This defines what constitutes competent performance.

(b) A **range statement.** This defines the situations, contexts, methods etc in which competence should be displayed.

(c) **Evidence requirements.** These state that competence must be demonstrated consistently, over an appropriate time scale with evidence of performance being provided from the appropriate sources.

(d) **Sources of evidence.** These are suggestions of ways in which you can find evidence to demonstrate that competence. These fall under the headings: 'observed performance; work produced by the candidate; authenticated testimonies from relevant witnesses; personal account of competence; other sources of evidence.'

The elements of competence for Unit 3 *Preparing Ledger Balances and an Initial Trial Balance* are set out below. Knowledge and understanding required for the unit as a whole are listed first, followed by the performance criteria and range statements for each element.

Unit 3: Preparing Ledger Balances and an Initial Trial Balance

What is the unit about?

This unit relates to the internal checks involved in an organisation's accounting processes. The first element is primarily concerned with comparing individual items on the bank statement with entries in the cash book, and identifying any discrepancies. This involves recording details from the relevant primary documentation in the cash book, manual and computerised, and calculating the totals and balances of receipts and payments. You are also required to identify any discrepancies, such as differences identified by the matching process.

The second element requires you to total the relevant accounts and to reconcile the control accounts, within a computerised and a manual accounting system. You are also required to resolve or refer any discrepancies and to ensure security and confidentiality.

The third element involves drafting an initial trial balance manually and producing a trial balance from a computerised accounting system. You will be expected to identify and rectify discrepancies, which may occur in a manual accounting system, and create a suspense account where necessary.

Knowledge and understanding

The business environment

1	Types of business transactions and the documents involved (Elements 3.1 & 3.2)
2	General principles of VAT (Element 3.1)
3	General bank services and operation of bank clearing system (Element 3.1)
4	Function and form of banking documentation (Element 3.1)

Accounting methods

5	Double entry bookkeeping, including balancing accounts (Elements 3.1, 3.2 & 3.3)
6	Methods of coding (Elements 3.1, 3.2 & 3.3)
7	Capital and revenue expenditure (Element 3.1)
8	Operation of manual accounting systems (Elements 3.1, 3.2 & 3.3)
9	Operation of computerised accounting systems including output (Elements 3.1, 3.2 & 3.3)
10	The use of the cash book and petty cash book as part of the double entry system or as books of prime entry (Elements 3.1, 3.2 & 3.3)
11	Identification of different types of errors (Element 3.1)
12	Relationship between the accounting system and the ledger (Elements 3.1 & 3.2)
13	Petty cash procedures: imprest and non imprest methods: analysis (Element 3.2)
14	Methods of posting from primary records to ledger accounts (Element 3.2)
15	Inter-relationship of accounts - double entry system (Elements 3.2 & 3.3)
16	Use of journals (Elements 3.2 & 3.3)
17	Reconciling control accounts with memorandum accounts (Element 3.2)
18	Function and form of the trial balance (Element 3.3)

The organisation

19	Relevant understanding of the organisation's accounting systems and administrative systems and procedures (Elements 3.1, 3.2 & 3.3)
20	The nature of the organisation's business transactions (Elements 3.1, 3.2 & 3.3)
21	Organisational procedures for filing source information (Elements 3.1, 3.2 & 3.3)

Element 3.1 Balance bank transactions

Performance criteria		Chapters in this Text
A	Record details from the relevant primary documentation in the cash book and ledgers	2,3
B	Correctly calculate totals and balances of receipts and payments	2,3
C	Compare individual items on the bank statement and in the cash book for accuracy	3
D	Identify discrepancies and prepare a bank reconciliation statement	3

Range statement

1	Primary documentation: credit transfer; standing order and direct debit schedules; bank statement
2	Cash book and ledgers: manual; computerised
3	Discrepancies: differences identified by the matching process
4	Bank reconciliation statement: manual; computerised

Element 3.2 Prepare ledger balances and control accounts

Performance criteria		**Chapters in this Text**
A	Make and record authorised adjustments	4,5,7
B	Total relevant accounts in the main ledger	4,5
C	Reconcile control accounts with the totals of the balance in the subsidiary ledger	4,5,6
D	Reconcile petty cash account with cash in hand and subsidiary records	6
E	Identify discrepancies arising from the reconciliation of control accounts and either resolve or refer to the appropriate person	4,5,6
F	Ensure documentation is stored securely and in line with the organisation's confidentiality requirements	9

Range statement

1	Record: manual journal; computerised journal
2	Adjustments: to correct errors; to write off bad debts
3	Control accounts: sales ledger; purchase ledger; non-trade debtors; manual; computerised
4	Discrepancies: manual sales ledger and manual purchases ledger control account not agreeing with subsidiary ledger; cash in hand not agreeing with subsidiary record or control account

Element 3.3 Draft an initial trial balance

Performance criteria		**Chapters in this Text**
A	Prepare the draft initial trial balance in line with the organisation's policies and procedures	8
B	Identify discrepancies in the balancing process	8
C	Identify reasons for imbalance and rectify them	8
D	Balance the trial balance	8

Range statement

1	Trial balance: manual; computerised
2	Discrepancies in a manual accounting system: incorrect double entries; missing entries and wrong calculations
3	Rectify imbalances in a manual accounting system by: adjusting errors; creating a suspense account

Exam Based Assessment technique

Completing exam based assessments successfully at this level is half about having the knowledge, and half about doing yourself full justice on the day. You must have the right **technique**.

The day of the exam based assessment

1   Set at least one **alarm** (or get an alarm call) for a morning exam.

2   Have **something to eat** but beware of eating too much; you may feel sleepy if your system is digesting a large meal.

3   Allow plenty of **time to get to where you are sitting the exam**; have your route worked out in advance and listen to news bulletins to check for potential travel problems.

4   **Don't forget** pens, pencils, rulers, erasers.

5   Put **new batteries** into your calculator and take a spare set (or a spare calculator).

6   **Avoid discussion** about the exam assessment with other candidates outside the venue.

Technique in the exam based assessment

1   **Read the instructions (the 'rubric') on the front of the assessment carefully**

Check that the format hasn't changed. It is surprising how often assessors' reports remark on the number of students who do not attempt all the tasks.

2   **Read the paper twice**

Read through the paper twice - don't forget that you are given 15 minutes' reading time. Check carefully that you have got the right end of the stick before putting pen to paper. Use your 15 minutes' reading time wisely. **From June 2003**, reading time can only be used for **reading**. You can not make notes or use a calculator during those 15 minutes.

3   **Check the time allocation for each section of the exam**

Time allocations are given for each section of the exam. When the time for a section is up, you should go on to the next section.

4   **Read the task carefully and plan your answer**

Read through the task again very carefully when you come to answer it. Plan your answer to ensure that you **keep to the point**. Two minutes of planning plus eight minutes of writing is virtually certain to produce a better answer than ten minutes of writing. Planning will also help you answer the assessment efficiently, for example by identifying workings that can be used for more than one task.

5   **Produce relevant answers**

Particularly with written answers, make sure you **answer what has been set**, and not what you would have preferred to have been set. Do not, for example, answer a question on **why** something is done with an explanation of **how** it is done.

6   **Work your way steadily through the exam**

Don't get bogged down in one task. If you are having problems with something, the chances are that everyone else is too.

7   **Produce an answer in the correct format**

The assessor will state **in the requirements** the format which should be used, for example in a report or memorandum.

8   **Do what the assessor wants**

You should ask yourself what the assessor is expecting in an answer; many tasks will demand a combination of technical knowledge and business commonsense. Be careful if you are required to give a decision or make a recommendation; you cannot just list the criteria you will use, but you will also have to say whether those criteria have been fulfilled.

9   **Lay out your numerical computations and use workings correctly**

Make sure the layout is in a style the assessor likes.

Show all your **workings** clearly and explain what they mean. Cross reference them to your answer. This will help the assessor to follow your method (this is of particular importance where there may be several possible answers).

10   **Present a tidy paper**

You are a professional, and it should show in the **presentation of your work**. You should make sure that you write legibly, label diagrams clearly and lay out your work neatly.

11   **Stay until the end of the exam**

Use any spare time **checking and rechecking** your script. Check that you have answered all the requirements of the task and that you have clearly labelled your work. Consider also whether your answer appears reasonable in the light of the information given in the question.

12   **Don't worry if you feel you have performed badly in the exam**

It is more than likely that the other candidates will have found the exam difficult too. As soon as you get up to leave the venue, **forget** that exam and think about the next - or, if it is the last one, celebrate!

13   **Don't discuss an exam with other candidates**

This is particularly the case if you **still have other exams to sit**. Even if you have finished, you should put it out of your mind until the day of the results. Forget about exams and relax!

Assessment strategy

This Unit is assessed by **skills based assessment** and **exam based assessment**.

Skills based assessment

Skills based assessment is a means of collecting evidence of your ability to **carry out practical activities** and to **operate effectively in the conditions of the workplace** to the standards required. Evidence may be collected at your place of work, or at an Approved Assessment Centre by means of simulations of workplace activity, or by a combination of these methods.

If the Approved Assessment Centre is a **workplace**, you may be observed carrying out accounting activities as part of your normal work routine. You should collect documentary evidence of the work you have done, or contributed to, in an **accounting portfolio**. Evidence collected in a portfolio can be assessed in addition to observed performance or where it is not possible to assess by observation.

Where the Approved Assessment Centre is a **college or training organisation**, devolved assessment will be by means of a combination of the following.

(a) Documentary evidence of activities carried out at the workplace, collected by you in an **accounting portfolio**.

(b) Realistic **simulations** of workplace activities. These simulations may take the form of case studies and in-tray exercises and involve the use of primary documents and reference sources.

(c) **Projects and assignments** designed to assess the Standards of Competence.

If you are unable to provide workplace evidence you will be able to complete the assessment requirements by the alternative methods listed above.

Possible assessment methods

Where possible, evidence should be collected in the workplace, but this may not be a practical prospect for you. Equally, where workplace evidence can be gathered it may not cover all elements. The AAT regards performance evidence from simulations, case studies, projects and assignments as an acceptable substitute for performance at work, provided that they are based on the Standards and, as far as possible, on workplace practice.

There are a number of methods of assessing accounting competence. The list below is not exhaustive, nor is it prescriptive. Some methods have limited applicability, but others are capable of being expanded to provide challenging tests of competence.

BPP)))
PROFESSIONAL EDUCATION

Assessment method	Suitable for assessing
Performance of an accounting task either in the workplace or by simulation: eg preparing and processing documents, posting entries, making adjustments, balancing, calculating, analysing information etc by manual or computerised processes	**Basic task competence**. Adding supplementary oral questioning may help to draw out underpinning knowledge and understanding and highlight your ability to deal with contingencies and unexpected occurrences
General case studies. These are broader than simulations. They include more background information about the system and business environment	Ability to **analyse a system** and suggest ways of modifying it. It could take the form of a written report, with or without the addition of oral or written questions
Accounting problems/cases: eg a list of balances that require adjustments and the preparation of final accounts	Understanding of the **general principles of accounting** as applied to a particular case or topic
Preparation of flowcharts/diagrams. To illustrate an actual (or simulated) accounting procedure	**Understanding of the logic** behind a procedure, of controls, and of relationships between departments and procedures. Questions on the flow chart or diagram can provide evidence of underpinning knowledge and understanding
Interpretation of accounting information from an actual or simulated situation. The assessment could include non-financial information and written or oral questioning	**Interpretative competence**
Preparation of written reports on an actual or simulated situation	**Written communication skills**
Analysis of critical incidents, problems encountered, achievements	Your ability to handle **contingencies**
Listing of likely errors eg preparing a list of the main types of errors likely to occur in an actual or simulated procedure	Appreciation of the range of **contingencies** likely to be encountered. Oral or written questioning would be a useful supplement to the list
Outlining the organisation's policies, guidelines and regulations	Performance criteria relating to these aspects of competence. It also provides evidence of competence in **researching information**
Objective tests and short-answer questions	**Specific knowledge**
In-tray exercises	Your **task-management ability** as well as technical competence
Supervisors' reports	**General job competence**, personal effectiveness, reliability, accuracy, and time management. Reports need to be related specifically to the Standards of Competence
Analysis of work logbooks/diaries	**Personal effectiveness**, time management etc. It may usefully be supplemented with oral questioning
Formal written answers to questions	**Knowledge and understanding** of the general accounting environment and its impact on particular units of competence
Oral questioning	**Knowledge and understanding** across the range of competence including organisational procedures, methods of dealing with unusual cases, contingencies and so on. It is often used in conjunction with other methods

Exam based assessment

An exam based assessment is a means of collecting evidence that you have the **essential knowledge and understanding** which underpins competence. It is also a means of collecting evidence across the **range of contexts** for the standards, and of your ability to **transfer skills**, knowledge and understanding to different situations. Thus, although exams contain practical tests linked to the performance criteria, they also focus on the underpinning knowledge and understanding. You should, in addition, expect each exam to contain tasks taken from across a broad range of the standards.

Unit 3 Ledger Balances and Initial Trial Balance

With the introduction of the New Standards for the Level 2 NVQ/SVQ in Accounting, there will be a single Exam Based Assessment which will be based on Unit 3 *Preparing Ledger Balances and an Initial Trial Balance.*

The exam will be in two sections and of three hours duration in total. In addition a reading time of 15 minutes will be allowed. It will be based on an organization which operates a manual accounting system consisting of a main ledger and subsidiary ledgers. The exam will always use the terms main ledger but other organisations may refer to it as the general ledger or nominal ledger. Equally, the subsidiary ledgers may be referred to as the sales and purchases ledgers in other organisations. The subsidiary ledger control accounts will be referred to as the sales ledger control account, purchases ledger control account and non-trade debtors control account in the exam. Candidates can assume that the control accounts will be contained in the main ledger forming part of the double entry. The individual accounts of debtors and creditors will be in the subsidiary ledgers and will therefore be regarded as memoranda accounts.

Section 1 will always ask candidates to enter opening balances into accounts, record transactions from books of prime entry, balance off accounts and complete an initial trial balance. The books of prime entry given could be a selection from sales and sales returns day books **or** purchases and purchases returns day books, cash book and journal. In the past feedback from Centres and candidates has indicated that it is confusing to include both sales and purchases day books as books of prime entry. As there is only enough room/time available to feature one subsidiary ledger, and in response to this feedback, the exam at Foundation level will give extracts from the sales/sales returns day books **or** purchases/purchases returns day books, but not both.

Centres and candidates should note that this section requires the candidate to balance all of the accounts, and so candidates should possess the necessary skills to produce neatly and accurately balanced accounts, with balances clearly labelled. In previous exams task 1.3 asked the candidate to 'balance the accounts showing clearly the balances carried down and brought down'. Now this instruction is split into two tasks. In task 1.3 the candidate will be required to balance the account showing clearly the balance carried down. Task 1.4 will ask the candidate to clearly show the balance brought down. This is indicative of the importance placed on this aspect of competence at this level.

The candidate will be asked to transfer the balances calculated in the first part of section 1 to the trial balance, and then to transfer the remaining balances from a given list. Candidates should total the debit and credit columns of the trial balance, which should be equal. A trial balance with an imbalance will never be tested in section 1, therefore the trial balance should always balance.

Candidates are advised to take 90 minutes to complete section 1. Whilst the aim should be to produce a trial balance with the total of the debit and credit columns equal, candidates should not sacrifice checking time, or time allocated for section 2, in an attempt to discover the reason for an imbalance. On completion of both sections, if the candidate is still within the three hours time allowed, it is at this point that they should revisit section 1 and make further checks for accuracy.

Section 2 will always contain a mixture of 10 questions and tasks, some of which will be short-answer, and some requiring a longer response. Typical examples of the tasks which a candidate can expect are, control account reconciliations, preparation of journal entries, creation or clearance of a suspense account either in an account or through the journal, completion of banking and business documentation and the preparation of a bank reconciliation statement. Centres should note that candidates will always be asked to start the bank reconciliation statement with the statement balance, and reconcile this to the balance in the cash book.

It should be noted that the following areas are included in the 2003 standards of competence for this unit, which were not included, or explicitly stated, in the previous standards (2000). This indicates that these topics are now examinable.

Performance criteria

- Bank reconciliation statement (3.1)

Range

- Direct debit schedules and bank statements as source documents (3.1)
- Non-trade debtors control account (3.2)
- Suspense account (3.3)

Knowledge and understanding

- General principles of VAT
- Methods of coding
- Capital and revenue expenditure
- The use of the cash book and petty cash book as part of the double entry system or as books of prime entry
- Petty cash procedures: imprest and non imprest methods; analysis

Building your portfolio

What is a portfolio?

A portfolio is a collection of work that demonstrates what the owner can do. In AAT language the portfolio demonstrates **competence**.

A painter will have a collection of his paintings to exhibit in a gallery, an advertising executive will have a range of advertisements and ideas that she has produced to show to a prospective client. Both the collection of paintings and the advertisements form the portfolio of that artist or advertising executive.

Your portfolio will be unique to you just as the portfolio of the artist will be unique because no one will paint the same range of pictures in the same way. It is a very personal collection of your work and should be treated as a **confidential** record.

What evidence should a portfolio include?

No two portfolios will be the same but by following some simple guidelines you can decide which of the following suggestions will be appropriate in your case.

(a)   **Your current CV**

This should be at the front. It will give your personal details as well as brief descriptions of posts you have held with the most recent one shown first.

(b)   **References and testimonials**

References from previous employers may be included especially those of which you are particularly proud.

(c)   **Your current job description**

You should emphasise financial **responsibilities and duties**.

(d)   **Your student record sheets**

These should be supplied by AAT when you begin your studies, and your training provider should also have some if necessary.

(e)   **Evidence from your current workplace**

This could take many forms including **letters, memos, reports** you have written, **copies of accounts** or **reconciliations** you have prepared, **discrepancies** you have investigated etc. Remember to obtain permission to include the evidence from your line manager because some records may be sensitive. Discuss the performance criteria that are listed in your Student Record Sheets with your training provider and employer, and think of other evidence that could be appropriate to you.

(f)   **Evidence from your social activities**

For example you may be the treasurer of a club in which case examples of your cash and banking records could be appropriate.

(g)   **Evidence from your studies**

Few students are able to satisfy all the requirements of competence by workplace evidence alone. They therefore rely on simulations to provide the remaining evidence to complete a unit. If you are not working or not working in a relevant post, then you may need to rely more heavily on simulations as a source of evidence.

(h) **Additional work**

Your training provider may give you work that specifically targets one or a group of performance criteria in order to complete a unit. It could take the form of questions, presentations or demonstrations. Each training provider will approach this in a different way.

(i) **Evidence from a previous workplace**

This evidence may be difficult to obtain and should be used with caution because it must satisfy the 'rules' of evidence, that is it must be current. Only rely on this as evidence if you have changed jobs recently.

(j) **Prior achievements**

For example you may have already completed the health and safety unit during a previous course of study, and therefore there is no need to repeat this work. Advise your training provider who will check to ensure that it is the same unit and record it as complete if appropriate.

How should it be presented?

As you assemble the evidence remember to **make a note** of it on your Student Record Sheet in the space provided and **cross reference** it. In this way it is easy to check to see if your evidence is **appropriate**. Remember one piece of evidence may satisfy a number of performance criteria so remember to check this thoroughly and discuss it with your training provider if in doubt.

To keep all your evidence together a ring binder or lever arch file is a good means of storage.

When should evidence be assembled?

You should begin to assemble evidence **as soon as you have registered as a student**. **Don't leave it all** until the last few weeks of your studies, because you may miss vital deadlines and your resulting certificate sent by the AAT may not include all the units you have completed. Give yourself and your training provider time to examine your portfolio and report your results to AAT at regular intervals. In this way the task of assembling the portfolio will be spread out over a longer period of time and will be presented in a more professional manner.

What are the key criteria that the portfolio must fulfil?

As you assemble your evidence bear in mind that it must be:

- **Valid**. It must relate to the Standards.
- **Authentic**. It must be your own work.
- **Current**. It must refer to your current or most recent job.
- **Sufficient**. It must meet all the performance criteria by the time you have completed your portfolio.

What are the most important elements in a portfolio that cover Unit 3?

You should remember that the unit is about **ledger balances** and **initial trial balance**. Therefore you need to produce evidence not only demonstrating that you can carry out certain tasks, but also you must show that you can supply the required information.

For Element 3.1 *Balance bank transactions* you need to show that you can deal with receipts and payments in the cash book in the correct manner. This will include, for example, being able to carry out a bank reconciliation.

To fulfil the requirements of Element 3.2 *Prepare ledger balances and control accounts* you need to demonstrate that you can identify and report on differences between the subsidiary ledger accounts and the control accounts in the main ledger, eg sales ledger control account and the sales ledger balances in the subsidiary ledger.

For Element 3.3 *Draft an initial trial balance* you need to show that you can balance off ledger accounts and then transfer the balances correctly to an initial trial balance. You also need to be able to identify errors and correct for wrong calculations, missing entries and incorrect double entry.

Finally

Remember that the portfolio is **your property** and **your responsibility**. Not only could it be presented to the external verifier before your award can be confirmed; it could be used when you are seeking **promotion** or applying for a more senior and better paid post elsewhere. How your portfolio is presented can say as much about you as the evidence inside.

> For further information on portfolio building, see the BPP Text *Building Your Portfolio*. This can be ordered using the form at the back of this Text or via the Internet: www.bpp.com/aat

P A R T A

Balance bank transactions

chapter 1

Revision of
basic bookkeeping

Contents

Knowledge and understanding

Important note

The knowledge and understanding points in Unit 3 are mainly the same as for Units 1 and 2. However do not neglect these knowledge and understanding points, as these subjects can be included in the Unit 3 exam eg methods of coding, general principles of VAT, filing.

1 Introduction

Most of the knowledge and understanding points in Unit 3 are duplicates of those in Units 1 and 2. This allows the examiner to **include them in the Unit 3 exam**.

Therefore do not overlook this chapter. It is **vital** if you are going to prove yourself **competent**. It also lays the foundations for more detailed topics later in this Combined Text and Kit.

If you have any problems understanding the material in this Chapter, please revise these topics in the BPP Interactive Text for Units 1 and 2.

2 Basics of double entry

2.1 The accounting equation

The accounting equation is the basis for the production of all accounts.

2.1.1 Capital

For accounting purposes, a business is treated as a **separate entity** from its owner(s).

Therefore the amount of money invested in the business by the owner(s) is a liability owed by the business to the owner(s). This liability is called **capital**.

2.2 Double entry

Assets are represented by **debits** and liabilities by **credits**. Therefore, from the accounting equation,

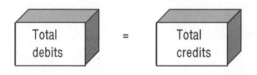

We will use this when preparing a trial balance in Part C. The following should be revision. If not, revise Chapter 5 of the BPP interactive Text for Units 1 and 2.

ASSET ACCOUNT	
DEBIT	**CREDIT**
Increase	Decrease

LIABILITY ACCOUNT	
DEBIT	**CREDIT**
Decrease	Increase

CAPITAL ACCOUNT	
DEBIT	**CREDIT**
Decrease	Increase

DRAWINGS	
DEBIT	**CREDIT**
Increase	Decrease

INCOME	
DEBIT	**CREDIT**
Decrease	Increase

EXPENDITURE	
DEBIT	**CREDIT**
Increase	Decrease

Remember the following:

Drawings decrease capital and so are **debits**.

Profit increases capital and so is a **credit**.

So **income** increases profit and is a **credit**.

Expenditure decreases profit and is a **debit**.

2.3 Double entry bookkeeping

Double entry bookkeeping is based on the idea that every transaction creates two entries: a debit and a credit.

If a bank accepts cash from a customer, two things happen: the bank's cash increases and the amount owed to a customer increases.

In accountancy terms, the entries are:

DEBIT: Cash
CREDIT: Amount owed to customers (creditors)

Activity 1.1

What are the entries for the following transactions? Ignore VAT for the moment.

Transactions	DEBIT (Dr)	CREDIT (Cr)
Owner puts £500 into the business		
Cash sales of £1,000		
Purchases of £2,500 made on credit		
Credit sales made totalling £5,000		
£2,000 received from debtor		
Business expenses paid of £750		
Drawings made of £1,000		

Tutorial note. If you find this activity difficult, postings are revised in Chapter 2.

3 Capital and revenue items

3.1 The balance sheet

A **balance sheet** is a statement of the assets, liabilities and capital of a business at a given moment in time.

The balance sheet is divided into two halves, showing **capital** in one half and **net assets** (**assets** less **liabilities**) in the other. It reflects the accounting equation, in that **one half must equal the other.**

```
NAME OF BUSINESS
BALANCE SHEET AS AT (DATE)                    £
Assets                                        X
Less liabilities                             (X)
Net assets                                    X

Capital                                       X
```

There are two types of assets.

Fixed asset	Current asset
For use in the business not sale	Generally for use within one year
Make a profit over more than one accounting period	Cash or other assets (stock, debtors) which can be turned into cash within a year

Liabilities in the balance sheet are either **current** (due to be paid within a short period, usually one year) or **long-term.**

3.2 The profit and loss account

The **profit and loss account** is a statement which matches the **income** earned in a period with the **expenses** incurred in earning it.

The profit and loss account consists of two different statements:

Sales	X	} Trading account
Less cost of sales	(X)	
Gross profit	X	
Expenses	(X)	} Profit and loss account
Net profit	X	

Activity 1.2

(a) What is the purpose of the balance sheet?

(b) What are:

    (i) Fixed assets?
    (ii) Current assets?

(c) What are:

    (i) Current liabilities?
    (ii) Long-term liabilities?

3.3 Capital and revenue expenditure

Some items appear in the balance sheet (**capital items**) and some appear in the profit and loss account (**revenue items**). You need to tell them apart.

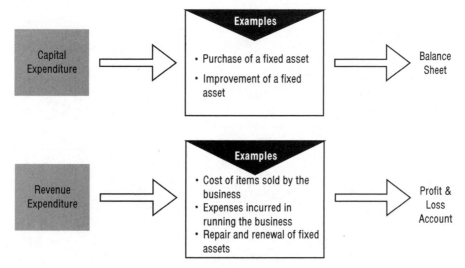

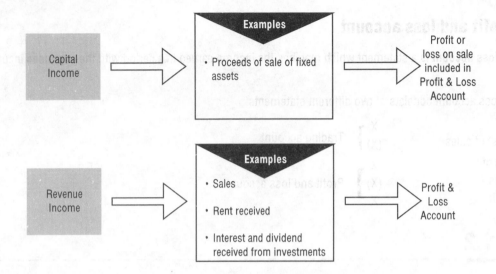

Activity 1.3

What is the difference between capital and revenue expenditure? Why is the distinction important?

Activity 1.4

Set out below are the balance sheet and trading, profit and loss account of Spock Enterprises as at 30 April 20X7.

SPOCK ENTERPRISES
BALANCE SHEET AS AT 30 APRIL 20X7

	£	£
Fixed assets		
Freehold premises		87,500
Fixtures and fittings		14,000
Motor vehicles		15,750
		X
Current assets		
Stocks	28,000	
Debtors	875	
Cash	700	
	X	
Current liabilities		
Bank overdraft	3,500	
Creditors	3,150	
Tax payable	6,125	
	X	
Net current assets		X
Total assets less current liabilities		X
Long-term liabilities		
Loan		43,750
Net assets		X
Capital		
Capital as at 1 May 20X6		76,300
Profit for the year		X
Capital as at 30 April 20X7		X

SPOCK ENTERPRISES

TRADING, PROFIT AND LOSS ACCOUNT
FOR THE YEAR ENDED 30 APRIL 20X7

	£	£
Sales		243,775
Cost of sales		152,425
Gross profit		X
Other income		3,500
		X
Selling and distribution expenses	25,725	
Administration expenses	25,900	
Finance expenses	29,225	
		X
Net profit		X

Task

Fill in the missing numbers in the spaces marked with an 'X'. Start with the balance sheet and work down as far as 'net assets'. Insert this figure in the space labelled 'capital as at 30 April 20X7'. You should then be able to work out the other missing numbers.

Tutorial note. Before looking at the solution, check for yourself whether your answer is right by comparing the 'net profit' figure in the profit and loss account with the 'profit for the year' figure in the balance sheet. If your answer is correct, the two figures should be the same.

4 Documenting business transactions

4.1 Documents

- Invoice
- Credit note
- Letter of enquiry
- Quotation
- Sales/purchase order
- Stock lists
- Supplier lists
- Staff time sheets
- Goods received/delivered notes
- Till receipts

These two are the most important. Learn their contents in detail. They may be used in multi-part stationery sets.

You will have met most of these documents in Units 1 and 2.

Activity 1.5

List the documents which you would expect to change hands when you have a new roof installed in your house.

The purpose of the **accounting system** is to record, summarise and present the information contained in the documents generated by transactions.

4.2 Discounts

There are two types of discount which you must be able to deal with.

- **Trade discounts** (a reduction in the cost of the goods)

- **Cash discounts** (a reduction in the amount payable for the goods)

Activity 1.6

John Smith, the proprietor of Smith Electrical, is interested in purchasing 60 halogen toasters. The toasters normally sell for £50 but you are able to offer a 20% trade discount and, in addition, a settlement discount of 5%, provided that payment is made within 14 days. John Smith asks you to give him a verbal quotation of exactly how much he would have to pay for the toasters.

Tasks

(a)   Clearly showing your workings, calculate how much in total Smith Electrical would have to pay for the toasters if payment was made within 14 days of the sale. Ignore VAT.

(b)   Calculate how much would have to be paid if payment was *not* made within 14 days. Ignore VAT.

4.3 VAT

Students often have problems with value added tax (VAT), but the rules for the types of transactions you will deal with are very straightforward.

Rule 1	There are three **rates** of VAT: standard rate (17½%), lower rate (5%) and zero rate. (Any task will always show the VAT rate to be used.)
Rule 2	**Input tax** is paid on goods and services bought by a business; **output tax** is charged on goods and services sold.
Rule 3	Some goods are **exempt** from VAT.
Rule 4	Gross price = net price + VAT.
Rule 5	VAT included in a gross price can be calculated using the VAT fraction: 17.5/117.5 or 7/47.
Rule 6	Total VAT shown on an invoice should be rounded **down** to the nearest 1p, so £32.439 would be shown as £32.43.

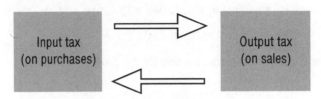

If output tax exceeds
input tax, balance paid to C+E

If input tax exceeds output
tax, balance repaid by C+E

4.3.1 VAT and discounts

When a cash discount is offered, VAT is computed on the amount of the invoice *less* the discount (at the highest rate offered), even if the discount is not taken.

Activity 1.7

Electromarket Ltd, an electrical goods retailer, ordered 20 clock radios from Timewatch Ltd. The radios cost £10 each, plus VAT at 17.5%. Timewatch Ltd offers a 5% discount for payment within 10 days. By mistake, Timewatch Ltd supplied 25 clock radios and issued an invoice for 25. On being informed of its mistake, Timewatch issued a credit note for the 5 radios which were returned.

Tasks

(a)   Calculate the VAT shown on the invoice.

(b)   Calculate the VAT shown on the credit note.

Key learning points

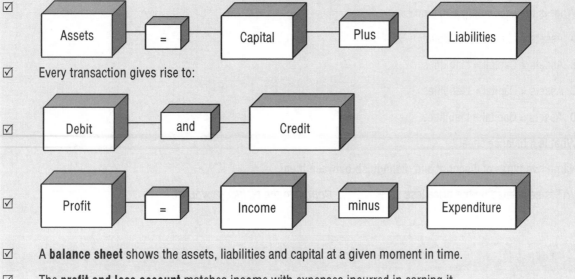

☑ Every transaction gives rise to:

☑ A **balance sheet** shows the assets, liabilities and capital at a given moment in time.

☑ The **profit and loss account** matches income with expenses incurred in earning it.

☑ **Capital expenditure** is expenditure to improve or acquire fixed assets. It creates or increases fixed assets in the balance sheet.

☑ **Revenue expenditure** is for maintenance or the trade of the business. It is charged to the profit and loss account.

☑ VAT on sales is **output tax**. VAT on purchases is **input tax**.

☑ If output tax exceeds input tax, balance is paid to C+E. If input tax exceeds output tax, balance is repaid by C+E to the business.

☑ VAT is **always** calculated on the **full discounted** price regardless of whether the discount is taken.

☑ **VAT** is collected by a business on behalf of HM Customs and Excise (C&E).

Quick quiz

1   What is the accounting equation?

    A Assets + Liabilities = Capital

    B Assets + Capital = Liabilities

    C Assets = Capital + Liabilities

    D Assets = Capital – Liabilities

2   What is a balance sheet?

3   Name two types of discount and distinguish between them.

4   VAT is calculated on the price less _____. *Complete the blanks (2 words).*

Answers to quick quiz

1   **C**   Assets = Capital + Liabilities

2   A balance sheet is a statement of the assets, liabilities and capital of a business at a given moment in time.

3   (i)   Trade discount is a reduction in the cost of goods.
    (ii)   Cash discount is a reduction in the amount payable for the goods.

4   VAT is calculated on the price less **cash discount**.

Activity checklist

This checklist shows which performance criteria, range statement or knowledge and understanding point is covered by each activity in this chapter. Tick off each activity as you complete it.

Activity

1.1		This activity deals with knowledge and understanding point 5: double entry bookkeeping.
1.2		This activity deals with knowledge and understanding point 7: capital and revenue expenditure.
1.3		This activity deals with knowledge and understanding point 7: capital and revenue expenditure.
1.4		This activity deals with knowledge and understanding point 7: capital and revenue expenditure.
1.5		This activity deals with knowledge and understanding point 1: types of business transactions and the documents involved.
1.6		This activity deals with knowledge and understanding point 1: types of business transactions.
1.7		This activity deals with knowledge and understanding point 2: general principles of VAT.

chapter 2

Recording, summarising and posting transactions

Contents

Performance criteria

3.1 .A   Record details from the relevant primary documentation in the cash book and ledgers

3.1.B   Correctly calculate the totals and balances of receipts and payments

Knowledge and understanding

5   Double entry bookkeeping, including balancing accounts

10   Use of the cash book and petty cash book as part of the double entry system or as books of prime entry

12   Relationship between the accounting system and the ledger

14   Methods of posting from primary records to ledger accounts

15   Inter-relationship of accounts – double entry system

19   Relevant understanding of the organisation's accounting systems

1 The problem

Any business produces a lot of documents in the course of trading.

- Invoices for sales and purchases
- Credit notes
- Remittance advices and cheques received
- Petty cash receipts
- Cheque stubs for payments
- Electronic receipts and payments

It is impossible to know how a business is performing by just looking at the **source documents** (the **primary documentation**).

2 The solution

- **Record** each transaction
- **Summarise** a period's transactions
- **Post** the summary to the ledger

This chapter is mainly revision of topics already dealt with in Units 1 and 2. However these subjects are vitally important if you are going to understand bank reconciliations (see Chapter 3) and control accounts (Part B). Finally a trial balance (Part C) could not be prepared without this knowledge.

3 Recording business transactions: an overview

3.1 Why do we need to record source documents?

A business sends out and receives *many* source documents.

The details on these source documents need to be recorded, otherwise the business might forget to ask for some money, or forget to pay some, or even accidentally pay something twice.

It needs to **keep records of source documents** - of transactions - so that it knows what is going on.

3.2 How do we record them?

Books of prime entry form the record of all the documents sent and received by the business.

Book of prime entry	Documents recorded	Summarised and posted to
Sales day book/Sales returns day book	Sales invoices, credit notes sent	Sales ledger/control account in main ledger
Purchase day book/Purchase returns day book	Purchase invoices, credit notes received	Purchase ledger/control account in main ledger
Cash book	Cash paid and received	Main ledger
Petty cash book	Notes and coin paid and received	Main ledger
Journal	Adjustments	Main ledger

The journal will be dealt with in Chapter 7.

Activity 2.1

State which books of prime entry the following transactions would be entered into.

(a)   Your business pays A Brown (a supplier) £450.
(b)   You send D Steptoe (a customer) an invoice for £650.
(c)   You receive an invoice from A Brown for £300.
(d)   You pay D Steptoe £500.
(e)   F Jones (a customer) returns goods to the value of £250.
(f)   You return goods to J Green to the value of £504.
(g)   F Jones pays you £500.

TERMINOLOGY ALERT

The AAT uses specific terminology.

Main ledger – this is the same as **general or nominal ledger**.

Subsidiary ledger – this is the same as:

- **Sales (debtors) ledger AND**

- **Purchases (creditors) ledger**

In this text we will use the terms sales ledger and purchases ledger rather than subsidiary ledger because you need to tell them apart. Be prepared to meet 'subsidiary ledger' in a simulation or exam.

3.3 Summarising source documents

Ledger used	Need for summary
Subsidiary ledgers	
Sales ledger Purchase ledger }	Summaries need to be kept of all the transactions undertaken with an **individual** supplier or customer - invoices, credit notes, cash - so that a net amount due or owed can be calculated.
Main ledger	
(a) Sales ledger control account	Summaries need to be kept of the **total** transactions undertaken with all suppliers and customers, so a total for debtors and a total for creditors can be calculated.
(b) Purchase ledger control account	

We will look at control accounts in more detail later in this Text.

3.4 Posting to the ledgers

Have a look at the diagram on the next page. It shows how items are **posted** to (**entered in**) the ledgers, ultimately to arrive at the financial statements.

Don't worry that some of the terms are unfamiliar. Keep referring back to this diagram as you work through the Text. It will soon make sense.

4 The sales day books

4.1 Sales Day book

The **sales day book** is a list of all invoices sent out to **customers** each day.

The following is an extract from a sales day book. Ignore VAT for the moment.

SALES DAY BOOK

Date 20X7	Invoice number (2)	Customer	Sales ledger folio (1)	Total amount invoiced £
Jan 10	247	James Ltd	SL14	105.00
	248	Steptoe & Son	SL 8	86.40
	249	Talbot & Co	SL 6	31.80
	250	John Silvertown	SL 9	1,264.60
				1,487.80

(1)   The column called 'sales ledger folio' is a reference to a page (by convention called a folio) for the individual customer in the **sales ledger**. It means, for example, that the sale to James Ltd for £105 is also recorded on page 14 of the sales ledger.

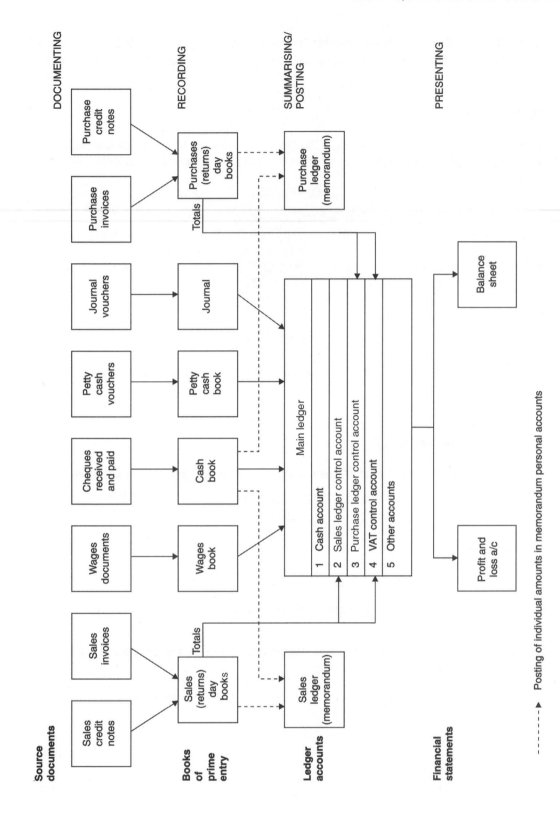

BPP
PROFESSIONAL EDUCATION

.(2)   The invoice number is the **unique number** given to each sales invoice by the business's sales system. Listing them out sequentially in the sales day book helps us to see that all the invoices are included.

4.2 Sales analysis

Most businesses 'analyse' their sales. The business, in this case, sells boots and shoes. The sale to Steptoe was entirely boots, the sale to Talbot was entirely shoes, and the other two sales were a mixture of both. VAT is at 17.5%.

SALES DAY BOOK

Date 20X7	Invoice	Customer	Sales ledger folio	Total amount invoiced £	Boot sales £	Shoe sales £	VAT £
Jan 10	247	James Ltd	SL 14	105.00	60.00	29.37	15.63
	248	Steptoe & Son	SL 8	86.40	73.54		12.86
	249	Talbot & Co	SL 6	31.80		27.07	4.73
	250	John Silvertown	SL 9	1,264.60	800.00	276.26	188.34
				1,487.80	933.54	332.70	221.56

This sort of analysis gives the managers of the business useful information which helps them to decide how best to run the business.

4.3 The sales returns day book

When customers return goods for some reason, the returns are recorded in the **sales returns day book**.

SALES RETURNS DAY BOOK

Date 20X7	Customer and goods	Sales ledger folio	Amount £
30 April	Owen Plenty		
	3 pairs 'Texas' boots	SL 82	135.00

Not all sales returns day books analyse what goods were returned, but it makes sense to keep as complete a record as possible.

If there are few returns, sales returns could be shown as **bracketed figures in the sales day book**. In this case, a sales returns day book would not be needed.

5 The purchase day books

5.1 Purchase day book

The **purchase day book** is the record of all the invoices received from **suppliers.**

An extract from a purchase day book might look like this (assuming VAT @ 17.5%).

PURCHASE DAY BOOK

Date	Supplier (2)	Purchase ledger folio (1)	Total amount invoiced	Purchases (3)	Expenses	VAT
20X7			£	£	£	£
Mar 15	Sugar & Spice	PL 31	315.00	268.09		46.91
	F Seager	PL 46	29.40	25.03		4.37
	ABC	PL 42	116.80		99.41	17.39
	Shabnum Rashid	PL 12	100.00	85.11		14.89
			561.20	378.23	99.41	83.56

(1) The 'purchase ledger folio' is a reference to a page for the individual supplier in the purchase ledger.

(2) There is no 'invoice number' column, because the purchase day book records **other people's invoices**, which have all sorts of different numbers. Sometimes, however, a purchase day book may allocate an internal number to an invoice.

(3) Like the sales day book, the purchase day book analyses the invoices which have been sent in. In this example, three of the invoices related to goods which the business intends to re-sell (called simply 'purchases') and the fourth invoice was for stationery.

5.2 The purchase returns day book

The **purchase returns day book** records credit notes received for goods sent back to the suppliers.

The business expects a **credit note** from the supplier. In the meantime it may send the supplier a **debit note**, indicating the amount it expects its total debt to be reduced.

An extract from the purchase returns day book might look like this.

PURCHASE RETURNS DAY BOOK

Date	Supplier and goods	Purchase ledger folio	Amount
20X7			£
29 April	Boxes Ltd		
	300 cardboard boxes	PL 123	46.60

Again, purchase returns could be shown as **bracketed figures** in the purchase day book.

6 The cash book

6.1 The cash book

The **cash book** is used to keep a cumulative record of money received and money paid out by the business **via its bank account**.

This could be money received **on the business premises** in notes, coins and cheques which are subsequently banked. There are also receipts and payments made by bank transfer, standing order, direct debit, BACS and, in the case of bank interest and charges, directly by the bank.

One part of the cash book is used to record **receipts**, and another part to **record payments**. Below is a summary of what a cash book looks like

LEFT HAND SIDE: RECEIPTS					RIGHT HAND SIDE: PAYMENTS				
Date	Narrative	Discount allowed	Total receipt	Analysis	Date	Narrative	Discount received	Total payment	Analysis
		£10	£100	£100			£7	£90	£90

Note the following points about this cash book.

(a)   It represents two sides of a **ledger account**: the left hand receipts side is DEBIT, the right hand payments side is CREDIT.

(b)   It is a **two-column cash book** - on the debit side there are two columns: one column for total receipts and one for discounts allowed; on the credit side there are also two columns – one for total payments and one for discounts received.

(c)   Discounts allowed and received are **memorandum columns** only - they do not represent cash movements.

(d)   On each side, the 'analysis' can be one or more columns; **the total of the analysis columns *always* equals the total column**.

The best way to see how the cash book works is to follow through an example. **Note that in this example we are going to ignore VAT,** in order to simplify the workings.

Example: Cash book

On 1 September 20X7, Liz Cullis had £900 in the bank. During the day, Liz had the following receipts and payments.

(a)   Cash sale: receipt of £80
(b)   Payment from credit customer Hay: £400 less discount allowed £20
(c)   Payment from credit customer Been: £720
(d)   Payment from credit customer Seed: £1,000 less discount allowed £40
(e)   Cash sale: receipt of £150
(f)   Cash received for sale of machine: £200

(g)	Payment to supplier Kew: £120
(h)	Payment to supplier Hare: £310
(i)	Payment of telephone bill: £400
(j)	Payment of gas bill: £280
(k)	Payment of £1,500 to Hess for new plant and machinery

If you look through these transactions, you will see that six of them are receipts and five of them are payments.

Solution

The cash book for Liz Cullis is shown on the following page.

6.2 Balancing the cash book

At the beginning of the day there is a debit **opening balance** of £900 on Liz Cullis's cash book. During the day, the total receipts and payments were as follows.

	£
Opening balance	900
Receipts (3,390 – 900)	2,490
	3,390
Payments	(2,610)
Closing balance	780

The **closing balance** of £780 represents the excess of receipts over payments. It means that Liz Cullis still has cash available at the end of the day, so she 'carries it down' at the end of 1 September from the payments side of the cash book, and 'brings it down' at the beginning of 2 September to the receipts side of the cash book.

In other words, the cash book is balanced just like any other ledger account, as we saw in Units 1 and 2.

LIZ CULLIS: CASH BOOK

RECEIPTS

Date 20X7	Narrative	Folio	Discount allowed £	Total £	Receipts from debtors £	Cash sales £	Other £
01-Sep	Balance b/d (= opening bal)			900			
	(a) Cash sale			80		80	
	(b) Debtor pays: Hay	SL96	20	380	380		
	(c) Debtor pays: Been	SL632		720	720		
	(d) Debtor pays: Seed	SL501	40	960	960		
	(e) Cash sale			150		150	
	(f) Fixed asset sale			200			200
			60	3,390	2,060	230	200
02-Sep	Balance b/d (= new opening bal)			780			

PAYMENTS

Date 20X7	Narrative	Folio	Total	Payments to creditors	Expenses	Fixed assets
01-Sep	(g) Creditor paid: Kew	PL543	120	120		
	(h) Creditor paid: Hare	PL76	310	310		
	(i) Telephone expense		400		400	
	(j) Gas expense		280		280	
	(k) Plant & machinery		1,500			1,500
			2,610	430	680	1,500
	Balance c/d (= closing bal)		780			
			3,390	430	680	1,500

6.3 Bank statements

Weekly or monthly, a business will receive a **bank statement**. Bank statements should be used to check that the amount shown as a balance in the cash book agrees with the amount on the bank statement, and that no cash has 'gone missing'.

This is called a **bank reconciliation** (see Chapter 3).

6.4 Petty cash book

The **petty cash book** keeps a cumulative record of the **small amounts** of cash received into and paid out of the cash float.

You have already covered it in Units 1 and 2.

7 The main ledger

7.1 The main ledger

The **main ledger** summarises the financial affairs of a business. It contains details of assets, liabilities and capital, income and expenditure and so profit and loss.

It consists of a large number of different **ledger accounts**, each account having its own purpose or 'name' and an identity or code. Other names for the main ledger are the **nominal ledger** or **general ledger**.

7.2 Posting to the main ledger

Transactions are **posted** to accounts in the main ledger from the books of prime entry.

Posting is often done in total (ie all sales invoices in the sales day book for a day are added up and the total is posted to the sales ledger control account). However individual transactions are also posted (eg purchase of fixed assets).

Here are some examples of ledger accounts in the main ledger.

Ledger account	Fixed asset	Current asset	Current liability	Long-term liability	Capital	Expense	Income
Plant and machinery at cost	√						
Motor vehicles at cost	√						
Proprietor's capital					√		
Purchases of raw materials						√	
Stock of raw materials		√					
Sales ledger control		√					
Purchase ledger control			√				
Wages and salaries						√	
Rent and rates						√	
Advertising expenses						√	
Bank charges						√	
Motor expenses						√	
Telephone expenses						√	
Sales	·						√
Cash		√					
Bank overdraft			√				
Bank loan				√			

7.3 The format of a ledger account

If a ledger account is kept in an actual book rather than as a computer record, it usually looks like this.

ADVERTISING EXPENSES

Date	Narrative	Folio	£	Date	Narrative	Folio	£
20X7							
15 April	AbFab Agency for quarter to 31 March	PL 348	2,500				

There are two sides to the account, and an account heading on top, and so it is convenient to think in terms of 'T' accounts.

NAME OF ACCOUNT

DEBIT SIDE	£	CREDIT SIDE	£

We have already seen this with Liz Cullis's cash book. We will now go on to use the cash book to demonstrate the double-entry bookkeeping.

8 Double entry book-keeping

8.1 Double entry

Every financial transaction gives rise to two accounting entries, one a debit and the other a credit.

DEBIT	CREDIT
To own/have	To owe
↓	↓
AN ASSET INCREASES eg new office furniture	AN ASSET DECREASES eg pay out cash
CAPITAL/ A LIABILITY DECREASES eg pay a creditor	CAPITAL/A LIABILITY INCREASES eg buy goods on credit
INCOME DECREASES eg cancel a sale	INCOME INCREASES eg make a sale
AN EXPENSE INCREASES eg incur advertising costs	AN EXPENSE DECREASES eg cancel a purchase
Left hand side	**Right hand side**

8.2 Cash transactions

The cash book is a good starting point for understanding double entry. Remember:

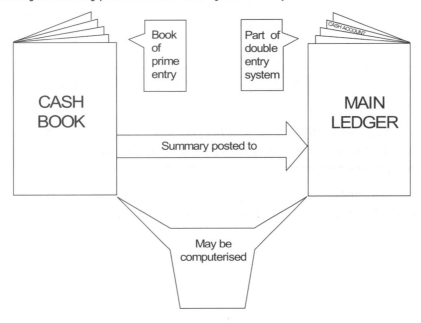

Here are the main cash transactions.

Cash transactions	DR	CR
Sell goods for cash	Cash	Sales
Buy goods for cash	Purchases	Cash
Pay an expense	Expense a/c	Cash

Example: Double entry for cash transactions

In the cash book of a business, the following transactions have been recorded.

(a)   A cash sale (ie a receipt) of £200

(b)   Payment of a rent bill totalling £150

(c)   Buying some goods for cash at £100

(d)   Buying some shelves for cash at £200

How would these four transactions be posted to the ledger accounts? For that matter, which ledger accounts should they be posted to? Don't forget that each transaction will be posted twice, in accordance with the rule of double entry.

Solution

(a)   The two sides of the transaction are:

(i)   Cash is received (**debit** entry in the cash account)
(ii)   Sales increase by £200 (**credit** entry in the sales account)

CASH ACCOUNT

	£		£
Sales a/c	200		

SALES ACCOUNT

	£		£
		Cash a/c	200

(Note how the entry in the cash account is cross-referenced to the sales account and vice-versa. This enables a person looking at one of the accounts to trace where the other half of the double entry can be found.)

(b)   The two sides of the transaction are:

(i)   Cash is paid (**credit** entry in the cash account)
(ii)   Rent expense increases by £150 (**debit** entry in the rent account)

CASH ACCOUNT

	£		£
		Rent a/c	150

RENT ACCOUNT

	£		£
Cash a/c	150		

(c)   The two sides of the transaction are:

(i)   Cash is paid (**credit** entry in the cash account)

(ii)   Purchases increase by £100 (**debit** entry in the purchases account)

CASH ACCOUNT

	£		£
		Purchases a/c	100

PURCHASES ACCOUNT

	£		£
Cash a/c	100		

(d)   The two sides of the transaction are:

(i)   Cash is paid (**credit** entry in the cash account)

(ii)   Assets – in this case, shelves – increase by £200 (**debit** entry in shelves account)

CASH ACCOUNT

	£		£
		Shelves a/c	200

SHELVES (ASSET) ACCOUNT

	£		£
Cash a/c	200		

If all four of these transactions related to the same business, the **summary cash account** would end up looking like this.

CASH ACCOUNT

	£		£
Sales a/c	200	Rent a/c	150
		Purchases a/c	100
		Shelves a/c	200

Activity 2.2

In the cash book of a business, the following transactions have been recorded on 7 April 20X7.

(a)   A cash sale (ie a receipt) of £60
(b)   Payment of rent totalling £4,500
(c)   Buying some goods for cash at £3,000
(d)   Buying some shelves for cash at £6,000

Task

Draw the appropriate ledger ('T') accounts and show how these four transactions would be posted to them.

8.3 Credit transactions

Not all transactions are settled immediately in cash.

(a)   A business purchases goods on **credit terms**, so that the suppliers are **creditors** of the business until settlement is made in cash.
(b)   The business grants credit terms to its customers, who are **debtors** of the business.

No entries can be made in the cash book, because initially no cash has been received or paid. Where then can the details of the transactions be posted?

The solution to this problem is to use **ledger accounts for debtors and creditors.**

CREDIT TRANSACTIONS	DR	CR
Sell goods on credit terms	Debtors	Sales
Receive cash from debtor	Cash	Debtors
Net effect = cash transaction	Cash	Sales
Buy goods on credit terms	Purchases	Creditors
Pay cash to creditor	Creditors	Cash
Net effect = cash transaction	Purchases	Cash

The net effect in the ledger accounts is the same as for a cash transaction - the only difference is that there has been a time delay during which the debtor/creditor accounts have been used.

Example: Credit transactions

(a) The business sells goods on credit to a customer Mr A for £2,000.
(b) The business buys goods on credit from a supplier B Ltd for £100.

How and where are these transactions posted in the ledger accounts?

Solution

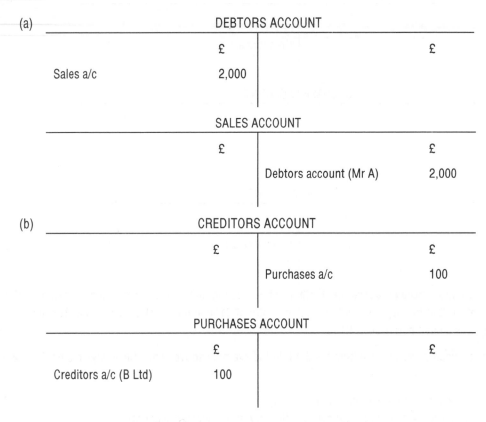

(a)
DEBTORS ACCOUNT

	£		£
Sales a/c	2,000		

SALES ACCOUNT

	£		£
		Debtors account (Mr A)	2,000

(b)
CREDITORS ACCOUNT

	£		£
		Purchases a/c	100

PURCHASES ACCOUNT

	£		£
Creditors a/c (B Ltd)	100		

Example continued: When cash is paid to creditors or by debtors

The business paid £100 to B Ltd one month after the goods were acquired. The two sides of this new transaction are:

(a) Cash is paid (**credit** entry in the cash account).
(b) The amount owing to creditors is reduced (**debit** entry in the creditors account).

CASH ACCOUNT

	£		£
		Creditors a/c (B Ltd)	100

CREDITORS ACCOUNT

	£		£
Cash a/c	100		

If we now bring together the two parts of this example, the original purchase of goods on credit and the eventual settlement in cash, we find that the accounts appear as follows.

CASH ACCOUNT

	£		£
		Creditors a/c	100

PURCHASES ACCOUNT

	£		£
Creditors a/c	100		

CREDITORS ACCOUNT

	£		£
Cash a/c	100	Purchases a/c	100

The **two entries in the creditors account cancel each other out**, indicating that no money is owing to creditors. We are left with a credit entry of £100 in the cash account and a debit entry of £100 in the purchases account. These are exactly the same entries as a **cash** purchase of £100.

Similar reasoning applies when a **customer settles his debt**. In the example above, when Mr A pays his debt of £2,000 the two sides of the transaction are:

- Cash is received (debit entry in the cash account)
- The amount owed by debtors is reduced (credit entry in the debtors account)

CASH ACCOUNT

	£		£
Debtors a/c (Mr A)	2,000		

DEBTORS ACCOUNT

	£		£
		Cash a/c	2,000

The accounts recording this sale to, and payment by, Mr A now appear as follows.

CASH ACCOUNT

	£		£
Debtors a/c	2,000		

SALES ACCOUNT

	£		£
		Debtors a/c	2,000

DEBTORS ACCOUNT

	£		£
Sales a/c	2,000	Cash a/c	2,000

The **two entries in the debtors account cancel each other out**, while the entries in the cash account and sales account reflect the same position as if the sale had been made for cash.

Activity 2.3

Identify the debit and credit entries in the following transactions.

(a) Bought a machine on credit from A, cost £8,000
(b) Bought goods on credit from B, cost £500
(c) Sold goods on credit to C, value £1,200
(d) Paid D (a creditor) £300
(e) Collected £180 from E, a debtor
(f) Paid wages £4,000
(g) Received rent bill of £700 from landlord G
(h) Paid rent of £700 to landlord G
(i) Paid insurance premium £90

Activity 2.4

Your business, which is not registered for VAT, has the following transactions.

- (a)   The sale of goods on credit
- (b)   Credit notes to credit customers upon the return of faulty goods
- (c)   Daily cash takings paid into the bank

Task

For each transaction complete the following grid:

Transaction	Original documents	Book of prime entry	Main ledger entry	
			Dr	Cr
(a)				
(b)				
(c)				

9 Posting from the day books

9.1 Sales day book to sales ledger control account

Earlier we used four transactions entered into the sales day book.

SALES DAY BOOK

Date	Invoice	Customer	Sales ledger folios	Total amount invoiced	Boot sales	Shoe sales	VAT
20X7				£	£	£	£
Jan 10	247	James Ltd	SL 14	105.00	60.00	29.37	15.63
	248	Steptoe & Son	SL 8	86.40	73.54		12.86
	249	Talbot & Co	SL 6	31.80		27.07	4.73
	250	John Silvertown	SL 9	1,264.60	800.00	276.26	188.34
				1,487.80	933.54	332.70	221.56

We post the total of the **total amount invoiced column** to the **debit** side of the **sales ledger control account.** The **credit** entries would be to the different **sales accounts,** (boot sales and shoe sales) and **VAT control account**.

SALES LEDGER CONTROL ACCOUNT (SLCA)

	£		£
Boot sales	933.54		
Shoes sales	332.70		
VAT Control	221.56		
	1,487.80		

BOOT SALES

	£		£
		SLCA	933.54

SHOE SALES

	£		£
		SLCA	332.70

VAT CONTROL

	£		£
		SLCA	221.56

That is why the analysis of sales is made, and why we analyse items in other books of prime entry.

Do we know how much we are owed by individual debtors? The answer is no. Therefore we keep two sets of accounts running in parallel – **sales ledger control account** in the main ledger and the memorandum **sales ledger** (individual debtor accounts).

REMEMBER!

Only the sales ledger control account is actually part of the double-entry system. The **individual** debtors' transactions are posted to the sales ledger from the sales day book, as a memorandum.

9.2 Purchase day book to purchase ledger control account

Here is the page of the purchase day book which we saw in Section 5.1.

PURCHASE DAY BOOK

Date	Supplier	Purchase ledger folio)	Total amount invoiced	Purchases	Expenses	VAT
20X7			£	£	£	£
Mar 15	Sugar & Spice	PL 31	315.00	268.09		46.91
	F Seager	PL 46	29.40	25.03		4.37
	ABC	PL 42	116.80		99.41	17.39
	Shabnum Rashid	PL 12	100.00	85.11		14.89
			561.20	378.23	99.41	83.56

This time we will post the total of the total amount invoiced column to the credit side of the purchase ledger control account. The debit entries are to the different expense accounts and VAT.

PURCHASE LEDGER CONTROL ACCOUNT (PLCA)

	£		£
		Purchases	378.23
		Stationery	99.41
		VAT	83.56
			561.20

PURCHASES

	£		£
PLCA	378.23		

STATIONERY

	£		£
PLCA	99.41		

VAT

	£		£
PLCA	83.56		

Again, we keep a separate record of how much we owe individual creditors by keeping two sets of accounts running in parallel - **the purchase ledger control account** in the main ledger, part of the double-entry system, and the memorandum **purchase ledger** (individual creditors' accounts). We enter individual creditors' transactions in their purchase ledger account from the purchase day book.

9.3 Section summary

CREDIT TRANSACTIONS	DR		CR	
	Memorandum	*Main ledger**	*Main ledger**	*Memorandum*
Sell goods to John Silvertown	Sales ledger: John Silvertown	SLCA (gross amount)	Sales (net) VAT	- -
Receive cash from John Silvertown	-	Cash a/c	SLCA	Sales ledger: John Silvertown
Buy goods from Sugar & Spice	-	Purchases (net) VAT	PLCA (gross amount)	Purchase ledger: Sugar & Spice
Pay cash to Sugar & Spice	Purchase ledger: Sugar & Spice	PLCA	Cash a/c	-

*Individual transactions included in **totals** posted from books of prime entry.

Note: When the cash is received from the debtor or paid to the creditor, the **total gross amount** is posted to the SLCA or PLCA. **No analysis of the VAT element** is needed in the cash book as this was done when the invoice was posted.

Activity 2.5

Jane Smith is a sole trader. The various accounts used in her business are held in a cash book, a sales ledger, a purchase ledger and a main ledger.

The following transactions take place.

- (a)   A cheque is issued to P Jones for £264 in payment for goods previously purchased on credit.
- (b)   An invoice for £850 is received from Davis Wholesalers Ltd relating to the supply of goods on credit.
- (c)   A credit note for £42 is received from K Williams in respect of goods returned.
- (d)   New fixtures costing £5,720 are purchased from Fixit Stores and paid for by cheque.
- (e)   An invoice for £25 relating to the delivery of the fixtures is received from Fixit Stores and settled immediately by cheque.
- (f)   G Cullis sells £85 of goods to Jane Smith for cash.
- (g)   An invoice is issued to R Newman for £340 relating to the purchase by him of goods on credit.
- (h)   An insurance premium of £64 is paid to Insureburn Ltd by cheque.
- (i)   A cheque for £40 received previously from J Baxter, a credit customer, is now returned unpaid by the bank.

Task

For each transaction in Jane Smith's books complete the following table:

	Main ledger		Subsidiary ledger	
	DR	CR	DR	CR
(a)				
(b)				
(c)				
(d)				
(e)				
(f)				
(g)				
(h)				
(i)				

Activity 2.6

Your business has the following transactions.

(a)   The purchase of goods on credit

(b)   Allowances to credit customers upon the return of faulty goods (sales returns)

(c)   Refund from petty cash to an employee of an amount spent on entertaining a client

Task

For each transaction identify clearly:

(i)   The original document(s)

(ii)   The book of prime entry for the transaction

(iii)   The postings in the double entry system

Key learning points

☑ Business transactions are initially recorded on **source documents**. Records of the details on these documents are made in books of prime entry.

☑ The main **books of prime entry** are as follows.

- Sales day book
- Purchase day book
- Cash book
- Petty cash book
- Journal

☑ Most accounts are contained in the **main ledger** (or **general or nominal ledger**).

☑ The rules of double entry state that every financial transaction gives rise to **two accounting entries**, one a **debit**, the other a **credit**. It is vital that you understand this principle.

☑ A **debit** is one of:

- An increase in an asset
- An increase in an expense
- A decrease in a liability

☑ A **credit** is one of:

- An increase in a liability
- An increase in income
- A decrease in an asset

☑ The **sales ledger** and **purchase ledger** are **subsidiary ledgers** which contain **memorandum** accounts for each individual debtor and creditor. They do not (usually) form part of the double entry system.

Quick quiz

1   Books of prime entry record all the documented _____ undertaken by the business. *Complete the blank.*

2   What is recorded in the sales day book?

3   A debit entry on an asset account decreases the asset. True or false?

4   What is the double entry when goods are sold for cash?

5   What is the double entry when goods are purchased on credit?

Answers to quick quiz

1   Books of prime entry record all the documented **transactions** undertaken by the business.

2   The sales day book records the invoices sent out to customers each day.

3   False. It increases the asset balance.

4   *Debit* Cash; *Credit* Sales.

5   *Debit* Purchases; *Credit* Purchase ledger control account.

Activity checklist

This checklist shows which performance criteria, range statement or knowledge and understanding point is covered by each activity in this chapter. Tick off each activity as you complete it.

Activity

2.1		This activity deals with knowledge and understanding point 19: relevant understanding of the organisation's accounting systems.
2.2		This activity deals with knowledge and understanding point 5: double entry bookkeeping and performance criteria 3.1.A
2.3		This activity deals with knowledge and understanding point 5: double entry bookkeeping and performance criteria 3.1.A
2.4		This activity deals with knowledge and understanding point 5: double entry bookkeeping and performance criteria 3.1.A
2.5		This activity deals with knowledge and understanding point 5: double entry bookkeeping and performance criteria 3.1.A
2.6		This activity deals with knowledge and understanding point 5: double entry bookkeeping and performance criteria 3.1.A

chapter 3

Bank
reconciliations

Contents

Performance criteria

3.1.A   Record details from the relevant primary documentation in the cash book and ledgers
3.1.B   Correctly calculate totals and balances of receipts and payments
3.1.C   Compare individual items on the bank statement and in the cash book for accuracy
3.1.D   Identify discrepancies and prepare a bank reconciliation statement

Range statement

3.1.1   Primary documentation: credit transfer; standing order and direct debit schedules; bank statement
3.1.2   Cash book and ledgers: manual; computerised
3.1.3   Discrepancies: differences identified by the matching process
3.1.4   Bank reconciliation statement: manual; computerised

Knowledge and understanding

3   General bank services and operation of bank clearing system
4   Function and form of banking documentation
11   Identification of different types of errors

1 The problem

By now you'll be familiar with the cash book. But this is a record of the amount of cash the business **thinks** it has in the bank.

You, too, may have an idea of what your bank balance should be. But then you get your bank statement, and the amount is rather different...

2 The solution

A bank reconciliation compares entries in the cash book and the bank statement and identifies differences.

3 Bank reconciliations

3.1 Why is a bank reconciliation necessary?

Why might your own estimate of your bank balance be different from the amount shown on your bank statement? There are three common explanations.

Cause of difference	Explanation
Errors	Errors in calculation, or in recording income and payments, are as likely to have been made by yourself as the bank. These **errors must be corrected**.
Bank charges or bank interest	The bank might deduct interest on an overdraft or charges for its services, which you are not informed about until you receive the bank statement. **These should be accounted for in your records**.
Timing differences	(a) **Cheques recorded as received** and paid-in but not yet 'cleared' and added to your account by the bank. This will be resolved in a very short time when the cheques are eventually cleared.
	(b) **Payments made by cheque** and recorded, but not yet banked by the payee. Even when they are banked, it takes a day or two for the banks to process them and for the money to be deducted from your account. These are known as **unpresented cheques**.

4 The bank statement

It is common practice for a bank to issue a monthly **statement** to each customer, itemising:

- The **balance** on the account **at the beginning** of the month
- Deposits and receipts due to the customer during the month
- **Payments** made by the customer during the month
- The **balance** the customer has on his account **at the end of the month**

REMEMBER!

If you have money in your account, **the bank owes you that money**, and you are a **creditor** of the bank. (If you are in 'credit', you have money in your bank account.)

However, in your books of account, if you have money in your account it is an asset (a **debit** balance) and the bank owes you that money (is your **debtor**).

If a business has £8,000 in the bank. It will have a debit balance in its own cash book, but the bank statement will show a credit balance of £8,000.

The bank's records are a 'mirror image' of the customer's own records, with debits and credits reversed. It is similar to a supplier's statement, which records the supplier's sales but the customer's purchases.

4.1 What does a bank statement look like?

An example of a bank statement is shown below; nearly all bank statements will look something like this.

Southern Bank — CONFIDENTIAL

200 BROMFORD AVENUE
LONDON
E11 8TH

Account: ABC & CO
4 THE MEWS
LONDON E4 2P2

SHEET NO   52 ⓓ

20X2

Telephone
020 8359 3100

Statement date 13 JUN 20X2 ⓐ

Account no   9309823 ⓑ

Date	Details	Withdrawals	Deposits	Balance (£)
ⓒ11MAY	Balance from Sheet no. 51 ⓓ			ⓕ 787.58
14MAY	000059 ⓖ	216.81		570.77
22MAY	000058	157.37		413.40
24MAY	000060	22.00		391.40
29MAY	LION INSURANCE DD ⓘ	87.32		
	CATS238/ 948392093 DD	1,140.10		
	LB HACKBETH CC SO ⓙ	54.69		
	COUNTER CREDIT 101479 ⓗ		469.86	
	INTEREST ⓛ	9.32		
	CHARGES ⓚ	30.00		460.17 O'D
13JUN	Balance to Sheet no. 53			ⓕ 460.17 O'D

ⓔ **Key**
SO Standing Order   DV Dividend   CC Cash &/or Cheques   Auto Withdrawals   { AC Automated cash   PY Payroll   **Interest –**
EC Eurocheque   TR Transfer   CP Card Purchases   { DD Direct Debit   OD Overdrawn   see over

---

Letter	Item	Explanation
(a)	Statement date	Only transactions which have passed through your account **up to this date** (and since the last statement date) will be shown on the statement.
(b)	Account number	This number is required on the statement, particularly if the bank's customer has **more than one account**.
(c)	Date	This shows the date any transaction **cleared** into or out of your account. You may have made the transaction earlier.
(d)	Sheet number	Each bank statement received will have a number. The numbers run in **sequential order**; this shows if a statement is missing.
(e)	Key	Not all bank statements will have a key to the abbreviations they use but it is helpful when one is provided. Note the following. • **Dividends** can be paid directly into a bank account. • **Automated cash** is a withdrawal from an automated teller machine - unusual for a business. • **Card purchase** is a purchase by debit card, again unusual for a business.
(f)	Balance	Most statements show a balance as at the end of each day's transactions.
(g)	Cheque numbers	The number is the same as that which appears on the individual cheque. Numbers are necessary to help you to **identify items** on the statement: you could not do so if only the amount of the cheque appeared.
(h)	Paying-in slip numbers	The need for these numbers is the same as for cheques.
(i)	Direct debit payments and receipts	The **recipient** of the direct debit payment is usually identified, either in words or by an account number.
(j)	Standing order payments and receipts	Again, the recipient is identifiable.
(k)	Charges	Based on the **number of transactions** (cheques, receipts and so on) which have been processed through your account in a given period (usually a quarter).
(l)	Interest	Interest is charged on the amount of an **overdrawn balance** for the period it is overdrawn.

Activity 3.1

The bank statement of Gary Jones Trading Ltd for the month of February 20X7 is shown below.

Task

You are required to explain briefly the shaded items on the statement.

Southern Bank   CONFIDENTIAL

Clapham Common Branch   Account   Gary Jones   SHEET NO   72
Clapham Common   Trading Ltd
London SW6   3 Barnes Street
                                            Clapham SW6

                    Telephone 020 7728 4213

20X7   Statement date   28 February 20X7   Account no   01140146

Date	Details		Withdrawals	Deposits	Balance (£)
	Balance brought forward				1,225.37
1 Feb	Cheque	800120	420.00		805.37
4 Feb	Cheque	800119	135.40		669.97
7 Feb	Bank giro credit	Pronto Motors		162.40	
7 Feb	Credit			380.75	
7 Feb	BACS	7492	124.20		1,088.92
9 Feb	Cheque	800121	824.70		264.22
11 Feb	Cheque	800122	323.25		59.03 OD
14 Feb	Credit			522.70	463.67
19 Feb	Credit			122.08	585.75
21 Feb	BACS		124.20		
21 Feb	Direct debit	Swingate Ltd	121.00		340.55
23 Feb	Bank giro credit	Bord & Sons		194.60	535.15
25 Feb	Cheque	800123	150.00		385.15
27 Feb	Credit			242.18	627.33
28 Feb	Bank charges		15.40		611.93
28 Feb	Balance to Sheet no.	73			611.93

5 How to perform a bank reconciliation

5.1 The reconciliation

The **cash book and bank statement will rarely agree at a given date**. Several procedures should be followed to ensure that the reconciliation between them is performed correctly.

Step 1   Identify the cash book balance and the bank balance (from the bank statement) on the date to which you wish to reconcile.

Step 2   Add up the cash book for the period since the last reconciliation and identify and note any errors found.

Step 3   Examine the bank statements for the same period and identify those items which appear on the bank statement but which have not been entered in the cash book.

- Standing orders and direct debits (into and out of the account)
- Dividend receipts from investments
- Bank charges and interest

Make a list of all those found.

Step 4   Identify all reconciling items due to timing differences.

(a)   Some cheque payments entered in the cash book have not yet been presented to the bank, or 'cleared', and so do not yet appear on the bank statement.

(b)   Cheques received, entered in the cash book and paid into the bank, but which have not yet been cleared and entered in the account by the bank, do not yet appear on the bank statement.

5.2 What does a bank reconciliation look like?

ADJUSTED CASH BOOK BALANCE

		£	£
Cash book balance brought down			X
Add:	correction of understatement	X	
	receipts not entered in cash book (standing orders, direct debits)	X	
			X
Less:	correction of overstatement	X	
	payments/charges not entered in cash book	X	
	(standing orders, direct debits)		
			(X)
Corrected cash book balance			A

BANK RECONCILIATION	£
Balance per bank statement	X
Add: cheques paid in and recorded in the cash book but not yet credited to the account by the bank (**outstanding lodgements**)	X
Less: cheques paid by the business but not yet presented to the business's bank for settlement (**unpresented cheques**)	(X)
Balance per cash book	A

Example: Bank reconciliation

At 30 September 20X3 the debit balance in the cash book of Dotcom Ltd was £805.15. A bank statement on 30 September 20X3 showed Dotcom Ltd to be in credit by £1,112.30.

On investigation of the difference between the two sums, three things come to light.

(a) The cash book had been added up wrongly on the debit side; it should have been £90.00 more.

(b) Cheques paid in but not yet credited by the bank amounted to £208.20.

(c) Cheques drawn but not yet presented to the bank amounted to £425.35.

We need to show the correction to the cash book and show a statement reconciling the balance per the bank statement to the balance in the cash book.

Solution

BANK RECONCILIATION 30.9.X3

	£	£
Cash book balance brought down		805.15
Add: correction of adding-up		90.00
Corrected balance		895.15
Balance per bank statement		1,112.30
Add: cheques paid in, recorded in the cash book, but not yet credited to the account by the bank	208.20	
Less: cheques paid by the company but not yet presented to the company's bank for settlement	(425.35)	
		(217.15)
Balance per cash book		895.15

The reconciling items noted here will often consist of several transactions which can either be listed on the face of the reconciliation or listed separately. In particular, there may be a **great many outstanding cheques** if this is a busy business account.

You can see here that the reconciliation falls into **two distinct steps**:

Step 1   Correct the cash book.

Step 2   Reconcile the bank balance to the corrected cash book balance.

Activity 3.2

The cash book of Gary Jones Trading Ltd for February 20X7 is set out below.

CASH BOOK

Receipts			Payments			
Date	Details		Date	Details	Cheq no	
20X7		£	20X7			£
1/2	Balance b/d	1,089.97	1/2	Rent	800120	420.00
3/2	Pronto Motors	162.40	4/2	R F Lessing	800121	824.70
3/2	Cash sales	380.75	4/2	Wages	BACS	124.20
11/2	Cash sales	522.70	11/2	British Gas plc	800122	323.25
16/2	Cash sales	122.08	18/2	D Waite	800123	150.00
24/2	Cash sales	242.18	18/2	Wages	BACS	124.20
28/2	Warley's Ltd	342.50	23/2	S Molesworth	800124	207.05
			25/2	Fogwell & Co	800125	92.44
			28/2	Balance c/d		596.74
		2,862.58				2,862.58
	Balance b/d	596.74				

Task

Using the information from the bank statement (Activity 3.1), complete the cash book entries for the month. (The transactions to be entered are those which appear on the bank statement but are not to be found in the cash book as shown above.) You do not need to reproduce the whole of the cash book given above. Use the balance b/d figure as your starting point.

The following additional information is available. The difference between the opening bank balance at 1 February per the cash book of £1,089.97 and the opening balance at 1 February per the bank statement of £1,225.37 CR is explained by the cheque number 800119 for £135.40 which was recorded in the cash book in January and presented on 7 February.

Activity 3.3

Prepare a bank reconciliation statement for Gary Jones Trading as at 28 February 20X7 using the information given in Activities 3.1 and 3.2.

5.3 Timing and frequency of the bank reconciliation

When and how often a company's bank reconciliation is performed depends on several factors.

Factor	Considerations
Frequency and volume of transactions	The more transactions there are, then the greater the likelihood of error.
Other controls	If there are very few checks on cash other than the reconciliation, then it should be performed quite often. (Other checks would include agreeing receipts to remittance advices.)
Cash flow	If the company has to keep a very close watch on its cash position then the reconciliation should be performed as often as the information on cash balances is required. Most companies do a reconciliation at the end of each month. If a company is very close to its overdraft limit, then it might need to do a weekly reconciliation.
Number of bank accounts	If, for some reason, a company has several bank accounts, all used regularly, then it may be impractical, or even impossible, to perform reconciliations very often.

Activity 3.4

At your firm, Gemfix Engineering Ltd, a new trainee has been asked to prepare a bank reconciliation statement as at the end of October 20X7. At 31 October 20X7, the company's bank statement shows an overdrawn balance of £142.50 DR and the cash book shows a favourable balance of £24.13.

You are concerned that the trainee has been asked to prepare the statement without proper training for the task. The trainee prepares the schedule below and asks you to look over it.

	£
Balance per bank statement (overdrawn)	142.50
Overdraft interest on bank statement, not in cash book	24.88
Unpresented cheques (total)	121.25
Cheque paid in, not credited on bank statement	(290.00)
Error in cash book*	27.00
	25.63
Unexplained difference	(1.50)
Balance per cash book	24.13

*Cheque issued for £136.00, shown as £163.00 in the cash book.

The trainee says that he was not able to reconcile the difference completely, but was pleased that he was able to 'get it down' to £1.50. He feels that there is no need to do any more work now since the difference remaining is so small. He suggests leaving the job on one side for a week or so in the hope that the necessary information will come to light during that period.

Tasks

    (a)   So that you can show the trainee how a bank reconciliation ought to be performed, prepare:

           (i)   A statement of adjustments to be made to the cash book balance

           (ii)   A corrected bank reconciliation statement as at 31 October 20X7

    (b)   Explain to the trainee why it is important to prepare bank reconciliations regularly and on time.

5.4 Stopped cheques

When you have received a cheque and banked it but it has already been stopped by the drawer, then the bank will not process it.

    (a)   You have already written the receipt in your cash book, but now it must be taken out again.

    (b)   This can be shown in the cash book as a deduction from receipts or an addition to payments, whichever is easier.

If you have written a cheque to someone and then subsequently you stop it, you must remove the payment from the cash book. If the reversal of the entry is not carried out then it will appear as a reconciling item on the bank reconciliation.

5.5 Out of date cheques

Banks consider cheques 'stale' after six months. Cheques which have been written but which have not been presented to the bank will continue to appear on a reconciliation month after month.

Step 1	Every time the reconciliation is performed you should check whether the oldest outstanding cheques are over six months old.
Step 2	Cancel or 'write back' such cheques in the cash book; they will then cease to be reconciling items.
Step 3	Notify the bank to stop the cheque as a precaution.
Step 4	Raise a new cheque.

5.6 Standing orders and direct debit schedule

Never just accept that a standing order or direct debit appearing on the bank statement is correct. The organisation must keep an up to date schedule of all current standing orders and direct debit.

Whenever a bank reconciliation is carried out, you must check all payments and/or receipts under standing order or direct debit to this schedule.

- The bank may use the wrong amount, particularly if the order or debit has been changed recently.
- The bank may pay an order or debit that has been recently cancelled.
- The bank may miss an order or debit that has been recently set up.
- The business may need to cancel an order or debit that has been overlooked.

Activity 3.5

On 1 October 20X0, Talbot Windows received a bank statement for the month of September 20X0.

(a) Update the cash book, checking items against the bank statement. Total the cash book, showing clearly the balance carried down.

(b) Prepare a reconciliation statement.

WEST BANK plc

220 High Street, Bolton, BL9 4BQ

To: Talbot Windows   Account No 48104039   30 September 20X0

STATEMENT OF ACCOUNT

DATE 20X0	DETAILS	DEBIT £	CREDIT £	BALANCE £
1 Sept	Balance b/f			13,400
4 Sept	Cheque No 108300	1,200		12,200
1 Sept	Counter credit		400	12,600
8 Sept	Credit transfer			
	Zebra Sales		4,000	16,600
10 Sept	Cheque No 108301	470		16,130
16 Sept	Standing order			
	West Council	300		15,830
24 Sept	Bank charges	132		15,698
25 Sept	Standing order			
	Any Bank	400		15,298
30 Sept	Cheque No 108303	160		15,138
30 Sept	Credit transfer			
	Bristol Ltd		2,000	17,138
30 Sept	Salaries	9,024		8,114

CASH BOOK

Date 20X0	Details	Bank £	Date 20X0	Cheque No	Details	Bank £
1 Sept	Balance b/f	13,400	1 Sept	108300	J Hibbert	1,200
1 Sept	L Peters	400	5 Sept	108301	Cleanglass	470
28 Sept	John Smith	2,400	25 Sept	108302	Denham Insurers	630
29 Sept	KKG Ltd	144	29 Sept	108303	Kelvin Ltd	160
					Salaries	9,024

Schedule of current standing orders

1. Monthly, on 16th of the month, £300.00 to West Council regarding rates.

2. Monthly, on 25th of month, £400.00 to Any Bank for hire purchase agreement.

J. Maclean

Chief Accountant

---

6 Reconciliations on a computerised system

In essence there is **no difference between reconciling a manual cash book and reconciling a computerised cash book**.

6.1 Computer controls over cash

In theory many of the same errors could occur in a computerised cash book as in a manual one. However, the computer will have **programme controls** built in to prevent or detect many of the errors.

Error	Programme control
Casting (addition)	Computers are programmed to add up correctly.
Updating from ledgers	When money is received from debtors, it will be posted to the sales ledger. The computer will then automatically update the bank account in the main ledger. This means that receipts and payments are unlikely to be confused.
Combined computer and manual cash books	The manual cash book reflects transactions generated by the computer system (for instance cheque payments from the purchase ledger), and also transactions initiated outside the computer system ('one-off' events such as the purchase of capital assets). The manual transactions will also be entered on to the computer. When a bank reconciliation is due to take place, the first job might be to make sure that the computer bank account and the cash book balances agree.

7 Bank services and types of account

7.1 Competition

Competition is fierce in the financial services industry. Banks must now compete against other kinds of financial institutions, such as building societies. As a result, the **range of services** and **types of account** offered to both personal and business customers has expanded.

7.2 Types of account

All the banks and building societies offer different types of account. The majority fall into one of these categories.

- Current account
- Deposit account
- Savings account
- Loan account
- Mortgage

All these accounts may be offered on different terms by different institutions, but they all offer a trade-off between:

- Minimum/maximum investment
- Charges/level of interest receivable or payable
- Withdrawal with or without penalties
- Minimum/maximum investment period
- Security required
- Maximum payment period (for loans/mortgage)

With such a wide range of accounts on offer, people can find the account which most suits their needs. It is worth visiting your local bank and building society offices and reading their literature on all the different accounts they offer.

7.3 Business accounts

The majority of businesses will only run a **current account**. Deposit accounts are also available as business current accounts will **not usually** pay interest if the balance is in credit.

If a business has excess cash for a certain period of time, then it may put the money on **short term deposit on the money market** to earn some interest.

7.4 Foreign exchange and related services

Compared to a personal customer, a business customer will have a very different requirement for foreign exchange services from a bank. Some of the services for both importers and exporters are highly specialised and we will not consider them in too much detail. The main services supplied will be:

- Foreign exchange
- Handling payments from buyers to suppliers
- The provision of finance
- The provision of information to exporters

7.5 Other services

Banks offer other services to business clients; the main ones are listed here.

Name of service	Nature of service
Safe custody services	Valuables, including deeds or share certificates, can be held in the vaults of the bank.
Insurance services	These might include insuring the business's buildings.
Business finance services	(a) **Discounting** and **factoring** involves administering the client's debts. (b) **Leasing** and **hire purchase** are forms of rental which help clients to buy large assets.
Home banking	Customers can control their banking needs from their own home or office by being connected directly to the bank's computer: (a) Using a television and telephone link (b) Using a computer This service is very useful for those who are either housebound or need constant access to their accounts but have no time to contact their bank personally.
CHAPS	This stands for **Clearing House Automated Payment System**. It was introduced to allow the clearing banks to transmit high value, guaranteed, sterling payments for same day settlement. This can only be done by computer. Security procedures are rigorous.
Pensions	Most banks now offer advice on pensions, for both directors and employees.

Key learning points

☑ A **bank reconciliation** is a comparison between the bank balance recorded in the books of a business and the balance appearing on the bank statement.

☑ The comparison may reveal **errors** or **omissions** in the records of the business, which should be corrected by appropriate adjustments in the cash book.

☑ Once the cash book has been corrected it should be possible to reconcile its balance with the bank statement balance by taking account of **timing differences**: payments made and cheques received which are recorded in the cash book but have not yet appeared on the bank statement.

☑ Banks offer a **wide range of services**, only some of which are relevant to the business customer.

Quick quiz

1   What are the three main reasons why a business's cash book balance might differ from the balance on a bank statement?

2   What is a bank reconciliation?

    A   Resolving a dispute between the bank and its customer
    B   Comparing the bank statement with the sales ledger
    C   Comparing the balance on the cash bank with the bank statement balance
    D   Comparing the cash book with the control accounts in the main ledger

3   What is a bank statement?

4   Cheque numbers are shown on the bank statement to aid _____. *Complete the blank.*

5   What are the two parts of a bank reconciliation statement?

6   Business bank accounts usually pay interest. True or false?

Answers to quick quiz

1   Reasons for disagreement are: errors; bank charges or interest; timing differences (for amounts to clear).

2   **C**. A bank reconciliation compares the balance of cash in the business's records to the balance held by the bank.

3   A bank statement is a document sent by a bank to its customers, itemising transactions over a certain period.

4   Cheque numbers are shown on the bank statement to aid **identification** (the amount only would not be enough).

5   (a) The adjustment of the cash book balance.
    (b) The reconciliation of the cash book balance to the bank statement.

6   False. Business bank accounts do not usually pay interest, but it depends on the individual business's arrangement with the bank.

Activity checklist

This checklist shows which performance criteria, range statement or knowledge and understanding point is covered by each activity in this chapter. Tick off each activity as you complete it.

Activity

3.1		This activity deals with range statement 3.1.1 primary documentation: bank statement
3.2		This activity deals with performance criteria 3.1.A and 3.1.B
3.3		This activity deals with performance criteria 3.1.C and 3.1.D
3.4		This activity deals with performance criteria 3.1.A, 3.1.B, 3.1.C and 3.1.D
3.5		This activity deals with performance criteria 3.1.A, 3.1.B, 3.1.C and 3.1.D, as well as range statement 3.1.1 primary documentation: standing order and direct debit schedules.

PART B

Control accounts

chapter 4

Sales ledger control account

Contents

Performance criteria

3.2.A   Make and record authorised adjustments

3.2.B   Total relevant accounts in the main ledger

3.2.C   Reconcile control accounts with the totals of the balance in the subsidiary ledger

3.2.E   Identify discrepancies arising from the reconciliation of control accounts and either resolve or refer to the appropriate person

Range statement

3.2.2.   Adjustments: to correct errors; to write off bad debts

3.2.3   Control accounts; sales ledger; manual; computerised

3.2.4   Discrepancies; manual sales ledger control account not agreeing with subsidiary ledger

Knowledge and understanding

12   Relationship between the accounting system and the ledger

17   Reconciling control accounts with memorandum accounts

1 The problem

In Chapter 2 we saw that:

   (a)   Sales invoices and cash received are logged in a **day book** or onto some equivalent listing or computer file which serves a similar purpose

   (b)   Each invoice and cash receipt is posted **singly** to an appropriate personal account in the sales ledger

But these personal accounts are for memorandum purposes only and do not form a part of the double entry system.

2 The solution

To record these transactions in the **double entry system** we do not need to deal with each invoice singly. Instead, the day books can be totalled at convenient intervals (eg daily, weekly or monthly) and these total amounts are recorded in the main ledger. For sales invoices, this means an accounting entry is made as follows.

DEBIT	Sales ledger control account (SLCA)	£1,175	
CREDIT	Sales account(s)		£1,0000
	VAT account		£175

This should be revision from Units 1 and 2.

3 Sales ledger control account

3.1 Control accounts

A control account is an (impersonal) ledger account which appears in the main ledger. The sales ledger control account (SLCA) records the total amounts owing to the business from its customers (debtors). The balance on the SLCA should be equal to the total of all the individual debtor balances in the sales ledger.

3.2 Control accounts and personal accounts

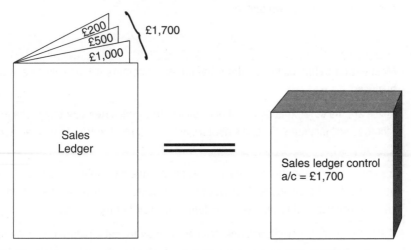

For example, if a business has three debtors, A Ashton who owes £80, B Bolton who owes £310 and C Collins who owes £200, the balances on the various accounts would be:

Sales ledger (personal accounts)

	£
A Ashton	80
B Bolton	310
C Collins	200
	590

All of these balances would be debit balances.

Main ledger: sales ledger control account   590

4 Posting to the sales ledger control account

This should be revision from your studies for Unit 1 and 2.

Typical entries in a SLCA are shown in the example below. The 'folio' reference 'Jnl' in this example indicates that this particular transaction is first **entered** in the **journal** before **posting** to the **control account** and other accounts indicated. The reference SDB is the sales day book, SRDB is the sales returns day book and CB is the cash book. We will deal with journals in Chapter 7.

SALES LEDGER CONTROL ACCOUNT

	Folio	£		Folio	£
Debit balances	b/d	7,000	Credit balances		200
Sales	SDB	52,390	Cash received	CB	52,250
Dishonoured cheques	Jnl	1,000	Discounts allowed	CB	1,250
Cash paid to clear			Returns inwards from		
credit balances	CB	110	debtors	SRDB	800
Credit balances	c/d	120	Bad debts	Jnl	300
			Debit balances	c/d	5,820
		60,620			60,620
Debit balances	b/d	5,820	Credit balances	b/d	120

Bad debts are dealt with in Section 5 of this chapter.

Note some points about the various kinds of entry shown above.

Debit entries	Points to note
Debit balances b/d	Most **debtor balances** will be **debit balances**: customers will usually owe money to the business.
Sales	These are the **sales** totals posted periodically from the **sales day book**. The amounts recorded will include VAT, since debtors are due to pay the VAT to us (see Section 2 of this chapter).
Dishonoured cheques	If a cheque is dishonoured, it means that the cheque has 'bounced' and the amount will not be paid to the business. A **debit entry** is necessary to 'reverse' the recording of the cheque received and to reinstate the debt. The **credit entry** is to cash.
Cash paid by us to clear credit balances	If a customer has a credit balance, **we owe money** to that customer, and we may clear the balance by paying money to the customer. The entry is **debit** SLCA; **credit** cash.
Credit balances c/d	Any closing credit balances are carried down.

Credit entries	Points to note
Credit balances b/d	**Credit balances** in the sales ledger control account can arise, for example, if goods which have already been paid for are **returned**, or if a customer has **overpaid**. Such balances will be unusual.
Cash received	**Cash received from debtors** will be posted **debit** cash; **credit** SLCA.
Discounts allowed	**Cash discounts allowed** may be recorded in a memorandum column in the cash book. They form a part of the amounts invoiced to customers, which we are 'allowing' them not to pay. A credit entry is needed to cancel that part of amounts invoiced. **Debit** discounts allowed: **credit** SLCA
Returns inwards	**Credit notes** for returns inwards must be posted from the **sales returns day book**. **Debit** sales (or sales returns if recorded separately); **credit** SLCA.
Bad debts	Bad debts written off need to be **cancelled** from the control account. **Debit** bad debts; **credit** SLCA.
Debit balances c/d	The bulk of sales ledger balances to carry forward will be debit balances.

Activity 4.1

Prepare a specimen sales ledger control account in T account form. Show clearly the information it would contain and the sources of this information.

Activity 4.2

Tick the items below which you would **not** expect to see as individual items in a sales ledger control account.

1   Credit balances on individual debtor accounts
2   Debit balances on individual debtor accounts
3   Cash sales
4   Sales on credit
5   Provision for bad and doubtful debts
6   Settlement discounts allowed
7   Trade discounts received
8   Cash receipts
9   Bad debts written off
10 Sales returns
11 Credit notes received
12 Credit notes issued

5 Bad debts

5.1 Bad debts

For some balances on the ledger, there may be little or no prospect of the business being paid.

- The customer is **bankrupt**
- The customer has gone **out of business**
- **Dishonesty** may be involved

For one reason or another, therefore, a business decides to give up expecting payment and to **write the debt off as a 'lost cause'**.

5.2 Bad debts written off: ledger accounting entries

For bad debts written off, there is a **bad debts account** in the main ledger. The double-entry bookkeeping is fairly straightforward. When it is decided that a particular debt will not be paid, the customer becomes a bad debt. We therefore:

DEBIT	Bad debts account (expense)	£100	
CREDIT	SLCA		£100

A write off of any bad debt will need the authorisation of a senior official in the organisation.

Example: Bad debts written off

At 1 October 20X1 a business had total outstanding debts of £8,600. During the year to 30 September 20X2:

(a) Credit sales amounted to £44,000.

(b) Payments from various debtors amounted to £49,000.

(c) Two debts, for £180 and £420 (both including VAT) were declared bad. These are to be written off.

We need to prepare the sales ledger control account and the bad debts account for the year.

Solution

SALES LEDGER CONTROL ACCOUNT

Date	Details	£	Date	Details	£
1.10.X1	Balance b/d	8,600		Cash	49,000
	Sales for the year	44,000	30.9.X2	Bad debts	180
			30.9.X2	Bad debts	420
			30.9.X2	Balance c/d	3,000
		52,600			52,600
	Balance b/d	3,000			

BAD DEBTS

Date	Details	£	Date	Details	£
30.9.X2	SLCA	180	30.9.X2	Balance	600
30.9.X2	SLCA	420			
		600			600

In the sales ledger, personal accounts of the customers whose debts are bad will be **taken off the ledger**. The business should then take steps to ensure that it does not sell goods to those customers again.

5.3 Bad debts and VAT

A business can claim relief from VAT on bad debts which:

- Are **at least six months old** (from the time of supply)
- Which have been **written off** in the accounts of the business

VAT bad debt relief is accounted for as follows:

DEBIT	VAT account	£17.50	
	Bad debts	£100.00	
CREDIT	SLCA		£117.50

Example: Bad debts and VAT

If both the debts written off in the example above were inclusive of VAT, the accounts would look as follows:

SALES LEGER CONTROL ACCOUNT – no change

BAD DEBTS

Date	Details	£	Date	Details	£
30.9.X2	SLCA	153.20	30.9.X2	Balance	510.65
30.9.X2	SLCA	357.45			
		510.65			510.65

VAT ACCOUNT (part)

Date	Details	£	Date	Details	£
30.9.X2	SLCA	26.80			
30.9.X2	SLCA	62.55			

5.4 Provision for doubtful debts: ledger accounting entries

A provision for doubtful debts is rather different from a bad debt written off. A business might know from past experience that, say, 2% of debtors' balances are unlikely to be collected. It would then be considered prudent to make a **general provision of 2% of total debtor balances.**

It may be that no particular customers are regarded as suspect and so it is not possible to write off any individual customer balances as bad debts.

The procedure is, then, to leave the sales ledger control account completely untouched, but to open up a provision account by the following entries:

DEBIT	Doubtful debts account (expense)	£250	
CREDIT	Provision for doubtful debts		£250

When giving a figure for debtors, the credit balance on the provision account is deducted from the debit balance on total debtors.

In **subsequent** years, adjustments may be needed to the amount of the provision. The procedure to be followed then is as follows.

Step 1	Calculate the **new provision** required.
Step 2	Compare it with the **existing balance** on the provision account (ie the balance b/f from the previous accounting period).
Step 3	Calculate the **increase or decrease** required.

(i)   If a higher provision is required now

DEBIT	Doubtful debts account (expense)	£X
CREDIT	Provision for doubtful debts	£X

with the amount of the increase.

(ii)   If a lower provision is needed now than before

DEBIT	Provision for doubtful debts	£X
CREDIT	Doubtful debts account (expense)	£X

with the amount of the decrease.

Example: Provision for doubtful debts

John Seager has total debtors' balances outstanding at 31 December 20X3 of £28,000. He believes that about 1% of these balances will not be paid and wishes to make an appropriate provision. Before now, he has not made any provision for doubtful debts at all.

On 31 December 20X4 his debtors' balances amount to £40,000. His experience during the year has convinced him that a provision of 5% should be made.

What accounting entries should John make on 31 December 20X3 and 31 December 20X4, and what will be his net figure for debtors at those dates?

Solution

At 31 December 20X3

Provision required = 1% × £28,000
= £280

Alex will make the following entries.

DEBIT	Doubtful debts account	£280	
CREDIT	Provision for doubtful debts		£280

The net debtors figure will be:

	£
Sales ledger balances	28,000
Less provision for doubtful debts	280
	27,720

At 31 December 20X4

Following the procedure described above, John will calculate:

	£
Provision required now (5% × £40,000)	2,000
Existing provision	(280)
Additional provision required	1,720

DEBIT	Doubtful debts account	£1,720
CREDIT	Provision for doubtful debts	£1,720

The provision account will appear as follows.

PROVISION FOR DOUBTFUL DEBTS

Date	Details	£	Date	Details	£
20X3			20X3		
31 Dec	Balance c/d	280	31 Dec	Doubtful debts account	280
20X4			20X4		
31 Dec	Balance c/d	2,000	1 Jan	Balance b/d	280
			31 Dec	Doubtful debts account	1,720
		2,000			2,000
			20X5		
			1 Jan	Balance b/d	2,000

Net debtors will be:

	£
Sales ledger balances/SLCA	40,000
Less provision for doubtful debts	2,000
	38,000

5.4.1 Doubtful debts and VAT

Because it is a general provision, the provision for doubtful debts has no effect whatsoever on VAT.

Activity 4.3

Gavin is a wholesaler and the following information relates to his accounting year ending 30 September 20X2.

(a) Goods are sold on credit terms, but some cash sales are also transacted.

(b) At 1 October 20X1 Gavin's trade debtors amounted to £30,000 against which he had set aside a provision for doubtful debts of 5%.

(c) On 15 January 20X2 Gavin was informed the Fall Ltd had gone into liquidation, owing him £2,000. This debt was outstanding from the previous year.

(d) Cash sales during the year totalled £46,800, whilst credit sales amounted to £187,800.

(e)   £182,500 was received from trade debtors.

(f)   Settlement discounts allowed to credit customers were £5,300.

(g)   Apart from Fall Ltd's bad debt, other certain bad debts amounted to £3,500.

(h)   Gavin intends to retain the provision for doubtful debts account at 5% of outstanding trade debtors as at the end of the year, and the necessary entry is to be made.

Task

Enter the above transactions in Gavin's ledger accounts and (apart from the cash and bank and profit and loss accounts) balance off the accounts and bring down the balances as at 1 October 20X2.

6 Comprehensive example: Accounting for debtors

This is a good point at which to go through the steps of how transactions involving debtors are **accounted for** in a comprehensive illustrative example. Folio numbers are shown in the accounts to illustrate the cross-referencing that is needed and in the example folio numbers begin with either:

(a)   SDB, referring to a page in the sales day book; or
(b)   SL, referring to a particular account in the sales ledger; or
(c)   GL, referring to a particular account in the main ledger; or
(d)   CB, referring to a page in the cash book.

At 1 July 20X7, the Software Design Company had no debtors at all. During July, the following transactions affecting credit sales and customers occurred. All sales figures are gross; VAT on sales is charged at 17.5%.

- July 3   Invoiced A Ashton for the sale on credit of hardware goods: £100.

- July 11 Invoiced B Bolton for the sale on credit of electrical goods: £150.

- July 15 Invoiced C Collins for the sale on credit of hardware goods: £250.

- July 17 Invoiced D Derby for the sale on credit of hardware goods: £400. Goods invoiced at £120 were returned for full credit on the next day.

- July 10 Received payment from A Ashton of £100, in settlement of his debt in full.

- July 18 Received a payment of £80 from B Bolton.

- July 28 Received a payment of £120 from C Collins.

- July 29 Received a payment of £280 from D Derby.

Cash sales in July amounted to £2,502, all including VAT. £976 was for hardware goods, the balance for electrical.

Account numbers are as follows.

SL4   Personal account A Ashton
SL9   Personal account B Bolton
SL13   Personal account C Collins

SL21   Personal account D Derby
GL6   Sales ledger control account
GL21   Sales – hardware
GL22   Sales – electrical
GL1   Cash account
GL2   VAT account

Solution

The recording entries, suitably dated, would be as follows.

			SALES DAY BOOK				SDB35
			Gross		Net	Hard-	Elect-
Date	Name	Folio	total	VAT	total	ware	rical
20X7			£	£	£	£	£
July 3	A Ashton	SL4 Dr	100.00	14.89	85.11	85.11	
July 11	B Bolton	SL9 Dr	150.00	22.34	127.66		127.66
July 15	C Collins	SL13 Dr	250.00	37.23	212.77	212.77	
July 17	D Derby	SL21 Dr	400.00	59.57	340.43	340.43	
July 18	D Derby	SL 21 Cr	(120.00)	(17.87)	(102.13)	(102.13)	
			780.00	116.16	663.84	536.18	127.66
			GL6 Dr	GL2 Cr		GL21 Cr	GL22 Cr

Note. The personal accounts in the sales ledger are debited on the day the invoices and credit notes are sent out. The double entry in the main ledger accounts might be made at the end of each day, week or month; here it is made at the end of the month, by posting from the sales day book as follows.

POSTING SUMMARY - SDB 35 31/7/X7

		Debit	Credit
		£	£
GL 6	SLCA	780.00	
GL21	Sales – hardware		536.18
GL22	Sales – electrical		127.66
GL2	VAT		116.16

CASH BOOK EXTRACT
RECEIPTS – JULY 20X7   CB 23

Date 20X7	Name	Folio	Gross total £	VAT £	Net total £	Debtors £	Hard-ware £	Elect-rical £
July 10	A Ashton	SL4 Cr	100.00		100.00	100.00		
July 18	B Bolton	SL9 Cr	80.00		80.00	80.00		
July 28	C Collins	SL13 Cr	120.00		120.00	120.00		
July 29	D Derby	SL 21 Cr	280.00		280.00	280.00		
July	Cash sales		2,502.00	372.63	2,129.37		830.64	1,298.73
			3,082.00	372.63	2,709.37	580.00	830.64	1,298.73
			GL1 Dr	GL2 Cr		GL 6 Cr	GL21 Cr	GL22 Cr

As with the sales day book, a posting summary to the main ledger needs to be drawn up for the cash book.

POSTING SUMMARY – CB 23 31/7/X7

		Debit £	Credit £
GL 1	Cash account	3,082.00	
GL 6	SLCA		580.00
GL 21	Sales – hardware		830.64
GL 22	Sales – electrical		1,298.73
GL 2	VAT		372.63

The personal accounts in the sales ledger are memorandum accounts, because they are not a part of the double entry system.

MEMORANDUM SALES LEDGER

A ASHTON   A/c no: SL4

Date 20X7	Narrative	Folio	£	Date 20X7	Narrative	Folio	£
July 3	Sales	SDB 35	100.00	July 10	Cash	CB 23	100.00
			100.00				100.00

B BOLTON   A/c no: SL9

Date 20X7	Narrative	Folio	£	Date 20X7	Narrative	Folio	£
July 11	Sales	SDB 35	150.00	July 18	Cash	CB 23	80.00
				July 31	Balance b/d		70.00
			150.00				150.00
Aug 1	Balance b/d		70.00				

C COLLINS   A/c no: SL13

Date 20X7	Narrative	Folio	£	Date 20X7	Narrative	Folio	£
July 15	Sales	SDB 35	250.00	July 28	Cash	CB 23	120.00
				July 31	Balance c/d		130.00
			250.00				250.00
Aug 1	Balance b/d		130.00				

D DERBY   A/c no: SL21

Date 20X7	Narrative	Folio	£	Date 20X7	Narrative	Folio	£
July 17	Sales	SDB 35	400.00	July 18	Returns	SDB 35	120.00
				July 29	Cash	CB 23	280.00
			400.00				400.00

In the main ledger, the accounting entries can be made from the books of prime entry to the ledger accounts, in this example at the end of the month.

MAIN LEDGER (EXTRACT)

SALES LEDGER CONTROL ACCOUNT   A/c no: GL6

Date 20X7	Narrative	Folio	£	Date 20X7	Narrative	Folio	£
July 31	Sales	SDB 35	780.00	July 31	Cash	CB 23	580.00
					Balance c/d		200.00
			780.00				780.00
Aug 1	Balance b/d		200.00				

Note. At 31 July the closing balance on the sales ledger control account (£200) is the same as the total of the individual balances on the personal accounts in the sales ledger (£0 + £70 + £130 + £0).

VAT   A/c no: GL 2

Date 20X7	Narrative	Folio	£	Date 20X7	Narrative	Folio	£
				July 31	SLCA	SDB 35	116.16
				July 31	Cash	CB 23	372.63

CASH ACCOUNT   A/c no: GL1

Date 20X7	Narrative	Folio	£	Date	Narrative	Folio	£
July 31	Cash received	CB 23	3,082.00				

				SALES – HARDWARE			A/c no: GL21
Date	Narrative	Folio	£	Date	Narrative	Folio	£
				20X7			
				July 31	SLCA	SDB 35	536.18
				July 31	Cash	CB 23	830.64

				SALES – ELECTRICAL			A/c no: GL22
Date	Narrative	Folio	£	Date	Narrative	Folio	£
				20X7			
				July 31	SLCA	SDB 35	127.66
				July 31	Cash	CB 23	1,298.73

Activity 4.4

Your supervisor informs you that the following information for the year ended 31 May 20X7 comes from the accounting records of Supernova Ltd.

	£
Sales ledger control account as at 1 June 20X6	
Debit balance	12,404.86
Credit balance	322.94
Credit sales	96,464.41
Goods returned from trade debtors	1,142.92
Payments received from trade debtors	94,648.71*
Discounts allowed to trade debtors	3,311.47**

* This figures includes cheques totalling £192.00 which were dishonoured before 31 May 20X7, the debts in respect of which remained outstanding at 31 May 20X7. The only sales ledger account with a credit balance at 31 May 20X7 was that of ENR Ltd with a balance of £337.75.

** The discounts are all settlement discounts, taken against invoice values.

You are told that, after the preparation of the sales ledger control account for the year ended 31 May 20X7 from the information given above, the following accounting errors were discovered.

(i)   In July 20X7, a debt due of £77.00 from PAL Ltd had been written off as bad. Whilst the correct entries have been made in PAL Ltd's personal account, no reference to the debt being written off has been made in the sales ledger control account.

(ii) Cash sales of £3,440.00 in November 20X6 have been included in the payments received from trade debtors of £94,648.71.

(iii) The sales day book for January 20X7 had been undercast by £427.80.

(iv) Credit sales £96,464.41 includes goods costing £3,711.86 returned to suppliers by Supernova Ltd.

(v)   No entries have been made in the personal accounts for goods returned from trade debtors of £1,142.92.

(vi) The debit side of FTR Ltd's personal account has been overcast by £71.66.

Tasks

(a)   Prepare the sales ledger control account for the year ended 31 May 20X7 as it would have been *before* the various accounting errors outlined above were discovered.

(b)   Prepare a computation of the amount arising from the sales ledger to be shown as trade debtors as at 31 May 20X7.

Tutorial note. Think carefully whether all the errors listed affect the control account.

7 Purpose of the sales ledger control account

There are a number of reasons for having a sales ledger control account, mainly to do with the usefulness of **reconciling the control account to the list of memorandum sales ledger balances.**

Purpose	Details
To check the accuracy of entries made in the personal accounts	Comparing the balance on the sales ledger control account with the total of individual balances on the sales ledger personal accounts means we can identify the fact that errors have been made.
To **trace errors**	By using the sales ledger control account, a comparison with the individual balances in the sales ledger can be made for **every week** or **day** of the month, and the error found much more quickly than if a control account like this did not exist.
To provide an **internal check**	The person posting entries to the sales ledger control account will act as a check on a different person whose job it is to post entries to the sales ledger accounts.
To provide a **debtors balance quickly**	This is useful when producing a trial balance.

8 Sales ledger control account reconciliation

8.1 Manual systems

The sales ledger control account should be **balanced regularly** (at least monthly), and the balance on the account **agreed to the sum of the individual debtors' balances** extracted from the sales ledger.

In practice, more often than not the balance on the control account does not agree with the sum of balances extracted, for one or more of the following reasons.

Reason for disagreement	How to correct
Miscast of the total in the book of prime entry (adding up incorrectly).	The main ledger debit and credit postings will balance, but the sales ledger control account balance will not agree with the sum of individual balances extracted from the (memorandum) sales ledger. A journal entry must then be made in the main ledger to correct the sales ledger control account and the corresponding sales account.
A **transposition error** in **posting** an individual's transaction from the book of prime entry to the memorandum ledger.	For example the sale to C Collins of £250 might be posted to his account as £520. The **sum of balances** extracted from the memorandum ledger **must be corrected**. No double entry would be required to do this, only alter the figure in C Collins' account.
Omission of a transaction from the sales ledger control account or the memorandum account, but not both.	A single entry will correct an omission from the memorandum account in the sales ledger. Where a transaction is missing from the sales ledger control account, then the double entry will have to be checked and corrected.
The **sum of balances** extracted from the sales ledger may be **incorrectly extracted** or **miscast**.	Correct the total of the balances.

Reconciling the sales ledger control account balance with the sum of the balances extracted from the (memorandum) sales ledger is an important procedure. It should be performed **regularly** so that any errors are revealed and appropriate action can be taken. The reconciliation should be done in five steps.

Step 1	Balance the accounts in the memorandum ledger, and review for errors.
Step 2	Correct the total of the balances extracted from the memorandum ledger.

	£	£
Sales ledger total		
Original total extracted		15,320
Add: difference arising from transposition error		
(£95 written as £59)		36
		15,356
Less:		
Credit balance of £60 extracted as a debit balance	120	
(£60 × 2)		
Overcast of list of balances	90	
		(210)
		15,146

Step 3	Balance the sales ledger control account, and review for errors.
Step 4	Adjust or post the sales ledger control account **with correcting entries.**

Step 5 Prepare a statement showing how the corrected sales ledger agrees to the corrected sales ledger control account.

SALES LEDGER CONTROL ACCOUNT

	£		£
Balance before adjustments	15,091	Returns inwards: individual posting omitted from control a/c	45
		Balance c/d	15,146
Undercast of total invoices issued in sales Day book	100	(now in agreement with the corrected total of individual balances above)	
	15,191		15,191
Balance b/d	15,146		

Once the five steps are completed, the total sales ledger balances should equal the sales ledger control account balance.

The sales ledger control account reconciliation will be carried out by the **sales ledger clerk** and reviewed and approved by a **senior member of staff**.

Activity 4.5

(a) You are an employee of Ultrabrite Ltd and have been asked to help prepare the end of year accounts for the period ended 30 November 20X7 by agreeing the figure for total debtors.

The following figures, relating to the financial year, have been obtained from the books of prime entry.

	£
Purchases for the year	361,947
Sales	472,185
Returns inwards	41,226
Returns outwards	16,979
Bad debts written off	1,914
Discounts allowed	2,672
Discounts received	1,864
Cheques paid to creditors	342,791
Cheques received from debtors	429,811
Customer cheques dishonoured	626

You discover that at the close of business on 30 November 20X6 the total of the debtors amounted to £50,241.

Task

Prepare Ultrabrite Ltd's sales ledger control account for the year ended 30 November 20X7.

(b) To give you some assistance, your rather inexperienced colleague, Peter Johnson, has attempted to extract and total the individual balances in the sales ledger. He provides you with the following listing which he has prepared.

	£
Bury plc	7,500
P Fox & Son (Swindon) Ltd	2,000
Frank Wendlebury & Co Ltd	4,297
D Richardson & Co Ltd	6,847
Ultra Ltd	783
Lawrenson Ltd	3,765
Walkers plc	4,091
P Fox & Son (Swindon) Ltd	2,000
Whitchurch Ltd	8,112
Ron Bradbury & Co Ltd	5,910
Anderson Ltd	1,442
	46,347

Subsequent to the drawing up of the list, the following errors have so far been found.

(i) A sales invoice for £267 sent to Whitchurch Ltd had been correctly entered in the day book but had not then been posted to the account for Whitchurch Ltd in the sales ledger.

(ii) One of the errors made by Peter Johnson (you suspect that his list may contain others) was to omit the £2,435 balance of Rectofon Ltd from the list.

(iii) A credit note for £95 sent to Bury plc had been correctly entered in the day book but was entered in the account in the sales ledger as £75.

Task

Prepare a statement reconciling the £46,347 total provided by Peter Johnson with the balance of your own sales ledger control account.

Tutorial note. Review Peter Johnson's list very carefully and check the casting.

8.2 Integrated accounting systems

In an **integrated system**, postings to the sales ledger are carried out automatically in the same way as the corresponding posting to the sales ledger control account in the main ledger.

(a) Differences between the sales ledger control account and the total of the individual sales ledger accounts might still arise, however. This is because, in any accounting system, adjustments may be made to accounts by the different method of using **the journal**.

(b) There will still then be a need to perform a sales ledger control account reconciliation.

In a computerised accounting system, different parts of the system (for example, the main ledger, the sales ledger and the purchase ledger) may be 'integrated'.

In a **non-integrated system**, the different operations involved are not combined.

(a)   A posting must be made to the sales ledger **and** a posting must also be made to the sales ledger control account in the main ledger.

(b)   This gives rise to the need for day books, which list and produce summary totals of transactions for posting in summarised form to the sales ledger control account.

(c)   A non-integrated system of ledgers may be either computer-based or manual.

The AAT have advised that all skills testing and exams will be based on a **non-integrated** system.

Key learning points

☑   A control account is an account which keeps a total record for a collective item (for example debtors) which in reality consists of many individual items (for example individual debtors). It is an impersonal account maintained in the main ledger.

☑   The sales ledger control account is a record of the total of the balances owed by customers. Postings are made from the sales and sales returns day books, the cash book and the journal, in order to maintain this record.

☑   Some debts may not be collectable and are written off as **bad debts**.

☑   If a proportion of debtor balances are unlikely to be collected, a **provision for doubtful debts** may be needed.

☑   The sales ledger control account serves a number of purposes.

–   It provides a check on the accuracy of entries made in the personal sales ledger accounts, and helps with the tracing of any errors which may have occurred.

–   It also provides an internal check on employees' work.

–   It gives a convenient total debtors balance when the time comes to produce a trial balance or a balance sheet.

☑   The balance on the sales ledger control account should be reconciled regularly with the sum of the memorandum sales ledger account balances so that any necessary action can be taken.

Quick quiz

1   What does the balance on the sales ledger control account represent?

2   A dishonoured cheque is a credit entry in the sales ledger control account. True or false?

3   How might a credit balance arise in the sales ledger control account?

4   Why might the balance on the sales ledger control account not agree with the total of the individual debtors' balances?

5   When setting up a provision for doubtful debts, the VAT should be written off. True or false?

Answers to quick quiz

1   The total amount due to the business from its debtors.

2   False. Cash received is a credit entry, therefore a dishonoured cheque must be a debit.

3   A customer may return goods or overpay his balance.

4   (i)   There may be a transposition error in posting an individual's transaction from the book of prime entry to the memorandum ledger.

     (ii)   The day book could be miscast.

     (iii)   A transaction may be omitted from the control account or the memorandum account.

     (iv)   The total may be incorrectly extracted.

5   False. It is a general provision and does not affect VAT.

Activity checklist

This checklist shows which performance criteria, range statement or knowledge and understanding point is covered by each activity in this chapter. Tick off each activity as you complete it.

Activity

4.1   ☐   This activity deals with range statement 3.2.3 control accounts: sales ledger.

4.2   ☐   This activity deals with range statement 3.2.3 control accounts: sales ledger.

4.3   ☐   This activity deals with performance criteria 3.2.A and 3.2.B.

4.4   ☐   This activity deals with performance criteria 3.2.A and 3.2.B.

4.5   ☐   This activity deals with performance criteria 3.2.A, 3.2.B, 3.2.C and 3.2.E

chapter 5

Purchase ledger
control account

Contents

Performance criteria

3.2.A   Make and record authorised adjustments

3.2.B   Total relevant accounts in the main ledger

3.2.C   Reconcile control accounts with the totals of the balances in the subsidiary ledger

3.2.E   Identify discrepancies arising from the reconciliation of control accounts and either resolve or refer to the appropriate person

Range statement

3.2.2   Adjustments to correct errors

3.2.3   Control accounts: purchase ledger; manual; computerised

3.2.4   Discrepancies: manual purchases ledger control account not agreeing with subsidiary ledger

Knowledge and understanding

12   Relationship between the accounting system and the ledger

13   Reconciling control accounts with memorandum accounts

1 The problem

As with the sales ledger, the memorandum purchase ledger is not part of the double entry system.

How do we record purchases in the main ledger?

2 Solution

The answer is by means of the purchase ledger control account, which you have already met in your studies for Units 1 and 2.

DEBIT	Purchases/expense accounts	£1,000	
	VAT account	£175	
CREDIT	Purchase ledger control account (PLCA)		£1,175

Now that you have seen how the sales ledger control account works (in Chapter 4), you should find the purchase ledger control account fairly straightforward.

3 Purpose of the purchase ledger control account

3.1 What is the purchase ledger control account?

The two control accounts which you will meet most often are the control accounts for sales ledger and for purchase ledger.

The balance on the sales ledger control account is the **total amount due to the business at that time from its debtors.**

Therefore the balance on the purchase ledger control account at any time is the **total amount owed by the business at that time to its creditors.**

The purchase ledger control account records all of the transactions involving the trade creditors of the business.

The purchase ledger control account, like the sales ledger control account, provides:

- A check on the **accuracy of entries** in the individual personal accounts
- Help in **locating errors**
- A form of **internal check**
- A total trade creditors' balance for when a **trial balance** or balance sheet needs to be prepared

3.2 How the control account works

It works very much like the sales ledger control account.

Step 1	The **purchase day book** records the individual purchase invoices which a business receives. There may also be a separate purchase returns day book for credit notes received.
Step 2	Each invoice and credit note is recorded individually in the appropriate personal account in the **purchase ledger** for the supplier.
Step 3	The personal accounts for creditors are, usually, **memorandum accounts** and do not form part of the double entry system.
Step 4	The total purchase invoice and credit note transactions shown in the day books can be posted to the main ledger using **double entry.**

Activity 5.1

Which one of the following statements describes the relationship between the **purchase ledger control account and the purchase ledger?**

A   The **purchase ledger control account** is where the corresponding debit side of credit entries to the **purchase ledger** are posted.

B   The **purchase ledger control account** is where invoices from customers for whom you have not set up an account in the **purchase ledger** are posted.

C   The **purchase ledger** is a memorandum list of invoices and related transactions analysed by supplier. The **purchase ledger control account** is the total of amounts owed to all creditors.

D   The **purchase ledger** forms part of the double entry. The **purchase ledger control account** is a memorandum control total used for internal checking purposes.

4 Posting to the purchase ledger control account

This section should be revision from your studies for Units 1 and 2.

Typical entries in the purchase ledger control account (PLCA) are shown in the example below. The references PDB and PRDB are to the purchase day book and purchase returns day book respectively.

PURCHASE LEDGER CONTROL ACCOUNT

	Folio	£		Folio	£
Opening debit balances	b/d	70	Opening credit balances	b/d	8,300
Cash paid	CB	29,840	Purchases and other		
Discounts received	CB	30	expenses	PDB	31,000
Returns outwards	PRDB	60	Cash received clearing		
Closing credit balances	c/d	9,400	debit balances	CB	20
			Closing debit balances	c/d	80
		39,400			39,400
Debit balances	b/d	80	Credit balances	b/d	9,400

Let's consider these entries in more detail.

Debit entries	Double entry
Opening debit balances	This is unusual, perhaps an overpayment to a creditor, or a deposit made before a supplier has sent an invoice.
Cash paid	**Debit** PLCA; **credit** cash.
Discounts received	The debit is the difference between the full amount invoiced by suppliers and the discounted amount which we paid. **Debit** PLCA; **credit** discounts received.
Returns outwards	These are returns of goods to suppliers recorded as credit notes received. **Debit** PLCA; **credit** purchases.
Closing credit balances	Represent the **total** of the creditors carried down.
Credit entries	Double entry
Opening credit balances	Represent total creditors brought down (disregarding any debit balances).
Purchases and other expenses	The amounts invoiced by suppliers. **Debit** purchases; **credit** PLCA.
Cash received clearing debit balances	An unusual item. **Debit** cash; **credit** PLCA.
Closing debit balances	Carried down separately from credit balances.

Example: Control accounts

On examining the books of Steps Ltd, you discover that on 1 October 20X1 the purchase ledger balances were £6,235 credit and £105 debit.

For the year ended 30 September 20X2 the following details are available.

	£
Sales	63,728
Purchases	39,974
Cash received from debtors	55,212
Cash paid to creditors	37,307
Discount received	1,475
Discount allowed	2,328
Returns inwards	1,002
Returns outwards	535
Bad debts written off	326
Cash received in respect of debit balances in purchase ledger	105
Amount due from customer as shown by sales ledger, offset against amount due to the same firm as shown by purchase ledger (settlement by contra)	434

On 30 September 20X2 there were no debit balances in the purchase ledger.

We need to write up the purchase ledger control account recording the above transactions and bringing down balances at 30 September 20X2 (note that assessments will often include extra information not needed in the solution).

Solution

PURCHASE LEDGER CONTROL ACCOUNT

20X1		£	20X1		£
Oct 1	Balances b/d	105	Oct 1	Balances b/d	6,235
20X2			20X2		
Sept 30	Cash paid to creditors	37,307	Sept 30	Purchases	39,974
	Discount received	1,475		Cash	105
	Returns outwards	535			
	Transfer SLCA	434			
	Balances c/d	6,458			
		46,314			46,314

5 Purchase ledger control account reconciliation

5.1 Manual systems

There are good reasons for performing this reconciliation.

(a)   The account should be **balanced regularly.**

(b)   The balance on the account should be agreed with the sum of the individual creditors' balances extracted from the purchase ledger.

As with the sales ledger control account, this routine will be carried out on a monthly basis in many businesses.

Items in the reconciliation are likely to arise from similar occurrences to those already identified in the case of the sales ledger control account discussed in Chapter 4.

Error	Affects
• Miscast of purchase day book or cash book	PLCA
• Transposition error in entry from day book to purchase ledger	Purchase ledger balances
• Missing entries in *either* purchase ledger *or* control account	*Either* purchase ledger *or* control account
• Miscast of total purchase ledger balances	Purchase ledger balances
• Miscast of PLCA	PLCA

The reconciliation of the purchase ledger control account should be carried out in five steps.

Step 1   Balance the accounts in the subsidiary ledger, and review for errors.

Step 2   Correct the total of the balances extracted from the subsidiary purchase ledger.

Step 3   Balance the purchase ledger control account, and review for errors.

Step 4   Adjust or post the necessary correcting entries to the control account.

Step 5   Prepare a statement showing how the corrected purchase ledger agrees to the corrected control account.

In the example below, it is necessary to write up the account for the year and then to prepare the **control account reconciliation statement.**

Example: Control account reconciliation

Minster plc at present makes use of a manual system of accounting consisting of a main ledger, a sales ledger and a purchase ledger together with books of prime entry. The various accounts within the ledgers are drawn up on ledger cards which are updated by hand from the books of prime entry when relevant transactions take place. The decision has now been taken to use a control account in the main ledger to help keep a check on the purchase ledger and the following figures relating to the financial year ended 31 October 20X1 have been extracted from the books of prime entry.

	£
Credit purchases	132,485
Cash purchases	18,917
Credit notes received from credit suppliers	2,361
Discounts received from credit suppliers	4,153
Cheques paid to credit suppliers	124,426
Balances in the sales ledger set off against balances in the purchase ledger	542

On 1 November 20X0 the total of the creditors was £28,603.

The purchase ledger accounts have been totalled at £28,185 as at 31 October 20X1.

Subsequent to the totalling procedure, the following matters are discovered.

(a)   Whilst the totalling was taking place, the chief accountant was reviewing the account of Peterbury Ltd, a supplier, and the ledger card was on his desk. The balance of the account at 31 October was £1,836.

(b)   A credit note for £387 issued by John Danbury Ltd, a credit supplier, was correctly entered in the day book but had not then been posted to John Danbury Ltd's account in the ledger.

(c)   An invoice for £1,204 issued by Hartley Ltd, a credit supplier, was correctly entered in the day book and was then entered in Hardy Ltd's account in the purchase ledger.

(d)   An invoice for £898 relating to a credit purchase from Intergram plc, although correctly entered in the day book, was posted to the supplier's account in the ledger as £889.

(e)   A discount for £37 allowed to Minster plc by the credit supplier K Barden Ltd, had been correctly entered in the cash book but was then omitted from the company's account in the ledger.

Tasks

(a)   Prepare Minster plc's purchase ledger control account for the year ended 31 October 20X1.

(b)   Prepare a statement reconciling the original total of the purchase ledger accounts with the balance of your purchase ledger control account.

Solution

Steps 1, 2 and 5		
	£	£
Balance as per listing of creditors' accounts		28,185
Add:		
Peterbury Ltd ledger card omitted	1,836	
Posting error (Intergram plc)	9	
		1,845
		30,030
Less:		
Credit note not posted (John Danbury Ltd)	387	
Discount received (K Barden Ltd)	37	
		424
Balance as per PLCA		29,606

Note. Item (c), the invoice from Hartley Ltd, although entered in the wrong personal account, is included in the purchase ledger listing and so does not affect the total.

Steps 3 and 4

PURCHASE LEDGERS CONTROL ACCOUNT

	£		£
Credit notes received	2,361	Balance b/d	28,603
Discounts received	4,153	Purchases	132,485
Bank	124,426		
Contra sales ledger	542		
Balance c/d	29,606		
	161,088		161,088

Activity 5.2

(a) Which, if any, of the following could you see in a reconciliation of the purchase ledger control account with the purchase ledger list of balances?

    (i) Mispostings of cash payments to suppliers
    (ii) Casting errors
    (iii) Transposition errors

(b) Which of the following would you not expect to see reflected in a purchase ledger control account?

    (i) Dividend payments
    (ii) Invoices received, in summary
    (iii) Drawings
    (iv) Cheque payments
    (v) Contras
    (vi) Returns to suppliers
    (vii) Debit notes to suppliers
    (viii) Discounts received

(c) You would never see a debit balance on a purchase ledger account.

	Tick
True	☐
False	☐

5.2 Integrated accounting systems

When we looked at the sales ledger control account in Chapter 4 we noted that, in a computerised system, different parts of the accounting system may be **'integrated'** together. Similar points apply to the purchase ledger as well.

BPP
PROFESSIONAL EDUCATION

Activity 5.3

A computerised accounting system contains three modules:

    (a)   Main ledger

    (b)   Purchase ledger

    (c)   Sales ledger

The system is an **integrated** one. This means that postings to the **main ledger** are made **automatically** from the sales and purchase ledgers.

In this situation, indicate whether the following statement is TRUE or FALSE.

		Tick
The purchase ledger control account total will *always* agree with the sum of the balances on the individual creditor accounts in the purchase ledger, and no disagreement is ever possible	True	☐
	False	☐

Activity 5.4

You are employed by Wallace & Grommet, a partnership. You have ascertained that as at 31 July 20X7 the purchase ledger control account balance of £57,997.34 does not agree with the total of the balances extracted from the purchase ledger of £54,842.40.

On investigation, some errors come to light.

    (a)   An account with a balance of £8,300.00 had been omitted from the purchase ledger balances.

    (b)   Purchases of £7,449.60 for June had not been credited to the purchase ledger control account.

    (c)   RNH Ltd's account in the purchase ledger had been undercast by £620.40.

    (d)   A van bought on credit for £6,400.00 had been credited to the purchase ledger control account.

    (e)   Returns outwards of £1,424.50 had been omitted from the purchase ledger control account.

    (f)   A cheque for £5,000.00 payable to SPL Ltd had not been debited to its account in the purchase ledger.

    (g)   Discounts received of £740.36 had been entered twice in the purchase ledger control account.

    (h)   A contra arrangement of £400.00 with a trade debtor had not been set off in the purchase ledger.

Tutorial note. With item (f), think carefully whether you are adding or deducting.

Task

Set out the necessary adjustments to:

    (a)   The schedule of balances as extracted from the purchase ledger

    (b)   The balance in the purchase ledger control account

5.3 And finally ...

Look back to the diagram in Section 3 of Chapter 2. Now you know about control accounts, it should all fall into place!

Key learning points

☑ The purchase ledger control account (PLCA) records the true total of the balances owed to credit suppliers. This record is prepared from postings from the purchase and purchase returns day books, the cash book and the journal.

☑ The PLCA acts as a check on the accuracy of individual suppliers' accounts in the purchase ledger, as well as acting as a form of internal check. If a trial balance or balance sheet is needed, a total trade creditors' balance can be extracted from the account.

☑ The balance on the PLCA should be reconciled regularly with the sum of the subsidiary purchase ledger account balances.

Quick quiz

1   What does the balance on the purchase ledger control account represent?

2   Name two uses of a purchase ledger control account.

3   Discounts received from suppliers are credited to the purchase ledger control account. True or false?

4   What is the double entry for cash received to clear a debit balance on the purchase ledger control account?

    A   Debit cash; credit PLCA
    B   Debit PLCA; credit cash
    C   Debit PLCA; credit SLCA
    D   Credit PLCA; debit SLCA

5   The purchase day book is miscast. Would this affect the purchase ledger control account or the purchase ledger?

6   An invoice has been incorrectly entered in the purchase day book. Would this give rise to a difference between the purchase ledger control account and the total of purchase ledger balances?

Answers to quick quiz

1   The total amount owed by the business to its creditors.

2   (i)   Checks accuracy of entries in the personal accounts.
    (ii)   Provides a total creditors figure for the balance sheet.

3   False. They are debited.

4   **A**   DEBIT   Cash
           CREDIT   Purchase ledger control account

5   The purchase ledger control account.

6   No. Both would be incorrect.

Activity checklist

This checklist shows which performance criteria, range statement or knowledge and understanding point is covered by each activity in this chapter. Tick off each activity as you complete it.

Activity

5.1 ☐ This activity deals with knowledge and understanding point 12: relationship between the accounting system and the ledger.

5.2 ☐ This activity deals with performance criteria 3.2.C.

5.3 ☐ This activity deals with range statement 3.2.3 control accounts: purchase ledger; computerised.

5.4 ☐ This activity deals with performance criteria 3.2.A, 3.2.B, 3.2.C and 3.2.E.

chapter 6

Other control accounts

Contents

Performance criteria

3.2.A   Make and record authorised adjustments

3.2.B   Total relevant accounts in the main ledger

3.2.D   Reconcile petty cash control account with cash in hand and subsidiary record

3.2.E   Identify discrepancies arising from the reconciliation of control accounts and either resolve or refer to the appropriate person

Range statement

3.2.2   Adjustments: to correct errors

3.2.3   Control accounts: non-trade debtors

3.2.4   Discrepancies: cash in hand not agreeing with subsidiary record and control account.

Knowledge and understanding

13   Petty cash procedures: imprest and non imprest methods; analysis

15   Inter-relationship of accounts – double entry system

19   Relevant understanding of the organisation's accounting systems and administrative systems and procedures

1 The problem

The most common control accounts are for the purchase ledger and the sales ledger.

However other items need to be controlled as well.

- Wages and salaries
- Cash in hand
- Cash at bank
- Stocks
- Sundry debtors

2 The solution

The wages and salaries control account was dealt with in detail in Units 1 and 2.

The stock control account will form part of your Unit 5 studies.

The other items form part of your Unit 3 studies.

- Cash in hand (petty cash: Units 1 and 2 and this chapter)
- Cash at bank (bank reconciliation – see Chapter 3)
- Sunday debtors (this chapter)

3 Other control accounts

3.1 Petty cash

You have covered petty cash payments and receipts in your studies for Units 1 and 2. A **cash control account** may be used with the petty cash book. In this case, the subsidiary account is the petty cash book.

A cash control account might look like this.

CASH CONTROL ACCOUNT

Date 20X1	Details	£	Date 20X1	Details	£
6 June	Balance b/d	100.00	12 June	Petty cash book (Note)	76.42
12 June	Bank	76.42	12 June	Balance c/d	100.00
		176.42			176.42
13 June	Balance b/d	100.00			

Note. £76.42 is the total of the analysis columns for the week. A transfer of £76.42 from the bank account is needed to restore the imprest amount to £100.

The cash control account forms **part of the double entry**. It should be agreed to the petty cash book (the subsidiary account) and the cash in hand at regular intervals. Any discrepancies need to be investigated and either resolved or referred to your supervisor.

To make sure you have understood the cash control account, try this activity.

Activity 6.1

A petty cash control account is kept in the main ledger of Astbury Ltd. The petty cash book is the subsidiary account. Astbury Ltd do not operate an imprest system. At the beginning of August there is a balance brought forward of £214.

During August £196 was spent from petty cash, and at the end of the month £200 was put into the petty cash box from the bank. The cash in hand at the end of the month is £212.00.

Task

Enter these transactions into the petty cash control account below, showing clearly the balance carried down. Identify any discrepancy to cash in hand.

PETTY CASH CONTROL ACCOUNT

Date 20X1	Details	£	Date 20X1	Details	£

Activity 6.2

Following the events in activity 6.1, you discover that an IOU for £2 was not included in the petty cash count of £212. Also a payment of £4 out of petty cash (supported by a valid petty cash voucher) had been omitted form the petty cash book and control account. Resolve the discrepancy found in activity 6.1.

3.2 Non-trade debtors

The sales ledger control account only deals with trade debtors.

There could also be amounts owed to the business from non-trade debtors.

- Amounts owed for sale of fixed assets.
- Rents receivable from letting part of the factory or office premises.
- Recovery of incorrect payments

These non-trade debtors can be kept track of by means of a non-trade debtors control account. It is a convenient way of bringing all non-trade debtor balances together.

Example: Non trade debtors

Macon Ltd lets part of its office premises to Chardonnay Ltd at a rent of £2,000 pa, payable quarterly in advance. At 1 January 20X5 Chardonnay Ltd owed £500 rent due on 31 December 20X4 and also £11,500 for second-hand office furniture bought from Macon Ltd. What is the balance on the non-trade debtors control account?

Solution

NON TRADE DEBTORS CONTROL ACCOUNT (NTDC)

	£		£
Rent receivable	500	Balance c/d	2,000
Sales of fixed assets	1,500		
	2,000		2,000
Balance b/f	2,000		

RENT RECEIVABLE

	£		£
Rent for year (P&L a/c)	2,000	Cash (3 × £500)	500
		NTDC	500
	2,000		2,000

SALE OF FIXED ASSETS

	£		£
Fixed assets disposal	1,500	NTDC	1,500

Key learning points

- ☑ **Petty cash** can be controlled by use of a control account and cash counts.

- ☑ Sundry **non-trade debtors** can be collected into one convenient total by means of a control account.

Quick quiz

1   A petty cash control account is not needed if an imprest system is used. True or false?

2   _____ debtors can be kept track of by using a control account. *Complete the blank.*

Answers to quick quiz

1   False. Even under an imprest system, checks need to be made that: cash in hand + IOUs + vouchers held = imprest amount.

2   **Non-trade** debtors can be kept track of by using a control account.

Activity checklist

This checklist shows which performance criteria, range statement or knowledge and understanding point is covered by each activity in this chapter. Tick off each activity as you complete it.

Activity

6.1   [　　　]   This activity deals with Performance criteria 3.2.B and 3.2.D.

6.2   [　　　]   This activity deals with performance criteria 3.2.A and 3.2.E.

P A R T   C

Initial trial balance

chapter 7

The correction
of errors

Contents

Performance criteria

3.2.A   Make and record authorised adjustments

Range statement

3.2.1   Record: manual journal; computerised journal
3.2.2   Adjustments: to correct errors
3.3.3   Rectify imbalances in an manual accounting system by: adjusting errors; creating a suspense account

Knowledge and understanding

11   Identification of different types of errors
16   Use of journals

1 The problem

Using control accounts, we have identified errors in the records. How do we document the corrections needed?

2 The solution

As with all accounting entries, we need documentation. In Chapter 2 the journal was mentioned as a book of prime entry.

The **journal** is a way of recording entries that do not go through the other books of prime entry e.g.

- Writing off bad debts (see Chapter 4)
- Setting up provision for doubtful debts (see Chapter 4)
- Correcting errors (this Chapter)

3 Types of error in accounting

You have already learned about errors which arise in the context of the cash book or the sales and purchase ledgers and their control accounts. Here we deal with errors that may be corrected by means of the **journal** or a **suspense account**.

It is not possible to draw up a complete list of all the errors which might be made by bookkeepers and accountants. If you tried, it is likely someone would commit a completely new error that you had not thought of.

However, it is possible to describe five **types of error** which cover most of the errors which can occur.

- Errors of **transposition**
- Errors of **omission**
- Errors of **principle**
- Errors of **commission**
- **Compensating** errors

Once an error has been detected, it needs to be put right.

If the error **involves a double entry** in the ledger accounts, then it is corrected using a **journal entry**.

When the error **breaks the rule of double entry**, then it is corrected by the use of a **suspense account** as well as a journal entry.

3.1 Errors of transposition

Transposition is when two digits are accidentally recorded the wrong way round.

Example: Transposition

A sale is recorded in the sales account as £11,279, but it has been incorrectly recorded in the sales ledger control account as £11,729. The error is the transposition of the **7** and the **2**. The consequence is that the debit will not be equal to the credit.

You can often detect a transposition error by checking whether the difference between debits and credits can be divided exactly by 9. For example, £11,729 – £11,279 = £450; £450 ÷ 9 = 50. (This only works, if transposition is the *only* problem!)

3.2 Errors of omission

An **error of omission** means failing to record a transaction at all, or making a debit or credit entry, but not the corresponding double entry.

Examples: Omission

If a business receives an invoice from a supplier for £1,350, the transaction might be omitted from the books entirely. As a result, both the total debits and the total credits of the business will be out by £1,350.

If a business receives an invoice from a supplier for £820, the purchase ledger control account might be credited, but the debit entry in the purchases account might be omitted. In this case, the total credits would not equal total debits (because total debits are £820 less than they ought to be).

3.3 Errors of principle

An **error of principle** involves making a double entry in the belief that the transaction is being entered in the correct accounts, but subsequently finding out that the accounting entry breaks the 'rules' of an accounting principle or concept.

Examples: Principle

Repairs to a machine costing £300 should be treated as revenue expenditure, and debited to a repairs account. If the repair costs are added to the cost of the fixed asset (capital expenditure) an error of principle has occurred. Although total debits equal total credits, the repairs account is £300 less than it should be and the cost of the fixed asset is £300 greater than it should be.

A proprietor sometimes takes cash for his personal use and during a certain year these drawings amount to £1,400. The bookkeeper reduces cash sales by £1,400 so that the cash book balances. This is an error of principle, and the result of it is the drawings account is understated by £1,400, and so is the total value of sales in the sales account.

3.4 Errors of commission

Errors of commission are where the bookkeeper makes a mistake in carrying out his or her task of recording transactions in the accounts.

Examples: Commission

Putting a debit entry or a credit entry in the wrong account. If telephone expenses of £342 are debited to the electricity expenses account, an error of commission has occurred. Although total debits and total credits balance, telephone expenses are understated by £342 and electricity expenses are overstated by £342.

Errors of casting (adding up). The total daily credit sales in the sales day book of a business should add up to £79,925, but are incorrectly added up as £79,325. The total sales in the sales day book are then used to credit total sales and debit sales ledger control account in the main ledger, so that total debits and total credits are still equal, although incorrect.

3.5 Compensating errors

Compensating errors are, coincidentally, equal and opposite to one another.

Example: Compensating errors

Two transposition errors of £360 might occur in extracting ledger balances, one on each side of the double entry. In the administration expenses account, £3,158 is written instead of £3,518, while in the sundry income account, £6,483 is written instead of £6,843. The debits and the credits are each £360 too low. Consequently, compensating errors hide the fact that there are errors.

4 The correction of errors: journal entries

4.1 Journals

Date	Folio	Debit	Credit
		£	£
Account to be debited		X	
Account to be credited			X
(Narrative to explain the transaction)			

The journal requires the debit and credit entries to be equal. You will notice that we have used the journal format to show double entry postings earlier in this text.

Assessors often ask you to 'journalise' a transaction (ie to show the postings in the form of a journal entry), even where there are no errors and journals are not normally used. This is because journals show that you understand the double entry postings involved.

4.2 Using journals to correct errors

£200 is misposted to the gas account instead of to the rent account. A journal entry is made to correct the misposting error as follows.

1.5.20X7

DEBIT	Rent account	£200	
CREDIT	Gas account		£200

To correct a misposting of £200 between the gas account and the rent account.

If total debits were equal to total credits before the journal, then they will still be equal after the journal is posted.

Suppose total debits were originally £100,000 but total credits were £99,520. If the same correcting journal is put through, total debits will remain £100,000 and total credits will remain £99,520. Total debits were different by £480 *before* the journal, and they are still different by £480 *after* the journal.

This means that journals can only be used to correct errors which require both a credit and (an equal) debit adjustment.

Example: Journal entries

Write out the journal entries which would correct these errors. Ignore VAT.

(a) A business receives an invoice for £1,350 from a supplier which was omitted from the books entirely.

(b) Repairs worth £300 were incorrectly debited to the fixed asset (machinery) account instead of the repairs account.

(c) The bookkeeper of a business reduces cash sales by £1,400 because he was not sure what the £1,400 represented. In fact, it was drawings.

(d) Telephone expenses of £342 are incorrectly debited to the electricity account.

(e) A page in the sales day book has been added up to £79,325 instead of £79,925.

Solution

(a)
DEBIT	Purchases	£1,350	
CREDIT	PLCA		£1,350

A transaction previously omitted.

(b)
DEBIT	Repairs account	£300	
CREDIT	Fixed asset (machinery) a/c		£300

The correction of an error of principle: repairs costs incorrectly added to fixed asset costs

(c)
DEBIT	Drawings	£1,400	
CREDIT	Sales		£1,400

An error of principle, in which sales were reduced to compensate for cash drawings not accounted for.

(d)	DEBIT	Telephone expenses	£342	
	CREDIT	Electricity expenses		£342

Correction of an error of commission; telephone expenses wrongly charged to the electricity account

(e)	DEBIT	SLCA	£600	
	CREDIT	Sales		£600

The correction of a casting error in the sales day book
(£79,925 − £79,325 = £600)

4.3 Computerised journals

Errors can be made on computerised systems just as easily as on manual ones. Computerised journals have the same format and use as manual ones.

5 The correction of errors: suspense accounts

5.1 What is a suspense account?

A suspense account is a **temporary** account which can be opened for a number of reasons. The most common reasons are as follows.

(a)   A trial balance is drawn up which **does not balance,** ie total debits do not equal total credits (see Chapter 8).

(b)   The bookkeeper knows where to post the credit side of a transaction, but **does not know where to post the debit (or vice versa)**. A cash payment might be made and must obviously be credited to cash. The bookkeeper may not know what the payment is for, and so will not know which account to debit.

In both these cases, the procedure is as follows:

Step 1   A temporary suspense account is opened up.

Step 2   Identify the problem and decide how to resolve it.

Step 3   Post the correcting entries using the journal.

5.2 Use of suspense account: when the trial balance does not balance

An error occurs which results in an **imbalance** between total debits and total credits in the ledger accounts. An accountant draws up a trial balance and finds that, for some reason total debits exceed total credits by £207.

Step 1	He knows that there is an error somewhere, but for the time being he opens a suspense account and enters a credit of £207 in it. This serves two purposes.
	(a) The accountant will not forget that there is an error to be sorted out.
	(b) Now that there is a credit of £207 in the suspense account, the total debits equal total credits.
Step 2	He finds that he had accidentally failed to make a credit of £207 to purchases.
Step 3	The journal entry would be:

DEBIT	Suspense a/c	£207	
CREDIT	Purchases		£207

To close off suspense a/c and correct error

When an error results in total debits not being equal to total credits, the first step an accountant makes is to open up a **suspense account**. Three more examples are given below.

Example: Transposition error

The bookkeeper of Remico made a transposition error when entering an amount for sales in the sales account. Instead of entering the correct amount of £49,287.90 he entered £49,827.90, transposing the **2** and **8**. The debtors were posted correctly, and so when total debits and credits on the ledger accounts were compared, it was found that credits exceeded debits by £(49,827.90 – 49,287.90) = £540.

Solution

The initial step is to equalise the total debits and credits by posting a debit of £540 to a suspense account. When the cause of the error is discovered, the double entry to correct it should be logged in the journal as:

DEBIT	Sales	£540	
CREDIT	Suspense a/c		£540

To close off suspense a/c and correct transposition error

Example: Error of omission

When Reckless Records paid the monthly salary cheques to its office staff, the payment of £21,372 was correctly entered in the cash account, but the bookkeeper omitted to debit the office salaries account. So the total debit and credit balances on the ledger accounts were not equal, and total credits exceeded total debits by £21,372.

Solution

The initial step in correcting the situation is to debit £21,372 to a suspense account, to equalise the total debits and total credits.

When the cause of the error is discovered, the double entry to correct it should be logged in the journal as:

DEBIT	Office salaries account	£21,372	
CREDIT	Suspense account		£21,372

To close off suspense account and correct error of omission

Example: Error of commission

A credit customer pays £1,220 of the £1,500 he owes to Polypaint Ltd, but Polypaint's bookkeeper has debited £1,220 on the sales ledger control account in the main ledger by mistake instead of crediting the payment received.

Solution

The total debit balances in Polypaint's ledger accounts now exceed the total credits by 2 × £1,220 = £2,440. The initial step would be to make a credit entry of £2,440 in a suspense account. When the cause of the error is discovered, it should be corrected as follows.

DEBIT	Suspense account	£2,440	
CREDIT	SLCA		£2,440

To close off suspense account and correct error of commission

In the sales ledger control account in the main ledger, the correction would appear as follows (assuming that this customer is the only customer for clarity).

SALES LEDGER CONTROL ACCOUNT

	£		£
Balance b/d	1,500	Suspense account: error corrected	2,440
Payment incorrectly debited	1,220	Balance c/d	280
	2,720		2,720

The balance carried forward of £280 represents the original debt (£1,500) less the payment received (£1,220).

5.3 Use of suspense account: not knowing where to post a transaction

The second use of suspense accounts is when a bookkeeper **does not know in which account to post one side of a transaction**. Until this is sorted out, the entry can be recorded in a suspense account. An example is when cash is received through the post from a source which cannot be determined. Another example is to credit proceeds on disposal of fixed assets to the suspense account instead of working out the profit or loss on disposal.

Example: Not knowing where to post a transaction

Conway received a cheque in the post for £350. The name on the cheque is B Down, but the staff have no idea who this is, nor why he should be sending £350. The bookkeeper opens a suspense account, so that the double entry for the transaction is:

DEBIT	Cash	£350	
CREDIT	Suspense account		£350

It turns out that the cheque was for a debt owed by Bob's Boutique and paid out of the proprietor's personal bank account. The suspense account can now be cleared.

DEBIT	Suspense account	£350	
CREDIT	SLCA		£350

(and the correct entry will also be put through the sales ledger account for Bob's Boutique).

5.4 Suspense accounts might contain several items

If more than one error or unidentifiable posting to a ledger account arises during an accounting period, they will all be **merged together** in the same suspense account. Indeed, until the causes of the errors are discovered, the bookkeepers are unlikely to know exactly how many errors there are.

Activity 7.1

You are assisting the accountant of Ranchurch Ltd in preparing the accounts for the year ended 31 December 20X7. You draw up a trial balance and you notice that the credit side is greater than the debit side by £5,607.82. You enter this difference in a suspense account.

On investigation, the following errors and omissions are found to have occurred.

(a) An invoice for £1,327.40 for general insurance has been posted to cash but not to the ledger account.

(b) A customer went into liquidation just before the year end, owing Ranchurch £428.52. The amount was taken off SLCA but the corresponding entry to expense the bad debt has not been made.

(c) A cheque paid for purchases has been posted to the purchases account as £5,296.38, when the cheque was made out for £5,926.38.

(d) A van was purchased during the year for £1,610.95, but this amount was credited to the motor vehicles account.

Task

Set up a suspense account and show the entries to clear it.

Tutorial note. As total credits exceed total debits, you are missing a debit of £5,607.82.

Activity 7.2

Using the information in activity 7.1, set out the journal needed to clear the suspense account.

5.5 Suspense accounts are temporary

A suspense account can only be **temporary**. Postings to a suspense account are only made when the bookkeeper doesn't know yet what to do, or when an error has occurred.

Mysteries must be solved, and errors must be corrected. Under no circumstances should there still be a suspense account when it comes to preparing the final accounts.

The suspense account **must be cleared** and all the correcting entries made before the final accounts are drawn up.

Key learning points

☑ There are five **types of error**.

- Errors of transposition
- Errors of omission
- Errors of principle
- Errors of commission
- Compensating errors

☑ Errors which leave total debits and total credits on the ledger accounts in balance can be corrected by using **journal entries**. Otherwise, a suspense account has to be opened first (and a journal entry used later to record the correction of the error, clearing the suspense account in the process).

☑ **Suspense accounts**, as well as being used to correct some errors, are also opened when it is not known immediately where to post an amount. When the mystery is solved, the suspense account is closed and the amount correctly posted using a journal entry.

☑ **Suspense accounts are only temporary**. None should exist when it comes to drawing up the financial statements at the end of the accounting period.

Quick quiz

1   What are the five main types of error which might occur in accounting?

2   The two common errors of commission are putting a debit or credit in the _____ account and errors of _____ (adding up). *Complete the blanks.*

3   What is a suspense account?

4   Suspense accounts are temporary. True or false?

Answers to quick quiz

1   Errors of transposition, omission, principle, commission and compensating errors.

2   The two common errors of commission are putting a debit entry or a credit entry in the **wrong** account and errors of **casting** (adding up).

3   A suspense account is an account showing a balance equal to the difference between total debits and total credits.

4   True. Suspense accounts must be cleared before the final accounts are drawn up.

Activity checklist

This checklist shows which performance criteria, range statement or knowledge and understanding point is covered by each activity in this chapter. Tick off each activity as you complete it.

Activity

7.1   [   ]   This activity deals with performance criteria 3.2.A and range statement 3.3.3 creating a suspense account.

7.2   [   ]   This activity deals with performance criteria 3.2.A and range statement 3.2.1 manual journal.

chapter 8

From ledger accounts to initial trial balance

Contents

Performance criteria

3.3.A Prepare the draft initial trial balance in line with the organisation's policies and procedures
3.3.B Identify discrepancies in the balancing process
3.3.C Identify reasons for imbalance and rectify them
3.2.D Balance the trial balance

Range statement

3.3.1 Trial balance: manual; computerised
3.3.2 Discrepancies in a manual accounting system: incorrect double entries; missing entries; wrong calculations
3.3.3 Rectify imbalances in a manual accounting system by: adjusting errors; creating a suspense account.

Knowledge and understanding

5	Double entry bookkeeping, including balancing accounts
8	Operation of manual accounting systems
9	Operation of computerised accounting systems, including output
15	Inter-relationship of accounts – double entry system
16	Use of journals
18	Function and form of the trial balance

1 The problem

So far we have concentrated on keeping the books of account. How do we get from the ledgers to the accounts?

2 The solution

This chapter takes you from the ledger accounts to the trial balance, which is the stage before the final accounts.

When you have worked through it, you will really feel that you are getting somewhere.

3 The initial trial balance

3.1 What is a trial balance?

There is no foolproof method for making sure that all entries have been posted to the correct ledger account, but a technique which shows up the more obvious mistakes is to prepare a **trial balance** (or list of account balances).

A **trial balance** is a list of ledger balances shown in debit and credit columns.

3.2 Collecting together the ledger accounts

Before you draw up a trial balance, you must have a **collection of ledger accounts**. These are the ledger accounts of Shabnum Rashid, a sole trader.

CASH

	£		£
Capital: Shabnum Rashid	10,000	Rent	4,200
Bank loan	3,000	Shop fittings	3,600
Sales	14,000	PLCA	7,000
SLCA	3,300	Bank loan interest	130
		Other expenses	2,200
		Drawings	1,800
			18,930
		Balancing figure: the amount of cash left over after payments have been made	11,370
	30,300		30,300
Balance b/d	11,370		

CAPITAL (SHABNUM RASHID)

	£		£
		Cash	10,000

BANK LOAN

	£		£
		Cash	3,000

PURCHASES

	£		£
PLCA	7,000		

PLCA

	£		£
Cash	7,000	Purchases	7,000

RENT

	£		£
Cash	4,200		

SHOP FITTINGS

	£		£
Cash	3,600		

SALES

	£		£
		Cash	14,000
Balance b/d	17,300	SLCA	3,300
	17,300		17,300
		Balance b/d	17,300

SLCA

	£		£
Sales	3,300	Cash	3,300

BANK LOAN INTEREST

	£		£
Cash	130		

OTHER EXPENSES

	£		£
Cash	2,200		

DRAWINGS ACCOUNT

	£		£
Cash	1,800		

The first step is to **'balance' each account**.

3.3 Balancing ledger accounts

At the end of an accounting period, a balance is struck on each account in turn. This means that all the **debits** on the account are totalled and so are all the **credits**.

- If the **total debits exceed the total credits** the account has a **debit balance**.
- If the **total credits exceed the total debits** then the account has a **credit balance**.

Let's see how this works with Shabnum Rashid's cash account.

Step 1	**Calculate a total** for **both sides** of **each ledger account**. Dr £30,300, Cr £18,930
Step 2	**Deduct** the **lower** total **from** the **higher** total. £(30,300 – 18,930) = £11,370
Step 3	**Insert the result of Step 2 as the balance c/d** on the side of the account with the lower total. Here it will go on the credit side, because the total credits on the account are less than the total debits.
Step 4	**Check** that the **totals on both sides** of the account are **now the same.** Dr £30,300, Cr £(18,930 + 11,370) = £30,300
Step 5	**Insert the amount of the balance c/d as the new balance b/d on the other side of the account**. The new balance b/d is the balance on the account. The balance b/d on the cash account is £11,370 Dr. ie £11,370 cash at bank.

In our simple example, there is very little balancing to do.

(a) Both the purchase ledger control account and the sales ledger control account balance off to zero.
(b) The cash account has a debit balance (the new balance b/d) of £11,370 (see above).
(c) The total on the sales account is £17,300, which is a credit balance.

The other accounts have only one entry each, so there is no totalling to do.

3.4 Collecting the balances on the ledger accounts

If the basic principle of double entry has been correctly applied throughout the period, the **credit balances will equal the debit balances** in total. This is illustrated by collecting together the balances on Shabnum Rashid's accounts.

	Debit £	Credit £
Cash	11,370	
Capital		10,000
Bank loan		3,000
Purchases	7,000	
PLCA	–	–
Rent	4,200	
Shop fittings	3,600	
Sales		17,300
SLCA	–	–
Bank loan interest	130	
Other expenses	2,200	
Drawings	1,800	
	30,300	30,300

The order of listing the various accounts listed in the **trial balance** does not matter. It is just a method used to test the accuracy of the double entry bookkeeping.

3.5 What if the trial balance shows unequal debit and credit balances?

If the trial balance does not **balance** there must be an **error in recording of transactions in the accounts**. A trial **balance** will **not** disclose the following types of errors.

Type 1	The **complete omission** of a transaction, because neither a debit nor a credit is made.
Type 2	A posting to the correct side of the ledger, but to a **wrong account** (also called errors of commission).
Type 3	**Compensating errors** (eg debit error of £100 is cancelled by credit £100 error elsewhere).
Type 4	**Errors of principle** (eg cash received from debtors being debited to the sales ledger control account and credited to cash instead of the other way round).

If the trial balance does not balance, the difference goes to a suspense account (see Chapter 7).

Example: Trial balance

As at the end of 29 November 20X1, your business High & Mighty has the following balances on its ledger accounts.

Accounts	Balance
	£
Bank loan	15,000
Cash	13,080
Capital	11,000
Rent	2,000
Purchase ledger control account (PLCA)	14,370
Purchases	16,200
Sales	18,900
Sundry creditors	2,310
Sales ledger control account (SLCA)	13,800
Bank loan interest	1,000
Other expenses	12,500
Vehicles	2,000

During 30 November the business made the following transactions.

(a) Bought materials for £1,400, half for cash and half on credit
(b) Made £1,610 sales, £1,050 of which were for credit
(c) Paid wages to shop assistants of £300 in cash

You are required to draw up a trial balance showing the balances as at the end of 30 November 20X1.

Solution

Put the opening balances into a trial balance, so decide which are debit and which are credit balances.

Account	Debit £	Credit £
Bank loan		15,000
Cash	13,080	
Capital		11,000
Rent	2,000	
PLCA		14,370
Purchases	16,200	
Sales		18,900
Sundry creditors		2,310
SLCA	13,800	
Bank loan interest	1,000	
Other expenses	12,500	
Vehicles	2,000	
	60,580	61,580
Suspense account	1,000	-
	61,580	61,580

Step 2 Take account of the effects of the three transactions which took place on 30 November 20X1.

			£	£
(a)	DEBIT	Purchases	1,400	
	CREDIT	Cash		700
		PLCA		700
(b)	DEBIT	Cash	560	
		SLCA	1,050	
	CREDIT	Sales		1,610
(c)	DEBIT	Other expenses	300	
	CREDIT	Cash		300

> **Step 3**   Amend the trial balance for these entries.

HIGH & MIGHTY: TRIAL BALANCE AT 30 NOVEMBER 20X1

	29/11/20X1		Transactions		30/11/20X1	
	DR	CR	DR	CR	DR	CR
Bank loan		15,000				15,000
Cash	13,080		(b) 560	1,000 (a)(c)	12,640	
Capital		11,000				11,000
Rent	2,000				2,000	
PLCA		14,370		700 (a)		15,070
Purchases	16,200		(a) 1,400		17,600	
Sales		18,900		1,610 (b)		20,510
Sundry creditors		2,310				2,310
SLCA	13,800		(b) 1,050		14,850	
Bank loan interest	1,000				1,000	
Other expenses	12,500		(c) 300		12,800	
Vehicles	2,000				2,000	
Suspense account	1,000				1,000	
	61,580	61,580	3,310	3,310	63,890	63,890

> **Step 4**   Identify the error(s) and clear the suspense account.

You discover that a vehicle was purchased for £3,000. The cash paid was correctly entered, but the entry to the vehicles account was debit £2,000.

SUSPENSE ACCOUNT

	£		£
Balance b/d	1,000	Vehicles	1,000

VEHICLES

	£		£
Balance b/d	2,000	Balance c/d	3,000
Suspense	1,000		
	3,000		3,000

Step 5	Revise the trial balance.

Trial balance at 30 November 20X1

Account	Debit £	Credit £
Bank loan		15,000
Cash	12,640	
Capital		11,000
Rent	2,000	
PLCA		15,070
Purchases	17,600	
Sales		20,510
Sundry creditors		2,310
SLCA	14,500	
Bank loan interest	1,000	
Other expenses	12,800	
Vehicles	3,000	
	63,890	63,890

Activity 8.1

Bailey Hughes started trading as a wholesale bookseller on 1 June 20X7 with capital of £10,000 with which he opened a bank account for his business.

During June the following transactions took place.

June		
	1	Bought warehouse shelving for cash from Warehouse Fitters Ltd for £3,500
	2	Purchased books on credit from Ransome House for £820
	4	Sold books on credit to Waterhouses for £1,200
	9	Purchased books on credit from Big, White for £450
	11	Sold books on credit to Books & Co for £740
	13	Paid cash sales of £310 from the warehouse shop intact into the bank
	16	Received cheque from Waterhouses in settlement of their account
	17	Purchased books on credit from RUP Ltd for £1,000
	18	Sold books on credit to R S Jones for £500
	19	Sent cheque to Ransome House in settlement of their account
	20	Paid rent of £300 by cheque
	21	Paid delivery expenses of £75 by cheque
	24	Received £350 from Books & Co on account
	30	Drew cheques for personal expenses of £270 and assistant's wages £400
	30	Settled the account of Big, White
	30	Received a mystery cheque for £500, post the other side of the entry to suspense

Tasks

(a) Record the foregoing in appropriate books of original entry.
(b) Post the entries to the ledger accounts.
(c) Balance the ledger accounts where necessary.
(d) Extract a trial balance at 30 June 20X7
(e) The cheque for £500 turned out to be from RS Jones. Clear the suspense account.

4 Computerised systems

So far we have looked at the way an accounting system is organised. You should note that all of the books of prime entry and the ledgers may be either **hand-written books** or **computer records.** Most businesses use computers, ranging from one **PC** to huge **mainframe computer systems**.

All computer activity can be divided into three processes.

Areas	Activity
Input	Entering data from original documents
Processing	Entering up books and ledgers and generally sorting the input information
Output	Producing any report desired by the managers of the business, including financial statements

Activity 8.2

Your friend Lou Dight believes that computerised accounting systems are more trouble than they are worth because 'you never know what is going on inside that funny box'.

Task

Explain briefly why computers might be useful in accounting.

4.1 Batch processing and control totals

Batch processing: similar transactions are gathered into batches, then sorted and processed by the computer.

Inputting individual invoices into a computer for processing (**transaction processing**), is time consuming and expensive. Invoices can be gathered into a **batch** and **input and processed all together**. Batches can vary in size, depending on the type and volume of transactions and on any limit imposed by the system on batch sizes.

Control totals are used to ensure there are no errors when the batch is input. They are used to ensure the total value of transactions input is the same as that previously calculated.

Say a batch of 30 sales invoices has a manually calculated total value of £42,378.47. When the batch is input, the computer adds up the total value of the invoices and produces a total of £42,378.47. The control totals agree, therefore no further action is required.

If the control total does **not agree,** then checks have to be carried out until the difference is found. An invoice might not have been entered or the manual total incorrectly calculated.

Key learning points

☑ Balances on ledger accounts can be collected on a trial balance. The debit and credit balances should be equal.

☑ Any imbalance on the trial balance should be posted to a **suspense account**.

☑ The suspense account is **temporary**. It must be **cleared** before final accounts are prepared.

☑ Computer accounting systems perform the same tasks as manual accounting systems, but they can cope with greater volumes of transactions and process them at a faster rate.

Quick quiz

1   What is the other name for a trial balance?

2   If the total debits in an account exceed the total credits, will there be a debit or credit balance on the account?

3   What types of error will not be discovered by drawing up a trial balance?

4   A suspense account on a trial balance can be ignored. True or false?

5   What are the advantages of batch processing?

Answers to quick quiz

1   The trial balance is also sometimes called the 'list of account balances'.

2   There will be a debit balance on the account.

3   There are four types, summarised as: complete omission; posted to wrong account; compensating errors; errors of principle.

4   False. The reason for the imbalance must be investigated and the suspense account cleared.

5   Batch processing is faster than transaction processing and checks on input can be made using control totals.

Activity checklist

This checklist shows which performance criteria, range statement or knowledge and understanding point is covered by each activity in this chapter. Tick off each activity as you complete it.

Activity

8.1   This activity deals with performance criteria 3.3.A, 3.3.B, 3.3.C and 3.3.D.

8.2   This activity deals with knowledge and understanding point 9: operation of computerised accounting systems, including output.

P A R T   D

Filing

chapter 9

Filing

Contents

Performance criteria

3.2.F   Ensure documentation is stored securely and in line with the organisation's confidentiality
        requirements

Knowledge and understanding

21   Organisational procedures for filing source information

1 Introduction

So far we have talked a lot about processing documents and the accounting system. In this chapter we will look at ways of storing the information which we are going to use.

2 Information storage

We are now going to look at the characteristics of a **filing system**, and at how files are organised and stored. This chapter should help you to deal with files in practice:

- Getting hold of them
- Finding documents within them
- Putting new documents into them

2.1 The features of an information storage system

Information for business users takes many forms. Whatever form documents and recorded information take, if they are to be of any use they must be maintained so that:

(a)   **Authorised people** (and only authorised people) can get to the information they require quickly and easily

(b)   Information can be **added to, updated and removed** as necessary

(c)   Information is **safe from fire, loss or handling damage** for as long as it is required (but not necessarily for ever)

(d)   Accessibility, flexibility and security are achieved as **cheaply** as possible

2.2 Files

A **file** is a collection of data records with similar characteristics.

Here are some examples of files.

(a)   A sales ledger
(b)   A purchase ledger
(c)   A cash book
(d)   Stock records
(e)   The nominal ledger
(f)   A price list
(g)   A collection of letters, memos and other papers all relating to the same matter, usually kept within a single folder

We will be talking mainly about **paper files** or **manual files** in this chapter; you should bear in mind, however, that **electronic files** can be created and used in a computer system as well.

Files of data may be temporary, permanent, active, and non-active.

(a) **Master files** and **reference files** are usually **permanent**, which means that they are never thrown away or scrapped. They will be **updated** from time to time, and so the information on the file might change, but the file itself will continue to exist.

(b) A **temporary file** is one that is eventually scrapped. Many **transaction files** are held for a very short time, until the transaction records have been processed, but are then thrown away. Other transaction files are permanent (for example a cash book) or are held for a considerable length of time before being scrapped.

(c) An **active file** is one that is frequently used. For example, sales invoice files relating to the current financial year, or correspondence files relating to current customers and suppliers.

(d) A **non-active file** is one that is no longer used on a day-to-day basis. For example, files that contain information relating to customers and suppliers who are no longer current, and purchase invoices relating to previous financial periods.

Apart from basic records which group items of information about personnel, sales or stock etc, there are huge amounts of information passing through organisations needing to be kept track of. Consider the following examples.

- Letters, memos, telegrams, telexes, emails
- Notes of phone calls and meetings
- Reports
- Advertising material and press cuttings
- Mailing lists
- Important/routine addresses and phone numbers
- Machinery documents such as guarantees or service logs
- Legal documents such as contracts, property deeds or insurance policies

2.3 Characteristics of a filing system

A 'good' file should possess some or all of the following characteristics.

(a) It should **contain all the information** you might want to look up.

(b) It should allow you to **find particular information easily**.

(c) It needs to be of a **convenient size**.

(d) It needs to have **room for expansion**.

(e) The file should be **stored close to you** and/or should be easy to get to when it is needed.

(f) The method used for storage should be **strong and secure** so that the file will not get damaged and information will not get lost.

A **filing system** for an entire organisation is not really much different. It should:

(a) **Contain all the information** that users might want

(b) Be classified and indexed in such as way as to make it **easy to find information** quickly

(c) Be **suited to the people who will use it**

(d) Be **reliable and secure**

(e) Be **flexible** enough to allow for expansion

(f) Be **cost-effective** to install and maintain. There is no point spending more to hold information on file than the information is actually worth

(g) Allow users to **retrieve information quickly**

Activity 9.1

Your organisation has just received the following letter. List the details that are likely to be used when deciding where it should be filed. What other department would you send a copy of the letter to?

SANDIMANS LTD

72 High Street, Epsom
Surrey EP12 4AB

Your reference: Z/0335/MJD
Our reference: BRC/1249/871

Mr G Latchmore
Purchasing Department
Lightfoot & Co
7 West Broughton St
LONDON W12 9LM

4 May 20X6

Dear Mr Latchmore

Stationery supplies

I refer to your letter of 11 April 20X6.

I am afraid that we are still unable to trace receipt of your payment of £473.20 in settlement of our invoice number 147829. I should be grateful if you would look into this and issue a fresh cheque if necessary.

Your sincerely

Mandy Sands

Mandy Sands

So, with all of this information floating around, how are we going to locate a particular item of information? We need to make sure that our information is held in an organised fashion, and that we have procedures in place so we can find what we are looking for quickly and easily.

3 Classifying, indexing and cross-referencing information

3.1 Classifying information

Information has to be filed in such a way that its **users know where it is and how to retrieve it** when it is needed. This means having different files for different types of information, and then **holding each file in a particular order.** Information in an individual file might be divided into categories and then held in a particular order within each category.

Classification is the process of grouping related items of information together into categories that reflect the relationship between them.

There are various ways in which information can be grouped together, or **classified**.

(a) By **name** (for example correspondence relating to a particular person or company).

(b) By **geography** (for example all documents relating to a particular country, area or city).

(c) By **subject matter** (for example all documents relating to a particular contract, transaction or type of problem).

(d) By **date** (for example all invoices for a certain month or year).

(e) By **department** (for example profits or costs for each department or employees of each department).

Once broad classifications are established, the material can be **put into a sequence** which will make individual items easier to retrieve. Again there are various systems for arranging files.

(a) **Alphabetical order** - for example customers listed in name order.

(b) **Numerical order** - for example invoices listed in numerical order of invoice numbers.

(c) **Alpha-numerical** (A1, A2, A3, B1, B2 and so on).

(d) **Chronological order** - for example letters within a subject file listed by the date they were written.

These ways of subdividing and arranging data in a logical way within suitable categories make it possible to store, find and also **index** or **cross-reference** information efficiently.

Let us have a look at some of these systems for arranging information.

3.2 Alphabetical classification

The most common means of classification is **alphabetical**. In an alphabetical name system, items are filed according to the first and then each following letter of a person's or company's name (for example in the phone book). This sounds simple enough, and indeed it is most of the time, but there are some rules which must be followed.

Surnames. The system works by surname. The hyphen is ignored in double-barrelled names. When surnames are the same, initials or first names are taken into account. All of this is illustrated below.

Dawson
Ullyott
Vivian
Watkins
Williams
Williamson
Winters, Douglas
Winters, George

Initials. Names made up of initials may come before whole-word names.

PBAB Parties Ltd
Party Time Ltd

Prefixes are included as part of the surname.

De Beauvoir
Le Bon
McVitee
Von Richthofen

Mc, Mac etc are all treated as if they were Mac, so:

McGraw
MacLaverty

and St is usually treated as Saint, so:

St Angela's Convent
Saint George's Chapel.

Titles and common words. Words such as 'Mr', 'Mrs', 'Sir', 'The', 'A' are ignored for filing purposes (or most names would be under M or T!) while departments, ministries, offices, local authorities and so on are filed under the key part of their name:

Stanwick, B (Mrs)	Bromley, London Borough of
Stock Exchange (The)	Fair Trading, Department of
Trend, N U (Prof)	Foreign Office
Finance, Ministry of	

Businesses with names like 'Phillip Smith Ltd', 'Frank Tilsley & Son, are sometimes listed under the first letter of the surname (as usual) but perhaps more often under the first letter of the whole name (P and F in the examples given).

Numbers which appear as names may also count as if they were spelled out as words:

84 Charing Cross Road (under 'E' for Eighty)
2001: A Space Odyssey (under 'T' for Two)
3i plc (under 'T' for Three).

You will find things arranged differently in some cases. Rules do vary from system to system. **Get to know the ones you have to work with in your organisation.**

The **alphabetical name system** is used, for example, in files of clients or customers, students, employees or members and also for index cards and cross-referencing (which we will come to later). It is simple to use and easily expandable: there is a 'right' place for files, so they can simply be taken out or slotted in as necessary.

3.3 Numerical classification

Numerical sequence is natural where standard documents are concerned. Invoices, for example, are numbered. So, if an invoice needs to be checked, its number need only be established (quoted by the enquirer, or looked up in the customer account) and it can be easily found. This is known as a **numerical-sequential** system.

Numerical classification is very **flexible**. Unlike the alphabetical method, you do not have to decide how much filing space to allocate to each letter, wasting space if you are too generous and having to shuffle the whole system along if you are too 'mean'. With numerical order, you simply give a new file the next number and position in the system.

On the other hand, numbers may not be very meaningful in isolation. A strict **alphabetical index** also has to be kept, and also a **numerical file list** or **accession register**, in order to establish the file number to look for. It also means that there is little room for subdivisions for easier identification and retrieval, although blocks of numbers can be allotted to different departments, say.

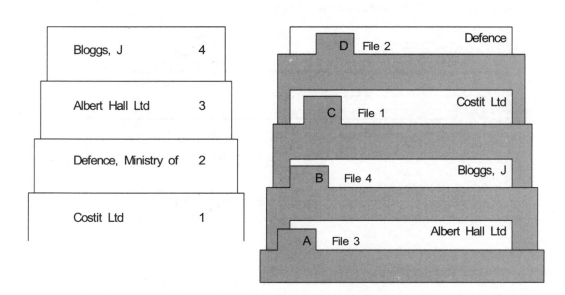

3.4 Alpha-numeric classification

In an **alpha-numeric system**, files are given a reference consisting of **letters** and **numbers**. For example a letter received from Mr Blotson about the purchase of a flat in Mayfair might be given the reference BLO/8745/99/1.

(a)   The system uses the first three letters of the correspondent's name and a number to distinguish him from anybody else called Blotson and/or to indicate that the subject matter is domestic property. The number 99 indicates that this correspondence began in 1999.

(b)   The 1 shows that it is the first file which has anything to do with this subject. If Mr Blotson's property deal fell through but he then found another flat, the correspondence relating to this would be kept in the separate but related file BLO/8745/99/2.

A system like this is most useful where there is a very large volume of correspondence on different but related topics. The Civil Service, for example, uses a system along these lines.

3.5 Other classifications

Using any of the above systems, bear in mind that you could group your files in any logical way. Common examples include:

(a)   **Subject classification**, where all material relating to a particular subject (client, contract, project, product and so on) is kept together. (You just need to title your subjects thoughtfully, otherwise you end up with a lot of 'miscellaneous' items that do not fit your subject categories)

(b)   **Geographical classification**, which is useful for sales, import/export and similar activities that may be organised by region or territory

Here is an example of geographical files, sub-classified by subject, in alphabetical order.

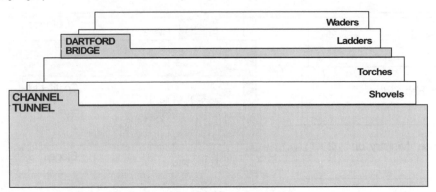

Activity 9.2

Listed below are details of thirty people who have written to your organisation.

	Name and address	Account	Date
1	Cottrell J, 5 Heathview Avenue, Bromley	–	2.6.96
2	Holden R, 27 Exning Road, Bexley	–	13.7.95
3	Williams J, 29 Gray Gardens, Dartford	100276	5.4.97
4	Bidwell D, 176 High Road, Dartford	–	16.5.98
5	Bexley J, 25 Romney Road, Orpington	400452	17.5.95

6	Maclean T, 1 Pitt Road, Orpington	400721	7.12.98
7	54321 Discos, 107 Warren Road, Bexley	300924	19.4.99
8	Dr J Crown, 20 Wimfred Street, Woolwich	–	1.1.96
9	Locke D, 22 Davis Street, Crayford	–	14.8.98
10	Sainton E, 15 Filmwell Close, Bromley	200516	3.5.99
11	Argent-Smith M, 17a Waterson Road, Bexley	–	7.8.99
12	Britton T, 81 Ward Avenue, Crayford	–	27.8.97
13	McLaughlin D, 80 Brookhill Road, Orpington	200435	4.3.97
14	Williams J A, 148 Godstow Road, Woolwich	–	6.6.99
15	O'Grady E, 40 Holborne Road, Sidcup	300989	4.4.94
16	Saint Francis Pet Shop, 14 Glenesh Road, Dartford	–	7.9.97
17	Emly P, 8 Faraday Avenue, Orpington	–	18.4.99
18	Harry Holden Ltd, 5 Clare Way, Bexley	100284	9.7.97
19	BRJ Plumbing, 132 Lodge Lane, Crayford	200223	25.11.98
20	Gisling B, 18 Dickens Avenue, Woolwich	–	6.3.99
21	Argentson S, 20 Porson Court, Dartford	400542	5.2.95
22	Kelsey L C, 58 Cudham Lane, Bromley	–	8.1.98
23	ILD Services Ltd, 4 Cobden Road, Orpington	200221	3.2.99
24	Van Saintby A, 69 Brookhill Close, Bromley	400693	5.2.99
25	Williams, John, 10 Buff Close, Dartford	–	2.12.98
26	Page W, 11 Leewood Place, Crayford	400442	9.7.96
27	Harrison P, Robinwood Drive, Dartford	101301	16.4.98
28	Briton N, 3 Chalet Close, Bexley	–	7.2.95
29	Richmond A, 9 Denham Close, Crayford	–	4.1.99
30	St Olave's Church, Church Way, Bromley	400371	21.2.98

Tasks

(a)   Referring to the documents by number (1-30), in what order would they appear if they were filed in date order?

(b)   Rearrange the names in alphabetical order, noting the reference number in brackets after the name.

(c)   In what order would those correspondents with accounts appear if they were filed in account number order?

(d)   Again referring to the documents by number, identify another sensible way of classifying them, and arrange them in this order.

Tutorial note. Use coloured highlighter pens!

4 Storing documents securely

4.1 Environment

It is vital that material containing information is stored in an appropriate location and that its condition does not deteriorate.

Documents containing information may be classified and indexed so that they are easily accessible, but unless they can be kept in **good condition**, with **economy of storage space and cost**, they will not fulfil our requirements for an effective and efficient filing system.

4.2 Keeping documents in good condition

Paper can very easily get screwed up, torn, stained, or otherwise damaged. This can result in its contents becoming difficult to read or even getting lost. For example tearing off the edge of a misaligned print-out could easily result in the final column of figures being thrown away.

Punching holes in a document so that it can be placed in some form of ring binder also needs to be carefully done so that vital numbers or words are not affected. A sensible way of achieving this is shown below.

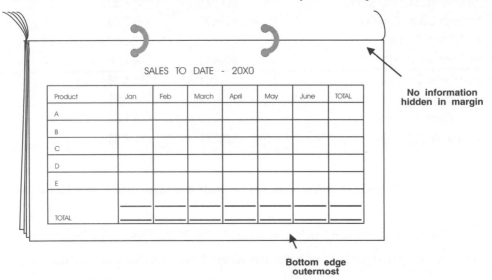

If **a file is too 'fat'** there is every likelihood that pages will get torn, fall out and get lost because of the difficulty of opening the file and keeping it open at the right page. If you need to be violent with a file it is not serving its purpose; you will be less inclined to consult the file and you run the risk of damaging its contents.

Obviously it is better not to let files get too fat in the first place, but if it is too late the best solution is to move some of the documents into a second volume. This may involve re-indexing the file or changing its title and altering any cross-references that have been made in the file itself or in other files.

Liquid and paper are not good friends: don't leave your coffee cup or your glass of water in places where you or somebody else is liable to knock them over.

4.3 Location

Most documents containing information will have to be placed in **folders** or **binders** before they can be housed in filing cabinets or other forms of storage. These come in a suitable range of sizes (for small pieces of paper or large computer printouts) and materials.

Plastic folders or **paper envelope (manila) folders** are the most common and cheapest methods. For larger volumes of information, there are **lever arch files** and **box files**. If information is to be kept for a long time but not referred to very frequently, then box files are useful. If they are to be referred to and updated more often, ring binders or lever arch files would provide security (there would be no loose bits of paper flying about) and accessibility.

4.4 Storage equipment

The following items of equipment are commonly used to store information.

- In-trays
- Pigeon-holes
- Filing cabinets
- Safes

An **in-tray** is a tray which lies horizontally, and is used to capture incoming documentation. If you have your own in-tray at work, you will know that it is best to sort through new information on a regular basis! When sorting through an in-tray it is usual to group documents which are **ready for filing, awaiting action**, or **for distribution**.

The main purpose of an in-tray is therefore **temporary storage** of information.

A **pigeon-hole** is very similar to an in-tray, but incoming documents are held in an upright, rather than a horizontal, position. In general, any incoming mail which is marked for your attention is placed in the first instance in your pigeon-hole. It is therefore also used as a **temporary store** for information.

Files containing information may be stored in an assortment of **filing cabinets**. The two main types of filing cabinet are **vertical suspension** and **lateral suspension**. The type of cabinet used will depend upon the space available in the office for such equipment, and the type of information to be stored.

4.5 Safes

A **safe** is a strong lockable cabinet which is used to store confidential or valuable information.

Most offices have some means of storing confidential or sensitive information. Safes normally have a **combination code** which must be entered correctly before they can be opened, and this code is normally known by one or two senior members of staff only.

Activity 9.3

Have a look around your office at work and look for examples of the different types of equipment that are used for storing and retrieving information.

4.6 Microfilm and microfiche

Microfilming is a particularly convenient means of information storage for saving space. Documents are photographed into a very much reduced ('micro') form. Microfilms are readable, but not to the unassisted naked eye, and a magnifying reading device (with a viewing screen) is needed by users. **Microfilm** is itself a **continuous strip** with images in frames along its length (like a photographic negative).

Micro film

Micro fiche

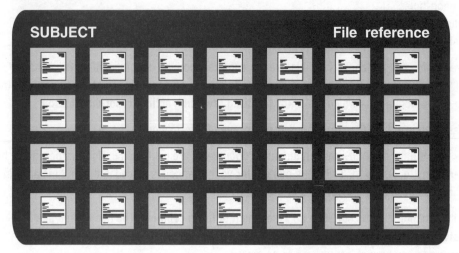

Microfiche is another method of storing information, but consists of **separate sheets of film**, rather than being a continuous strip like microfilm is. Microfiche is read by placing the fiche between two glass plates and moving a pointer (which is attached to the lens) across a grid. If you have never used a microfiche reader, see whether your local library has one, and have a practice.

Microfilm and microfiche need **special devices** in order to be read, updated or corrected. (If your organisation has 'computer aided retrieval' readers, see if you can get some coaching and practice on one.) However, they do offer very space-saving, durable and secure information storage.

4.7 File security and confidentiality

If files are **confidential** or **secret**, they will be 'classified', which means that access will be limited to authorised people. A list of classified files will be required and a policy must be drawn up stipulating **conditions of access** (for example who keeps the keys to the security cabinet, and whether files may be copied or taken out of the filing room) and specifying who has clearance to consult classified material.

Circumstances in which files may become classified include the following.

(a) Where they contain **information of a personal nature**, for example personnel files, files about customers' credit status or (in a solicitor's office, say) details of a client's domestic circumstances.

(b) Where they contain **product or service information** which may be exploited by a competitor, like designs or marketing programmes.

(c) Where they contain **information concerning legal or financial deals**, the outcome of which could be affected by public knowledge of the details (for example when companies are considering merging or one is trying to take over another).

You can probably think of information which is '**sensitive**' in your organisation in that it could be misused to the organisation's disadvantage if it got into the wrong hands. If you are working on a 'classified' file, or if you have any reason to think documents in your possession may be of a sensitive nature, take care.

(a) Do not leave them lying around on your desk. **Put them away out of sight** when you are not using them, and lock them up if you have to leave your desk.

(b) Do not forget to **lock up secure cabinets** when you have finished with them, and return the keys to the authorised holder.

(c) **Do not send out copies** of potentially confidential material without checking with a superior that it is safe to do so.

(d) Do not leave confidential documents in the photocopier!

(e) **Respect the privacy of others**, just as you would expect them to respect yours.

Activity 9.4

Your manager is out of the office. He has phoned in and asked you to find a letter which is 'somewhere' on his desk and fax through a copy to him.

As you are searching for the letter you notice the following documents.

1 An electricity bill for £372.97 addressed to D Glover (your manager) at his home address.

2 A letter from a building society asking for a reference for one of your firm's clients.

3 A report entitled 'Potential Merger - Initial considerations'.

4 A mass of figures with your organisation's name at the head and the title 'Draft Budget'.

5 A staff appraisal report about you.

6 A thick sheaf of correspondence - the top sheet is signed 'Love, Nancy'.

7 A letter from P Glover asking for details about your organisation's services.

8 A *very* strongly worded letter of complaint from a Mrs Paribus.

9 A series of cuttings about your organisation from a trade journal.

10 A list of your organisation's directors with their addresses, telephone numbers and ages noted alongside.

Tasks

(a)   Identify which, if any, of these documents you think should be filed away confidentially. Give reasons.

(b)   Suppose that the letter that you had to fax was document 8 above. What would you do?

Key learning points

☑ Information is generally held on **files**. **Filing** is an integral part of creating information.

☑ A file is a collection of data records with similar characteristics. Files of data may be **temporary**, **permanent**, **active or non-active**.

☑ Characteristics of a **'good' file** are as follows.

   – It should contain all the information you may need
   – The information should be found easily
   – It should be of a convenient size
   – It should be capable of expansion
   – It should be easily accessible
   – It should be stored under suitable conditions so that it won't get damaged or lose its information

☑ An **index** is something which makes it easier to locate information or records.

☑ **Cross-referencing** information is commonly carried out when items of information could be filed in more than one place, or could be needed in connection with more than one enquiry.

☑ The three main systems for **classifying information** are **alphabetical**, **numerical** and **alpha-numerical**.

Quick quiz

1   A file is a collection of _____ with similar characteristics. *Complete the blank*
2   List four systems used for arranging files.
3   What procedures might be followed when adding new information to a filing system?
4   How is information that is no longer needed on a regular basis dealt with?
5   What are classified files?

Note: Questions 3 and 4 are revision of material from Units 1 and 2.

Answers to quick quiz

1   A collection of **data records** with similar characteristics.
2   Alphabetical order, numerical order, alpha-numerical, chronological order.
3   Indicate that document is ready for filing, remove any paperclips and binders, place documents at random in a filing tray, determine a reference number for the document if it does not already have one, determine into which file the document is to be inserted, sort batches of documents and insert into appropriate place in appropriate files.
4   • Microfilmed or microfiched
    • Archived
    • Destroyed
5   Confidential or secret.

Activity checklist

This checklist shows which performance criteria, range statement or knowledge and understanding point is covered by each activity in this chapter. Tick off each activity as you complete it.

Activity

9.1   [ ]   This activity deals with knowledge and understanding point 21: organisational procedures for filing source information.

9.2   [ ]   This activity deals with performance criteria 3.2.F.

9.3   [ ]   This activity deals with knowledge and understanding point 21 with regard to your own organisation.

9.4   [ ]   This activity deals with performance criteria 3.2.F.

PART E

Answers to Activities

Answers to activities

Chapter 1

Answer 1.1

Transaction	Dr £	Cr £
Owner puts £500 into the business	Cash £500	Capital £500
Cash sales of £1,000	Cash £1,000	Sales £1,000
Purchases of £2,500 made on credit	Purchases £2,500	Creditors £2,500
Credit sales made totalling £5,000	Debtors £5,000	Sales £5,000
£2,000 received from debtor	Cash £2,000	Debtors £2,000
Business expenses paid of £750	Expenses £750	Cash £750
Drawing made of £1,000	Drawings £1,000	Cash £1,000

Note: Instead of debtors, you may have used the Sales Ledger Control Account and instead of creditors, you may have used the Purchase Ledger Control Account. If so, well done. We will be looking at Control Accounts in more detail in Part B.

Answer 1.2

(a)   A balance sheet is a statement of the liabilities, capital and assets of a business at a given moment in time. It is like a 'snapshot' photograph, since it captures on paper a still image, frozen at a single moment in time, of something which is continually changing. The balance sheet will usually show the position on the date which is the end of the **accounting period** of the business; an accounting period is usually one year.

(b)   (i)   **Fixed assets** are assets acquired for use within the business, rather than for selling to a customer. It must have a 'life' in use of more than one year.

      (ii)   **Current assets** are:

- Items owned by the business with the intention of turning them into cash within one year
- Cash, including money in the bank, owned by the business

(c)   (i)   **Current liabilities** are debts of the business that must be paid within a year. This will normally include the bank overdraft, as overdrafts are repayable on demand unless special terms are negotiated.

      (ii)   **Long-term liabilities** are debts which are not payable until some time after one year from the accounting date.

Answer 1.3

Revenue expenditure is the purchase of goods and services that will:

(a)   Be used fully in the accounting period in which they are purchased, and so be a cost or expense in the profit and loss account

(b)   Result in a current asset as at the end of the accounting period (because the goods or services have not yet been used or sold)

Capital expenditure is the purchase or improvement of fixed assets. These assets will provide benefits to the business in more than one accounting period and are not acquired to be resold in the normal course of trade. The cost of purchasing fixed assets is not charged in full to the profit and loss account. Instead, the fixed asset is gradually depreciated in the profit and loss accounts of a number of accounting periods. (Depreciation is dealt with later in your studies, in Unit 5.)

Since revenue items and capital items are accounted for in different ways, the correct and consistent calculation of profit for any accounting period depends on the correct and consistent classification of items as revenue or capital.

Answer 1.4

Tutorial note. The profit of £14,000 in the profit and loss account should be the balancing figure in the balance sheet.

SPOCK ENTERPRISES
BALANCE SHEET AS AT 30 APRIL 20X7

	£	£
Fixed assets		
Freehold premises		87,500
Fixtures and fittings		14,000
Motor vehicles		15,750
		117,250
Current assets		
Stocks	28,000	
Debtors	875	
Cash	700	
	29,575	
Current liabilities		
Bank overdraft	3,500	
Creditors	3,150	
Tax payable	6,125	
	12,775	
Net current assets		16,800
Total assets less current liabilities		134,050
Long-term liabilities		
Loan		43,750
Net assets		90,300
Capital		
Capital as at 1 May 20X6		76,300
Profit for the year		14,000
Capital as at 30 April 20X7		90,300

SPOCK ENTERPRISES
TRADING, PROFIT AND LOSS ACCOUNT
FOR THE YEAR ENDED 30 APRIL 20X7

	£	£
Sales		243,775
Cost of sales		152,425
Gross profit		91,350
Other income		3,500
		94,850
Selling and distribution expenses	25,725	
Administration expenses	25,900	
Finance expenses	29,225	
		80,850
Net profit		14,000

Answer 1.5

You would normally expect the following documents to be involved in such a transaction.

- (a) A letter of enquiry
- (b) A quotation
- (c) An order or letter of acceptance
- (d) An order acknowledgement
- (e) A delivery note
- (f) An invoice
- (g) A warranty or guarantee for the work performed (normally for a specified period of time)

Answer 1.6

Tutorial note. A trade discount is used to calculate the price at which goods change hands. In this question the price of the goods was £3,000 less a £600 trade discount, giving £2,400. The cash discount is then calculated on this figure, ie 5% of £2,400 = £120.

	£
60 toasters @ £50 each	3,000
Less 20% trade discount	600
Trade price	2,400
Less 5% settlement discount (if taken)	120
	2,280

- (a) From the above, if payment is made within 14 days, the total Smith Electrical would pay is £2,280.

- (b) If payment is not made within 14 days, Smith Electrical can not take advantage of the cash discount and so would pay £2,400.

Answer 1.7

(a)

	£
Net amount (25 × £10)	250.00
Discount (5% × £250)	(12.50)
Net amount after discount	237.50
VAT @ 17.5% on £237.50	41.56

(b)

	£
Net amount (5 × £10)	50.00
Discount (5% × £50)	(2.50)
Net amount after discount	47.50
VAT @ 17.5% on £47.50	8.31

Remember VAT is **always** charged on the discounted price, even if the discount is not taken. Therefore VAT on any credit note should also be based on the full discounted price.

Chapter 2

Answer 2.1

(a)   Cash book
(b)   Sales day book
(c)   Purchase day book
(d)   Cash book
(e)   Sales returns day book
(f)   Purchase returns day book
(g)   Cash book

Answer 2.2

(a)   The two sides of the transaction are:

   (i)   Cash is received (debit cash account).
   (ii)   Sales increase by £60 (**credit** sales account).

CASH ACCOUNT

		£		£
07.04.X7	Sales a/c	60		

PROFESSIONAL EDUCATION

SALES ACCOUNT

			£
	07.04.X7	Cash a/c	60

(b) The two sides of the transaction are:
    (i) Cash is paid (**credit** cash account).
    (ii) Rent expense increases by £4,500 (**debit** rent account).

CASH ACCOUNT

	£			£
		07.04.X7	Rent a/c	4,500

RENT ACCOUNT

		£		£
07.04.X7	Cash a/c	4,500		

(c) The two sides of the transaction are:
    (i) Cash is paid (credit cash account).
    (ii) Purchases increase by £3,000 (debit purchases account).

CASH ACCOUNT

	£			£
		07.04.X7	Purchases a/c	3,000

PURCHASES ACCOUNT

		£		£
07.04.X7	Cash a/c	3,000		

(d) The two sides of the transaction are:
    (i) Cash is paid (credit cash account).
    (ii) Assets – in this case, shelves - increase by £6,000 (debit shelves account).

CASH ACCOUNT

	£			£
		07.04.X7	Shelves a/c	6,000

SHELVES (ASSET) ACCOUNT

		£		£
07.04.X7	Cash a/c	6,000		

Tutorial note. If all four of these transactions related to the same business, the cash account of that business would end up looking as follows.

CASH ACCOUNT

		£			£
07.04.X7	Sales a/c	60	07.04.X7	Rent a/c	4,500
				Purchases a/c	3,000
				Shelves a/c	6,000

Answer 2.3

(a)	DEBIT	Machine (fixed asset)	£8,000	
	CREDIT	Creditors (A)		£8,000
(b)	DEBIT	Purchases	£500	
	CREDIT	Creditors (B)		£500
(c)	DEBIT	Debtors (C)	£1,200	
	CREDIT	Sales		£1,200
(d)	DEBIT	Creditors (D)	£300	
	CREDIT	Cash		£300
(e)	DEBIT	Cash	£180	
	CREDIT	Debtors (E)		£180
(f)	DEBIT	Wages expense	£4,000	
	CREDIT	Cash		£4,000
(g)	DEBIT	Rent expense	£700	
	CREDIT	Creditors (G)		£700
(h)	DEBIT	Creditors (G)	£700	
	CREDIT	Cash		£700
(i)	DEBIT	Insurance expense	£90	
	CREDIT	Cash		£90

Answer 2.4

	Original document	Book of prime entry	Accounts in main ledger to be posted to	
			Dr	Cr
(a)	Sales invoice	Sales day book	Debtors	Sales
(b)	Credit note	Sales returns day book	Sales/Returns inward	Debtors
(c)	Till rolls and/or sales invoices and receipts, bank paying-in book	Cash book	Cash	Sales

All these transactions would be entered into the double entry system by means of periodic postings from the books of prime entry to the main ledger.

Answer 2.5

	Main ledger		Subsidiary ledger	
	Dr	*Cr*	*Dr*	*Cr*
(a)	PLCA	Cash	PL – Jones	-
(b)	Purchases	PLCA	-	PL – Davis Wholesalers Ltd
(c)	PLCA	Purchases	PL – K Williams	-
(d)	Fixtures a/c	Cash	-	-
(e)	Fixtures a/c	Cash	-	-
(f)	Cash	Sales	-	-
(g)	SLCA	Sales	SL – R Newman	-
(h)	Insurance a/c	Cash	-	-
(i)	SLCA	Cash	SL – J Baxter	-

SLCA = Sales ledger control account
PLCA = Purchase ledger control account
SL = Sales ledger
PL = Purchase ledger

Answer 2.6

(a) *Purchase of goods on credit*

    (i)   The supplier's invoice would be the original document.
    (ii)   The original entry would be made in the purchase day book.
    (iii) The entries made would be:

    DEBIT   Purchases
    CREDIT   Purchase ledger control account

(b) *Allowances to credit customers on the return of faulty goods*

    (i)   The usual documentation is a credit note.
    (ii)   The book of original entry would be the sales returns day book.
    (iii) The double entry would be:

    DEBIT   Sales (or sales returns)
    CREDIT   Sales ledger control account/individual debtor's account in the sales ledger

(c) *Petty cash reimbursement*

    (i)   The original documents for the data would be receipts and a petty cash voucher.

(ii)   The transaction would be entered in the petty cash book.

(iii)   The double entry would be:

DEBIT   Entertaining expenses
CREDIT   Petty cash

Chapter 3

Answer 3.1

(a)   **Sheet number 72**. The bank numbers each statement sheet issued for the account. Transactions from 1 March 20X7 onwards will be shown on statement number 73, and so on. Numbering the statements in this way allows the customer to check that none of its bank statements are missing.

(b)   **Bank giro credit**. The bank giro credit system enables money to be paid in to any bank for the credit of a third party's account at another bank. Pronto Motors has paid in £162.40 for the credit of Gary Jones Trading's account at Southern Bank. A bank giro credit may take around two or three days for the banks to process.

(c)   **£59.03 OD**. This shows that there is a debit balance (an overdraft) of £59.03 at the bank on 11 February 20X7. Gary Jones Trading is at that point a *debtor* of the bank; the bank is a *creditor* of Gary Jones Trading.

(d)   **Direct debit**. Swingate Ltd must have authority (by means of a direct debit mandate signed on behalf of Gary Jones Trading Ltd) to take a direct debit from its account. This arrangement allows payments to be made to a third party without a cheque having to be sent.

(e)   **Bank charges**. The bank may make various charges to cover its costs in providing bank services to the customer. The bank will be able to explain how its charges are calculated.

Answer 3.2

CASH BOOK

Receipts			Payments		
Date	Details		Date	Details	
20X7		£	*20X7*		£
	Balance b/d	596.74	21 Feb	Swingate	121.00
23 Feb	Bord & Sons	194.60	28 Feb	Bank charges	15.40
			28 Feb	Balance c/d	654.94
		791.34			791.34

Answer 3.3

GARY JONES TRADING LIMITED
BANK RECONCILIATION STATEMENT AS AT 28 FEBRUARY 20X7

	£	£
Balance per bank statement		611.93
Add outstanding lodgement (Warleys Ltd)		342.50
		954.43
Less: unpresented cheques		
800124	207.05	
800125	92.44	
		(299.49)
Balance per cash book		654.94

Answer 3.4

(a) (i) CASH BOOK

	£		£
Uncorrected balance b/d	24.13	Overdraft interest	24.88
Error in cash book	27.00	Balance c/d	26.25
	51.13		51.13

(ii) GEMFIX ENGINEERING LIMITED
BANK RECONCILIATION STATEMENT AS AT 31 OCTOBER 20X7

	£
Balance as per bank statement (overdrawn)	(142.50)
Less unpresented cheques (total)	(121.25)
	(263.75)
Add cheque paid in, not yet credited on bank statement	290.00
Balance as per cash book	26.25

(b) There are three reasons why bank reconciliation statements should be prepared regularly and on time.

(i) The company's records should be updated for items such as bank charges and dishonoured cheques so that managers are not working with an incorrect figure for the bank balance.

(ii) Errors should be identified and corrected as soon as possible, whether they are made by the company or by the bank.

(iii) Checks should be made on the time delay between cheques being written and their presentation for payment, and to check the time taken for cheques and cash paid in to be credited to the account. A better understanding of such timing differences will help managers to improve their cash planning.

Answer 3.5

(a)

CASH BOOK

Date 20X0	Details	Bank £	Date 20X0	Cheque No	Details	Bank £
1 Sept	Balance b/f	13,400	1 Sept	108300	J Hibbert	1,200
1 Sept	L Peters	400	5 Sept	108301	Cleanglass	470
28 Sept	John Smith	2,400	25 Sept	108302	Denham Insurers	630
29 Sept	KKG Ltd	144	29 Sept	108303	Kelvin Ltd	160
8 Sept	Zebra Sales	4,000			Salaries	9,024
30 Sept	Bristol Ltd	2,000			West Council	300
					Any Bank	400
					Bank charges	132
					Balance c/d	10,028
		22,344				22,344
	Balance b/d	10,028				

(b)   BANK RECONCILIATION AT 30 SEPTEMBER 20X0

	£
Balance per bank statement	8,114
Less unpresented cheque 108302	(630)
	7,484
Add uncleared receipts (2,400 + 144)	2,544
Balance per cash book	10,028

Chapter 4

Answer 4.1

SALES LEDGER CONTROL ACCOUNT

		£			£
Debit balances b/d	(1)	X	Credit balances b/d	(1)	X
Sales	(2)	X	Cash receipts	(3)	X
Bank (refunds)	(3) or (5)	X	Credit notes	(4)	X
Bank (dishonoured cheques)	(3) or (5)	X	Bad debt expense	(5)	X
Credit balances c/d	(6)	X	Discount allowed*	(3)	X
			Debit balances c/d	(6)	X
		X			X

Sources of entries

    (1)   Brought down from previous period's control account once closed off.
    (2)   Sales day book.
    (3)   Cash book and petty cash book.
    (4)   Sales returns day book.
    (5)   Journal.
    (6)   Calculated and reconciled with sales ledger total of balances.

Tutorial note

*   Discounts allowed reflects only cash or settlement discounts, not trade discounts.

** Individual entries to the account would be dated and would have folio references to the appropriate book of prime entry/journal. These details have been omitted for the purposes of clarity.

Answer 4.2

ITEMS NOT APPEARING IN THE SALES LEDGER CONTROL ACCOUNT

1 and 2 Credit and debit balances on individual debtor account

Individual debtors accounts do not appear in the sales ledger control account, although the transactions which give rise to them (sales, cash receipts etc) do. The sales ledger control account is a total account.

3 Cash sales

The sales ledger control account deals with sales made on credit. Cash sales (*Debit* Cash; *Credit* Sales) have nothing to do with it.

5 Provision for bad and doubtful debts

This is a *separate account* from the sales ledger control account, even though it has the overall effect of reducing the value of the assets represented by the sales ledger control account.

7 Trade discounts received

These are discounts on what has been purchased, so have nothing to do with sales.

11 Credit notes received

These have the effect of reducing what *we* owe to other people, so they have nothing to do with the sales ledger control account.

ITEMS THAT DO APPEAR IN THE SALES LEDGER CONTROL ACCOUNT

4 Sales on credit

This should need no explaining.

6 Settlement discounts allowed

A settlement discount is given to a debtor who pays early, and so reduces the value of the debt. If someone owes £100, but you say that you'll reduce the amount to £95 if they pay within 2 weeks, then you have given a settlement discount of £5. The whole of the original debt is cleared - of the £100 owed, your customer has paid £95, and you have basically written off £5 to the profit and loss account.

8 Cash receipts

These are payments from debtors. They reduce the debt.

9 Bad debts written off

Writing off a bad debt involves removing the debt from the sales ledger and making a corresponding entry to the sales ledger control account, and then the profit and loss account.

10 Sales returns

These arise when sold goods are returned and the return is accepted. The debtor no longer owes the money, so the debt is cancelled. Sales returns would be posted from the sales returns day book as a total, a method similar to the way in which total sales are posted from the sales day book.

12 Credit notes issued

A credit note can be issued to reduce the value of the debt. This might be the result of a sales return, or correction of an error. (Note that if separate records of sales returns are processed, credit notes would only be processed in respect of other items, so as to avoid any double counting.)

Answer 4.3

SLCA

		£			£
1.10.X1	Balance b/f (b)	30,000	15.1.X2	Bad debts-Fall Ltd (c)	2,000
30.9.X2	Sales (d)	187,800	30.9.X2	Cash (e)	182,500
				Discounts allowed (f)	5,300
				Bad debts (g)	3,500
				Balance c/d	24,500
		217,800			217,800
1.10.X2	Balance b/d	24,500			

SALES ACCOUNT

		£			£
30.9.X2	Trading P & L a/c	234,600	30.9.X2	Cash (d)	46,800
				SLCA (d)	187,800
		234,600			234,600

BAD DEBTS ACCOUNT

		£			£
15.1.X2	SLCA-Fall Ltd (c)	2,000	30.9.X2	Trading P & L a/c	5,500
30.9.X2	SLCA (g)	3,500			
		5,500			5,500

PROVISION FOR DOUBTFUL DEBTS ACCOUNT

		£				£
30.9.X2	Balance c/d (h) 5% × £24,500 Trading P & L a/c - reduction in provision	1,225 275	1.10.X1	Balance b/f (b) 5% × £30,000		1,500
		1,500				1,500
			1.10.X2	Balance b/d		1,225

DISCOUNTS ALLOWED ACCOUNT

		£			£
30.9.X2	SLCA(f)	5,300	30.9.X2	Trading P & L a/c	5,300

CASH ACCOUNT (EXTRACT)

		£	
30.9.X2	SLCA(e) Sales(d)	182,500 46,800	

TRADING PROFIT AND LOSS (EXTRACT)

		£			£
30.9.X2	Bad debts Discounts allowed	5,500 5,300	30.9.X2	Sales Provision for doubtful debts	234,600 275

Answer 4.4

(a) UNADJUSTED SALES LEDGER CONTROL ACCOUNT

	£		£
Balance b/d	12,404.86	Balance b/d	322.94
Sales	96,464.41	Returns inwards	1,142.92
Bank: cheques dishonoured	192.00	Bank	94,648.71
Balance c/d	337.75	Discounts allowed	3,311.47
		Balance c/d	9,972.98
	109,399.02		109,399.02
Balance b/d	9,972.98	Balance b/d	337.75

(b) ADJUSTED SALES LEDGER CONTROL ACCOUNT

	£		£
Unadjusted balance b/d	9,972.98	Unadjusted balance b/d	337.75
Sales: receipts from cash sales		Bad debt written off	77.00
wrongly credited to debtors	3,440.00	Returns outwards: returns to	
Sales day book undercast	427.80	suppliers wrongly debited to	
Balance c/d	337.75	debtors	3,711.86
		Balance c/d	10,051.92
	14,178.53		14,178.53
Balance b/d	10,051.92	Balance b/d	337.75

Supernova Ltd has debtors of £10,051.92. It also has a creditor of £337.75.

Errors (v) and (vi) relate to entries in **individual customer accounts** in the sales ledger and have no effect on the control account in the main ledger.

Answer 4.5

(a)   SALES LEDGER CONTROL

		£			£
1.12.X6	Balance b/d	50,241	20X7	Returns inwards	41,226
20X7	Sales	472,185		Bad debts written off	1,914
	Cheques dishonoured	626		Discounts allowed	2,672
				Cheques received	429,811
			30.11	Balance c/d	47,429
		523,052			523,052

(b)

	£	£
Balance per P Johnson		46,347
Add: Whitchurch Ltd invoice, previously omitted from ledger	267	
Rectofon Ltd balance, previously omitted from list	2,435	
Casting error in list total (£46,747, not £46,347)	400	
		3,102
		49,449
Less: Error on posting of Bury plc's credit note to ledger	20	
P Fox & Son (Swindon) Ltd's balance included twice	2,000	
		2,020
Balance per sales ledger control account		47,429

Chapter 5

Answer 5.1

Answer C is correct.

Helping hand. Computerisation has meant that a number of different ways of processing creditors can be implemented. Some of these you might encounter in your work. Two examples are given below.

(a)   A separate purchase ledger module is *not* maintained. There is no purchase ledger control account. Instead there is a separate account for every creditor in the main ledger.

(b)   A separate purchase ledger module is maintained, but the role of the purchase day book is different in that each invoice is posted individually to the purchase ledger control account, VAT account, and purchase ledger account (ie the posting to the purchase ledger control account is not on a summary basis). The control account is still only a total account, however.

The use of the purchase day book and the purchase ledger, as separate from the main ledger to which summary postings are made, is merely for *convenience*.

Answer 5.2

(a)   All of them.

    (i)   Not all cash payments are to trade creditors, so a payment could be given a wrong main ledger account code.

    (ii)   These could be found in a manual system, or could be caused by a fault in a computer program.

    (iii)   Transposition errors could be caused if the purchase ledger, main ledger and purchase day book were separate, and there were manual postings.

(b)   (i)   Dividend payments and (iii) drawings do not relate in any way to trade creditors.

(c)   FALSE. You might overpay a supplier, or pay before the goods have been received and invoiced, or pay the wrong supplier.

Answer 5.3

FALSE

In any accounting system, whether computerised or manual, accounts can be altered by use of the journal. It would be quite possible to make adjustments to the purchase ledger control account which, for whatever reason, are not reflected in the purchase ledger. So, while the purchase ledger updates the purchase ledger control account, there might be other differences.

It depends on which type of accounting system is used.

Answer 5.4

WALLACE AND GROMMET
RECONCILIATION OF PURCHASE LEDGER BALANCES WITH THE PURCHASE LEDGER CONTROL ACCOUNT AS AT 31 JULY 20X7

		£	£
(a)	Balances according to purchase ledger		54,842.40
	Add: Account omitted (a)	8,300.00	
	RNH's account undercast (c)	620.40	
			8,920.40
			63,762.80
	Deduct: Cheque not debited to SPL's account (f)	5,000.00	
	Contra arrangement omitted (h)	400.00	
			5,400.00
	Amended balance as at 31 July 20X7		58,362.80

Tutorial note. The cheque for £5,000 is deducted. If it had been properly debited in the first place it would have **reduced** SPL's balance.

		£	£
(b)	Balance according to the purchase ledger control account		57,997.34
	Add: Discounts received entered twice (g)	740.36	
	Purchases for June (b)	7,449.60	
			8,189.96
			66,187.30
	Deduct: Vehicle erroneously entered as purchases (d)	6,400.00	
	Returns outward omitted from account (e)	1,424.50	
			7,824.50
	Amended balance as at 31 July 20X7		58,362.80

Chapter 6

Answer 6.1

PETTY CASH CONTROL

Date 20X1	Details	£	Date 20X1	Details	£
1 Aug	Balance b/f	214	31 Aug	Petty cash	196
31 Aug	Bank	200	31 Aug	Balance c/d	218
		414			414
1 Sept	Balance b/d	218			

RECONCILIATION

	£
Balance per petty cash control account	218
Cash in hand	212
Discrepancy (to be investigated)	£6

Answer 6.2

	£
Balance per petty cash control account (as above)	218
Less: payment omitted from the analysis	(4)
Balance of cash in hand per accounts	214
Cash in hand (as above)	212
IOU omitted	2
Balance of cash in hand	214

Chapter 7

Answer 7.1

SUSPENSE ACCOUNT

	£		£
Balance b/d	5,607.82	Insurance	1,327.40
		Bad debt expense	428.52
		Purchases (£5,926.38 – £5,296.38)	630.00
		Motor vehicles (£1,610.95 □ 2)	3,221.90
	5,607.82		5,607.82

Tutorial note. The van should be **debited** to the motor vehicles account, but it has been credited in error. Therefore we need **two debit** entries in the **motor vehicles account** – one to cancel the original posting and the second to complete the correct double entry. The two credit entries are to suspense.

Answer 7.2

		£	£
DEBIT	Insurance	1,327.40	
	Bad debt expense	428.52	
	Purchases	630.00	
	Motor vehicles	3,221.90	
CREDIT	Suspense account		5,607.82

Correction of errors and clearance of suspense account.

Chapter 8

Answer 8.1

(a) The relevant books of prime entry are the cash book, the sales day book and the purchase day book.

CASH BOOK (RECEIPTS)

Date June	Narrative	Total £	Capital £	Sales £	Debtors £	Suspense £
1	Capital	10,000	10,000			
13	Sales	310		310		
16	Waterhouses	1,200			1,200	
24	Books & Co	350			350	
30	Unknown receipt	500				500
		12,360	10,000	310	1,550	500

CASH BOOK (PAYMENTS)

Date June	Narrative	Total £	Fixtures and fittings £	Creditors £	Rent £	Delivery expenses £	Drawings £	Wages £
1	Warehouse Fittings Ltd	3,500	3,500					
19	Ransome House	820		820				
20	Rent	300			300			
21	Delivery expenses	75				75		
30	Drawings	270					270	
30	Wages	400						400
30	Big, White	450		450				
		5,815	3,500	1,270	300	75	270	400

SALES DAY BOOK

Date June	Customer	Amount £
4	Waterhouses	1,200
11	Books & Co	740
18	R S Jones	500
		2,440

PURCHASE DAY BOOK

Date June	Supplier	Amount £
2	Ransome House	820
9	Big, White	450
17	RUP Ltd	1,000
		2,270

(b) and (c)

The relevant ledger accounts are for cash, sales, purchases, creditors, debtors, capital, fixtures and fittings, rent, delivery expenses, drawings and wages.

CASH ACCOUNT

	£		£
June receipts	12,360	June payments	5,815
		Balance c/d	6,545
	12,360		12,360
Balance b/d	6,545		

SALES ACCOUNT

	£		£
		Cash	310
Balance c/d	2,750	SLCA	2,440
	2,750		2,750
		Balance b/d	2,750

PURCHASES ACCOUNT

	£		£
PLCA	2,270	Balance c/d	2,270
Balance b/d	2,270		

SLCA

	£		£
Sales	2,440	Cash	1,550
		Balance c/d	890
	2,440		2,440
Balance b/d	890		

PLCA

	£		£
Cash	1,270	Purchases	2,270
Balance c/d	1,000		
	2,270		2,270
		Balance b/d	1,000

CAPITAL ACCOUNT

	£		£
Balance c/d	10,000	Cash	10,000
		Balance b/d	10,000

FIXTURES AND FITTINGS ACCOUNT

	£		£
Cash	3,500	Balance c/d	3,500
Balance b/d	3,500		

RENT ACCOUNT

	£		£
Cash	300	Balance c/d	300
Balance b/d	300		

DELIVERY EXPENSES ACCOUNT

	£		£
Cash	75	Balance c/d	75
Balance b/d	75		

DRAWINGS ACCOUNT

	£		£
Cash	270	Balance c/d	270
Balance b/d	270		

WAGES ACCOUNT

	£		£
Cash	400	Balance c/d	400
Balance b/d	400		

SUSPENSE ACCOUNT

	£		£
Balance c/d	500	Cash	500
		Balance b/d	500

(d)   TRIAL BALANCE AS AT 30 JUNE 20X7

Account	Dr £	Cr £
Cash	6,545	
Sales		2,750
Purchases	2,270	
Debtors	890	
Creditors		1,000
Capital		10,000
Fixtures and fittings	3,500	
Rent	300	
Delivery expenses	75	
Drawings	270	
Wages	400	
Suspense		500
	14,250	14,250

(e)

SUSPENSE ACCOUNT

	£		£
SLCA	500	Balance c/d	500

SLCA

	£		£
Balance b/d	890	Suspense	500
		Balance c/d	390
	890		890

Tutorial note. The examiner for Unit 3 has indicated that you will usually be given the suspense account figure (as in Activity 3.1) and then asked to clear it.

Answer 8.2

The main advantage of computerised accounting systems is that a large amount of data can be processed very quickly. A further advantage is that computerised systems are more accurate than manual systems.

Lou's comment that 'you never know what is going on in that funny box' might be better expressed as 'lack of audit trail'. If a mistake occurs somewhere in the system it is not always easy to identify where and how it happened.

Chapter 9

Answer 9.1

You should have noted the following details.

Our (Lightfoot & Co's) reference:	Z/0335/MJD
Department:	Purchasing
Supplier name:	Sandimans Ltd
Previous correspondence:	11 April 20X6
Present correspondence:	4 May 20X6
Subject:	Stationery (invoice 147829)

It is most unlikely that details like the geographical source of the letter or the name of its writer would be needed for filing purposes.

The accounts department should be sent a copy so that they can chase up the cheque that has not been received.

Answer 9.2

(a) The order would be: 15, 21, 28, 2, 8, 1, 18 and 26, 16, 13, 3, 12, 22, 30, 27, 4, 5, 9, 19, 25, 6, 29, 23, 24, 20, 17, 7, 10, 14, 11.

Tutorial note. A good approach would have been to highlight all the documents of the same year in the same colour, thereby breaking down the task into more manageable portions.

(b) 54321 Discos (7)
Argent-Smith M (11)
Argentson S (21)
Bexley J (5)
Bidwell D (4)
Briton N (28)
Britton T (12)
BRJ Plumbing (19)
Cottrell J (1)
Crown Dr J (8)
Emly P (17)
Gisling B (20)

Harrison P (27)
Harry Holden Ltd (18)
Holden R (2)
ILD Services Ltd (23)
Kelsey L C (22)
Locke D (9)
McLaughlin D (13)
Maclean T (6)
O'Grady E (15)
Page W (26)
Richmond A (29)
Saint Francis Pet Shop (16)
Sainton E (10)
St Olave's Church (30)
Van Saintby A (24)
Williams J (3)
Williams J A (14)
Williams John (25)

Tutorial note. Slight variations are possible, for example with the treatment of numbers and initials, depending upon the policy of the organisation.

(c)   The order would be: 3, 18, 27, 23, 19, 13, 10, 7, 15, 30, 26, 5, 21, 24, 6.

(d)   Geographical classification by towns gives the following results.

Bexley:	2, 7, 11, 18, 28
Bromley:	1, 10, 22, 24, 30
Crayford:	9, 12, 19, 26, 29
Dartford:	3, 4, 16, 21, 25, 27
Orpington:	5, 6, 13, 17, 23
Sidcup:	15
Woolwich:	8, 14, 20

Answer 9.3

You were asked for relevant examples from your own workplace.

Answer 9.4

(a)   There is room for some flexibility in answers here - what follows is very much a suggestion.

1   The bill is not confidential if Mr Glover chooses not to keep it so. It is nothing to do with your organisation anyway.

2   Not confidential. The reference that was given might be, but this is not mentioned.

3   This is probably very confidential: public knowledge of merger proposals could affect the outcome of the negotiations.

4   This may or may not be confidential depending upon your own organisation's policy. The general view is that budgeting should be done with the involvement of staff, so we are inclined to say that this is not, on the face of it, a confidential document.

5   This is obviously a highly personal document: it should be filed away in your personnel file.

6   This is probably not confidential. The familiarity of the signature is most likely to be due to the length of time your manager and 'Nancy' have been dealing with each other. If not, your manager is not ashamed of it and what business is it of yours anyway?

7   There is nothing confidential about this: the surname is irrelevant.

8   Mrs Paribus's letter is probably not particularly confidential although the nature of her complaint might make it so. To preserve the reputation of your organisation it might be better to shut it away in a file to stop cleaners, caterers or other external parties reading it.

9   This material is published: it is clearly not confidential.

10   There is no reason why personal details of directors should be confidential. If the list or an item on it had a heading or note such as 'Do not disclose to anyone below the level of Senior Manager', however, your manager should be ensuring that it does not fall into the wrong hands.

To summarise, documents 3 and 5 are definitely confidential, and documents 2, 7 and 9 are definitely not. The remainder may or may not be confidential depending on the circumstances, and whose point of view you are considering the matter from.

(b)   The danger here is that your fax will be collected by someone other than your manager. Its contents seem as if they might be damaging to your organisation in the wrong hands. You should therefore ring your manager and discuss the problem with him. The best solution is probably for him to stand over the receiving fax machine until your fax is received.

Index

PART F

Practice Activities

chapter 1

Revision of
basic bookkeeping

This checklist shows which performance criteria, range statement or knowledge and understanding point is covered by each activity in this chapter. Tick off each activity as you complete it.

Activity

1		This activity deals with knowledge and understanding point 7: capital and revenue expenditure.
2		This activity deals with knowledge and understanding point 1: types of business transactions and the documents involved.
3		This activity deals with knowledge and understanding point 7: capital and revenue expenditure.
4		This activity deals with knowledge and understanding point 1: types of business transactions and the documents involved.
5		This activity deals with knowledge and understanding point 1: types of business transactions and the documents involved.

1 Stock or asset

Comart Supplies Ltd has recently purchased five computers. Would the purchase be regarded as capital expenditure or revenue expenditure if:

    (a)   The computers are to be used for data processing by the company?

           Capital/Revenue

    (b)   The computers are to be held as stock for sale to customers?

           Capital/Revenue

2 Advice note

An advice note is a document sent to a customer acknowledging that an order has been received.

True/False

3 Redecoration

Mary Chang has decided that some of the offices are looking rather shabby. She arranges for the walls to be redecorated and for the purchase of some new office furniture.

    (a)   Is the cost of the redecoration capital or revenue expenditure?

           Capital/Revenue

    (b)   Is the cost of the new office furniture capital or revenue expenditure?

           Capital/Revenue

4 Remittance advice

A remittance advice is a document sent by a supplier to a customer to advise the customer that goods ordered have been sent off to the customer.

True/False

5 Business documentation

What would be the appropriate document to be used in each of the following cases?

    (a)   MEL Motor Factors Ltd sends out a document to a credit customer on a monthly basis summarising the transactions that have taken place and showing the amount owed by the customer.

(b)   MEL Motor Factors Ltd sends out a document to a credit customer in order to correct an error where the customer has been overcharged on an invoice.

(c)   MEL Motor Factors Ltd wishes to buy certain goods from a supplier and sends a document requesting that those goods should be supplied.

chapter 2

Recording, summarising and posting transactions

Activity checklist

This checklist shows which performance criteria, range statement or knowledge and understanding point is covered by each activity in this chapter. Tick off each activity as you complete it.

Activity

6   [ ]   This activity deals with knowledge and understanding point 12: relationships between the accounting system and the ledger.

7   [ ]   This activity deals with knowledge and understanding point 13: petty cash procedures.

8   [ ]   This activity deals with knowledge and understanding point 19: relevant understanding of the organisation's accounting systems.

9   [ ]   This activity deals with knowledge and understanding points 1: documentation, 2: general principles of VAT and 5: double entry book keeping

10   [ ]   This activity deals with knowledge and understanding point 12: relationship between the accounting system and the ledger.

11   [ ]   This activity deals with knowledge and understanding points 5: double entry bookkeeping and 2: general principles of VAT.

6 Which ledger?

Would the following accounts be found in the main ledger, the purchase or the sales ledger?

(a)   Sales ledger control account
(b)   Sales account
(c)   Shop fitting repairs account
(d)   Customer personal accounts

7 Delivery van

MEL Motor Factors is about to purchase a new delivery van costing £7,821.

(a)   Would it normally be appropriate to make a purchase of this kind out of petty cash?
(b)   Explain, briefly, the reason for your answer.

8 Classifying accounts

Classify the balance on each of the following main ledger accounts as an asset, a liability, an expense or revenue.

(a)   Advertising
(b)   Discount received
(c)   Sales ledger control
(d)   VAT (credit balance)
(e)   Postage and stationery

9 Entries

The credit balance of £92 (including VAT @ 17.5%) on the debtor's account of Euro Hair Style Ltd on 1 March arose because of an overcharge on a sales invoice which was subsequently corrected. However, Euro Hair Style has paid the original amount shown on the invoice.

(a)   What document would have been sent to Euro Hair Style when the overcharge was corrected?

(b)   Show the entries in the main ledger accounts, including amounts, made when this document was issued.

Debit	£	Credit	£

10 Whereabouts

Would the following accounts be found in the main ledger, the purchase ledger or the sales ledger?

(a)   Exotic Blooms Ltd (a credit supplier) ....

(b)   Salaries and wages ....

(c)   Motor vehicles ....

11 Main ledger entries

What bookkeeping entries would be required in the **main ledger** to correct the following error?

A credit note for £160 plus £28 VAT issued to a customer has been treated as if it were a credit note received.

Debit	Amount £	Credit	Amount £
. . . .	. . . .	. . . .	. . . .
. . . .	. . . .	. . . .	. . . .
. . . .	. . . .	. . . .	. . . .
. . . .	. . . .	. . . .	. . . .
. . . .	. . . .	. . . .	. . . .
. . . .	. . . .	. . . .	. . . .

chapter 3

Bank reconciliations

12 Standing orders

Today's date is 1 May 20X1 and you are currently checking the month end balances on the ledger accounts as at 30 April 20X1. You have in front of you the authorised standing order and direct debits schedule and note the following standing orders that have not yet been entered into the accounting records.

25th of each month	Standing order	District Council (council tax)	£140
28th of each month	Standing order	Friendly Insurance Company	£80
30th of each month	Standing order	Telephone Corporation	£125

What is the double entry for each of these standing orders?

13 Journals

When the bank statement is received by your business for the month ending 30 June 20X0 three items appear on the bank statement which are not in the cash book:

14 June	Bank giro credit receipt	Johnson & Co (a debtor)	£1,245
30 June	Direct debit	English Gas Co	£330
30 June	Bank charges		£40

Prepare journal entries for each of these amounts showing the double entry required in the main ledger and a brief narrative explaining the entries.

14 Bank statement entries

When looking at the bank statement for your business for the month of January 20X1 you note the following entries.

		Debit £	Credit £
14 January	CR Cheque paid in		156.50
20 January	DR Returned cheque	156.50	

What do these entries in the bank statement mean and what further action should be taken?

15 Update

Given below is the cash book for your business for the month of June 20X1.

CASH BOOK						
RECEIPTS			**PAYMENTS**			
Date	*Detail*	*£*	*Date*	*Detail*	*Cheque no*	*£*
1 June	Bal b/d	572	5 June	J Taylor	013647	334
8 June	Hardy & Co	493	16 June	K Filter	013648	127
12 June	T Roberts	525	22 June	B Gas	013649	200
18 June	D Smith	617	28 June	Wages	BACS	940
25 June	Garnet Bros	369	29 June	D Perez	013650	317

You are also given the bank statement for the same period.

CENTRAL BANK
43, Main Street
York
YK2 3PT

CHEQUE ACCOUNT   Lenten Trading   Account number 19785682

SHEET 0141

		Paid out £	Paid in £	Balance £
1 June	Opening balance			572
4 June	Bank giro credit - A Hammond		136	708
11 June	Cheque 013647	334		374
12 June	Credit		493	867
16 June	Credit		525	1,392
18 June	DD – Telephone Company	146		1,246
22 June	Credit		617	1,863
27 June	Cheque 013649	200		1,663
28 June	BACS	940		723
30 June	Bank interest		11	734

Tasks

(a)   Check the bank statement and the cash book and update the cash book for any missing entries.
(b)   Balance the amended cash book.
(c)   Explain what the reason for cheque numbers 013648 and 013650 not appearing on the bank statement might be.

16 Compare

Given below is the cash book for your business for the month of February 20X1.

CASH BOOK						
RECEIPTS			**PAYMENTS**			
Date	*Detail*	*£*	*Date*	*Detail*	*Cheque no*	*£*
2 Feb	Davis & Co	183	1 Feb	Balance b/d		306
7 Feb	A Thomas	179	4 Feb	J L Pedro	000351	169
14 Feb	K Sinders	146	11 Feb	P Gecko	000352	104
21 Feb	H Harvey	162	15 Feb	F Dimpner	000353	217
27 Feb	A Watts	180	23 Feb	O Roup	000354	258

You are also given the bank statement for the month.

EASTERN BANK
20/24 Miles Square
Huddersfield
LD3 5FS

CHEQUE ACCOUNT   L Arnold   Account number 29785643

SHEET 0298

		Paid out £	Paid in £	Balance £	
1 February	Opening balance			306	O/D
8 Feb	Credit		183	123	O/D
12 Feb	Credit		179	56	
15 Feb	SO – Telephone	65			
	000352	104		113	O/D
20 Feb	Credit		146	33	
	000353	217		184	O/D
24 Feb	DD - Electricity	30		214	O/D
26 Feb	Credit		162		
	000351	169		221	O/D
28 Feb	Interest	15		236	O/D

PROFESSIONAL EDUCATION

Tasks

(a)   Compare the bank statement to the cash book and amend the cash book accordingly.

(b)   Find the closing balance on the amended cash book and state whether this would be a debit or a credit balance in the trial balance.

(c)   Prepare a bank reconciliation statement.

17 Balance

Given below is the cash book for your organisation for the month of January 20X1.

CASH BOOK						
RECEIPTS			**PAYMENTS**			
Date	*Detail*	*£*	*Date*	*Detail*	*Cheque no*	*£*
1 Jan	Balance b/d	1,035	2 Jan	O J Trading	02475	368
2 Jan	Filter Bros	115	4 Jan	K D Partners	02476	463
8 Jan	Headway Ltd	640	7 Jan	L T Engineers	02477	874
15 Jan	Letterhead Ltd	409	14 Jan	R Trent	02478	315
22 Jan	Leaden Partners	265	20 Jan	I Rain	02479	85
			25 Jan	TDC	SO	150
			28 Jan	Wages	02480	490

You are also given the bank statement for the month.

WESTERN BANK
Bank House
Leeds Road
Halifax
LD3 5FS

CHEQUE ACCOUNT   Frant & Co   Account number 43709436

SHEET 0276

		Paid out £	Paid in £	Balance £
1 Jan	Opening balance			1,035
6 Jan	CR		115	
	CH 02475	368		782
12 Jan	CR		640	
	CH 02477	784		638
19 Jan	CR		409	1,047
20 Jan	BGC – T Elliot		161	
	CH 02478	315		893
23 Jan	CH 02476	463		430
25 Jan	SO – TDC	150		280
28 Jan	CR		265	
	Charges	10		535

Tasks

(a)   Compare the cash book to the bank statement and amend the cash book appropriately.
(b)   Balance the amended cash book.
(c)   Prepare a bank reconciliation statement.

BPP
PROFESSIONAL EDUCATION

chapter 4

Sales ledger
control account

Activity checklist

This checklist shows which performance criteria, range statement or knowledge and understanding point is covered by each activity in this chapter. Tick off each activity as you complete it.

Activity

18 ☐ This activity deals with knowledge and understanding point 5: double entry bookkeeping, and point 2: general principles of VAT.

19 ☐ This activity deals with performance criteria 3.2.A.

20 ☐ This activity deals with performance criteria 3.2.A.

21 ☐ This activity deals with knowledge and understanding points 11: errors and 17: reconciling control accounts with memorandum accounts.

22 ☐ This activity deals with performance criteria 3.2.B, 3.2.C and 3.2.E.

18 Recording transaction

Software has been sold on credit by Comart Computers Ltd to Softsell Ltd, a new small business which is not registered for VAT. The invoice issued shows the cost of the software as £160 plus £28 VAT giving a total of £188. In recording the transaction, which main ledger account(s) will be debited and which will be credited:

(a) In the books of Comart Computers Ltd?

Debit   Credit

....

....

(b) In the books of Softsell Ltd?

Debit   Credit

....

....

19 Errors cause a difference

Would the following errors cause a difference to occur between the balance of the sales ledger control account and the total of the balances in the sales ledger?

(a) The total column of the sales day book was overcast by £100.

Yes/No

(b) In error H Lambert's account in the sales ledger was debited with £175 instead of M Lambert's account.

Yes/No

(c) An invoice for £76 was recorded in the sales day book as £67.

Yes/No

20 Set off

Gift Box is both a supplier to and a customer of Bloomers Ltd. It has been agreed that a debt of £75 owing to Gift Box is to be set off against the balance of £300 owed by Gift Box.

What entries would be required in the main ledger to record this set off?

Debit	Amount £	Credit	Amount £

21 Three reasons

List three reasons for maintaining a sales ledger control account.

22 Sales ledger control account reconciliation

Using the summary of activity shown below, complete the sales ledger control account showing clearly the balance carried down. Use the list of balances in the subsidiary (sales) ledger to reconcile this balance with the sales ledger control account. If there is an imbalance, make a note to your supervisor suggesting where the error might be.

SALES LEDGER CONTROL ACCOUNT

Date 20X0	Details	Amount £	Date 20X0	Details	Amount £

Details for reconciliation of the sales ledger control account

Summary of activity

	£
Opening balance at 1 August 20X0	182,806
Sales in August	82,250
Sales returns in August	2,352
Discounts allowed	100
Bank receipts from debtors	73,648

Balances in subsidiary (sales) ledger

	£
Tadman Ltd	29,142
Silvertown & Co	16,000
Talbot & Co	38,400
Hibbert Industries	46,036
Galactic Cleaners	30,034
Smith Ltd	(448)
Waldon & Co	28,896

PRACTICE ACTIVITIES

RECONCILIATION OF SALES LEDGER CONTROL ACCOUNT WITH SUBIDIARY (SALES) LEDGER
AT 31 AUGUST 20X0

£

Closing balance of sales ledger control account
Total balance of accounts in subsidiary (sales) ledger
Imbalance

NOTE TO SUPERVISOR

chapter 5

Purchase ledger control account

23 Balance of PLCA

Would the following errors cause a difference to occur between the balance of the purchase ledger control account and the total of the balances in the purchases ledger?

(a)   A creditor's account has been balanced incorrectly.

   Yes/No

(b)   An invoice for £37 has been entered into the purchases day book as £39.

Yes/No

(c)   An invoice has, in error, been omitted from the purchases day book.

Yes/No

24 Another set off

Which account in the main ledger would you debit and which account in the main ledger would you credit in respect of the following.

(a)   A set-off is to be made between Peter Allen's account in the sales ledger, which has a balance of £200, and his account in the purchase ledger, which has a balance of £450.

Debit   *Credit*

(b)   The correction of an error where it has been found that an invoice for £36, received from Allied Brokers Ltd for insurance, has been entered in the various columns of the purchase day book as £63. (*Note.* Ignore VAT)

Debit   *Credit*

(c)   The correction of an error where it has been discovered that the purchase of £10 of stationery has been debited to the purchases account.

Debit   *Credit*

25 Transactions with suppliers

Which main ledger account would be debited and which main ledger account credited in respect of each of the following transactions?

(a)   Bought office furniture on credit from Crome Supplies Ltd.
(b)   Credit note sent to Jean Crane & Co.
(c)   Paid by cheque a credit account 'Alf Green & Sons' for last month's van repairs.

Account to be debited   *Account to be credited*

(a)   _____   _____

(b)   _____   _____

(c)   _____   _____

26 More differences

Would each of the following cause a difference between the totals of the main ledger debit and credit account balances at 31 March?

(a)   A purchase invoice for £36 from P Smith was entered into P Short's account in the purchase ledger.

   Yes/No

(b)   A purchase invoice for £96 was not entered in the purchase day book.

   Yes/No

(c)   The total column of the purchase day book was undercast by £20.

   Yes/No

(d)   A purchase invoice from Short & Long for £42 for the goods for resale was entered as £24 in the purchase day book.

   Yes/No

27 Purchase ledger control account reconciliation

A list of subsidiary ledger balances is shown below, together with a summary of activity in the month of August 20X0. Prepare a purchase ledger control account as at 31 August 20X0, showing clearly the balance carried down. Reconcile this balance with the list of balances in the subsidiary (purchase) ledger. Comment on any imbalance.

Details for reconciliation of the purchase ledger control account

Summary of activity

	£
Opening balance at 1 August 20X0	67,200
Purchases in August	63,450
Purchases returns in August	1,880
Discounts received	200
Bank payments to creditors	68,310

PURCHASE LEDGER CONTROL ACCOUNT

Date	Details	Amount £	Date	Details	Amount £

Balances in subsidiary (purchases) ledger

	£
Donna Ltd	19,270
ABC Controls	14,100
Alex & John	11,750
S Rashid	9,400
XYZ Ltd	5,740

RECONCILIATION OF PURCHASE LEDGER CONTROL ACCOUNT WITH SUBSIDIARY
(PURCHASES) LEDGER AT 31 AUGUST 20X0

	£
Closing balance of purchase ledger control account	
Total balance of accounts in subsidiary (purchases) ledger	_____
Imbalance	_____

chapter 6

Other control accounts

28 Cash control 1

A petty cash control account is kept in the main ledger of Coulthurst Ltd. The petty cash book is the subsidiary account. At the beginning of August there is a balance brought forward of £175.

During August £125 was spent from petty cash, and at the end of the month, £150 was put into the petty cash box from the bank.

Task

Enter these transactions into the petty cash control account below, showing clearly the balance carried down. What does this balance represent?

PETTY CASH CONTROL ACCOUNT

Date 20X1	Details	Amount £	Date 20X1	Details	Amount £

29 Cash control 2

A petty cash control account is kept in the main ledger of Wye Ltd. The petty cash book is the subsidiary account. At the beginning of June there is a balance brought forward of £150.

During June £100 was spent from petty cash, and at the end of the month, £200 was put into the petty cash box from the bank.

Tasks

(a)   Enter these transactions into the petty cash control account below, showing clearly the balance carried down.

PETTY CASH CONTROL ACCOUNT

Date 20X1	Details	Amount £	Date 20X1	Details	Amount £

(b)   If Wye Ltd operated an imprest system, what would be the payment from the bank at the end of the month if it was decided to increase the imprest to £200.

30 Cash control 3

A petty cash control account is kept in the main ledger of Fabien Ltd. The petty cash book is the subsidiary account. At the beginning of April there is a balance brought forward of £232.

During April £210 was spent from petty cash, and at the end of the month, there was £2 cash in hand.

Tasks

(a)   Enter these transactions into the petty cash control account below, showing clearly the balance carried down.

(b)   Carry out a petty cash reconciliation.

(c)   If there was an IOU for £18 in the petty cash box plus an unrecorded voucher for £2, reconcile the petty cash balance at the end of April.

PETTY CASH CONTROL ACCOUNT

Date 20X1	Details	Amount £	Date 20X1	Details	Amount £

31 Non-trade debtors 1

At 1 April 20X1, the balance on non-trade debtors control account was £2,500. During April, further debts were due of £2,000 and cash was received of £4,000.

Task

Write up the non-trade debtors control account and show the balance carried forward.

NON-TRADE DEBTORS CONTROL ACCOUNT

Date 20X1	Details	Amount £	Date 20X1	Details	Amount £

32 Non-trade debtors 2

Using the details in activity 31 above, write up the non-trade debtors control account for May 20X1.

(a) Further debts were incurred of £4,000.
(b) Cash received was £2,500.
(c) An amount of £2,000 included in (a), should be included in the sales ledger control account.

NON-TRADE DEBTORS CONTROL ACCOUNT

Date 20X1	Details	Amount £	Date 20X1	Details	Amount £

chapter 7

The correction of errors

Activity checklist

This checklist shows which performance criteria, range statement or knowledge and understanding point is covered by each activity in this chapter. Tick off each activity as you complete it.

Activity

33		This activity deals with performance criteria 3.3.C.
34		This activity deals with performance criteria 3.3.C.
35		This activity deals with performance criteria 3.3.C.

33 Errors 1

Show the journal to correct the following error. An invoice received from Smith's Electrics Ltd had been entered in the day book correctly but the VAT element of £14 had been omitted.

34 Errors 2

The total of £98 discounts allowed column in the cash book had been wrongly posted to discounts received. Show the correcting journal.

35 Errors 3

A credit note issued to a customer for £23 plus VAT £4 had been posted to the main ledger as if it was a invoice issued. Show the correcting journal.

chapter 8

From ledger accounts to initial trial balance

36 MEL Factors

MEL Factors has the following balances at 30 April 20X1.

	£
Sales	10,000
Purchases	5,000
Expenses	2,000
Capital	20,000
Sales ledger control account	2,000
Purchase ledger control account	1,500
Cash in bank and in hand	3,000
Fixed assets	19,500

Task

Prepare an initial trial balance.

37 Comart Supplies

Comart's initial trial balance shows debits totalling £12,000 and credits totalling £14,500.

Tasks

(a)   How would you deal with this discrepancy?

(b)   Subsequently you discover that the sales ledger control account omits sales of £3,000 and that the purchase ledger control account omits purchases of £500. Show the suspense account and the journal to clear it.

chapter 9

Filing

38 Documents for trial balance

When preparing a trial balance at the end of an accounting period there will be a number of documents and reconciliations that you will need to be able to find from the filing system. List the documents and reconciliations that you will need to access before completing the initial trial balance.

39 Filing correspondence

A small business has always filed its correspondence with customers and suppliers in date order. However, as the business has grown, the owner has found that it is harder to locate the correspondence required from the filing system.

Suggest a different method of filing that might make accessing the required correspondence easier.

40 Storage

You are the bookkeeper in a small business and your office currently has no facility for storing the ledger accounts and other accounting records which you work on, including the wages book. These are all left on your desk when you are not in the office. You are to write a memo to the owner of the business expressing any concerns you may have about this system and suggesting ways of improving it. Today's date is 4 May 20X1.

41 Creditors' accounts

The creditors' accounts in the purchases ledger are filed in alphabetical order. In what order would the following creditors' accounts be filed?

- Smithson Ltd
- Sonic Partners
- Skelton Engineers
- Snipe Associates
- Spartan & Co
- Souter Finance

42 Accounts personnel

A fairly large engineering business has the following accounts personnel.

- Chief accountant
- Cashier
- Petty cashier and bookkeeper
- Sales ledger clerk
- Purchases ledger clerk
- Wages clerk

With which of these personnel are you likely to find the following?

- Wages book
- Aged debtor analysis
- Purchase ledger
- Bank statement
- Petty cash book
- Credit limits for customers
- Standing order schedule

Answers to
Practice Activities

Answers to practice activities

Chapter 1: Revision of basic bookkeeping

1 Stock or asset

   (a)   Capital
   (b)   Revenue

2 Advice note

False. An advice note is usually sent out with the delivery of goods to the customer.

3 Redecoration

   (a)   Revenue
   (b)   Capital

4 Remittance advice

False. A remittance advice is sent by a customer with their payment, detailing which invoices are being paid.

5 Business documentation

   (a)   Monthly statement of account
   (b)   Credit note
   (c)   Purchase order

Chapter 2: Recording, summarising and posting transactions

6 Which ledger?

(a)	Main ledger
(b)	Main ledger
(c)	Main ledger
(d)	Sales ledger

7 Delivery van

(a)   No

(b)   The amount of money kept in petty cash should be kept to a minimum to prevent fraud and theft. The amount would be far too large to keep in petty cash.

8 Classifying accounts

(a)	Expense
(b)	Revenue
(c)	Asset
(d)	Liability
(e)	Expense

9 Entries

(a)   A credit note

(b)

		£	£
DEBIT	Sales	78.30	
	VAT	13.70	
CREDIT	Sales ledger control account		92.00

10 Whereabouts

(a)	Purchase ledger
(b)	Main ledger
(c)	Main ledger

11 Main ledger entries

		£	£
DEBIT	VAT	28	
DEBIT	Returns inwards	160	
CREDIT	Purchase ledger control		188

Reversal of incorrect entry

		£	£
DEBIT	VAT	28	
DEBIT	Returns outwards	160	
CREDIT	Sales ledger control		188

Posting correct entry

Chapter 3: Bank reconciliations

12 Standing orders

		£	£
District Council:			
DEBIT	Council tax account	140	
CREDIT	Bank account		140
Friendly Insurance Company:			
DEBIT	Insurance account	80	
CREDIT	Bank account		80
Telephone Corporation:			
DEBIT	Telephone account	125	
CREDIT	Bank account		125

13 Journals

		Dr	Cr
		£	£
DEBIT	Bank account	1,245	
CREDIT	Sales ledger control account		1,245
	Being bank giro credit from Johnson & Co		
DEBIT	Gas account	330	
CREDIT	Bank account		330
	Being direct debit payment to English Gas Co		
DEBIT	Bank charges account	40	
CREDIT	Bank account		40
	Being bank charges for the period		

14 Bank statement entries

A cheque for £156.50 was received from a customer and paid into your bank account on 14 January. The cheque then went through the bank clearing system but the bank was unable to clear the cheque, either due to the fact that the cheque was not correctly drawn up or the drawee did not have sufficient funds in his account. Therefore, the cheque will have been returned to you marked 'refer to drawer'.

The cash book must be amended as it will currently show a receipt for £156.50. However, the money has not been received and therefore a credit entry is needed in the bank account (debit: sales ledger control account; credit: cash). The cheque should be returned to the customer with a request for a replacement cheque.

15 Update

(a)/(b)

CASH BOOK						
RECEIPTS			**PAYMENTS**			
Date	*Detail*	£	*Date*	*Detail*	*Cheque no*	£
1 June	Balance b/d	572	5 June	J Taylor	013647	334
8 June	Hardy & Co	493	16 June	K Filter	013648	127
12 June	T Roberts	525	22 June	B Gas	013649	200
18 June	D Smith	617	28 June	Wages	BACS	940
25 June	Garnet Bros	369	29 June	D Perez	013650	317
4 June	A Hammond – BGC	136	18 June	Telephone DD		146
30 June	Bank interest	11	30 June	Balance c/d		659
		2,723				2,723

(c) Cheque number 013650 was not written until 29 June and therefore could not possibly reach the supplier, be paid into the supplier's bank account and work its way through the bank clearing system by 30 June.

Cheque number 013648 was written into the cash book on 16 June and therefore, theoretically, should have cleared through the banking system by the end of the month. However, there may have been a delay in sending the cheque out to the payee or the payee may have delayed in paying the cheque into his bank account, meaning that by 30 June the cheque has still not cleared.

16 Compare

(a)

CASH BOOK						
RECEIPTS			**PAYMENTS**			
Date	Detail	£	*Date*	*Detail*	*Cheque no*	£
2 Feb	Davis & Co	183	1 Feb	Balance b/d		306
7 Feb	A Thomas	179	4 Feb	J L Pedro	000351	169
14 Feb	K Sinders	146	11 Feb	P Gecko	000352	104
21 Feb	H Harvey	162	15 Feb	F Dimpner	000353	217
27 Feb	A Watts	180	23 Feb	O Roup	000354	258
			15 Feb	Telephone	SO	65
			24 Feb	Electricity	DD	30
28 Feb	Balance c/d	314	28 Feb	Interest		15
		1,164				1,164

(b) This is a debit balance carried down and so a credit balance brought down, representing an overdraft. This will appear in the trial balance as a credit balance.

BANK RECONCILIATION AS AT 28 FEBRUARY 20X1

	£
Balance per bank statement – overdrawn	(236)
Add: outstanding lodgement (A Watts)	180
	(56)
Less: outstanding cheque (000354)	(258)
Balance per amended cash book	(314)

17 Balance

(a)(b)

CASH BOOK							
RECEIPTS				**PAYMENTS**			
Date	*Detail*	*£*		*Date*	*Detail*	*Cheque no*	*£*
1 Jan	Balance b/d	1,035		2 Jan	O J Trading	02475	368
2 Jan	Filter Bros	115		4 Jan	K D Partners	02476	463
8 Jan	Headway Ltd	640		7 Jan	L T Engineers	02477	874
15 Jan	Letterhead Ltd	409		14 Jan	R Trent	02478	315
22 Jan	Leaden Partners	265		20 Jan	I Rain	02479	85
20 Jan	BGC - T Elliot	161		25 Jan	TDC	SO	150
31 Jan	Adjustment to			28 Jan	Wages	02480	490
	cheque no 02477	90		28 Jan	Bank charges		10
31 Jan	Balance c/d	40					
		2,755					2,755

Tutorial note. Cheque 02477 has been recorded in the cash bank as £874 but the bank statement shows £784, the difference of £90 needs to be adjusted.

BANK RECONCILIATION STATEMENT AT 31 JANUARY 20X1

	£	£
Balance per bank statement		535
Less outstanding lodgements:		
02479	85	
02480	490	
		575
Balance per amended cash book (overdrawn)		(40)

Chapter 4: Sales ledger control account

18 Recording transaction

(a)	DEBIT	Sales ledger control a/c	£188	
	CREDIT	Sales		£160
	CREDIT	VAT		£28
(b)	DEBIT	Purchases	£188	
	CREDIT	Purchase ledger control a/c		£188

Tutorial note. Softsell is not registered for VAT and so cannot reclaim input VAT. The VAT, therefore, forms part of the cost of the purchase.

19 Errors cause a difference

(a) Yes
(b) No
(c) No. The same mistake would be processed in the sales ledger and the sales ledger control account.

20 Set off

DEBIT	Purchase ledger control a/c	£75	
CREDIT	Sales ledger control a/c		£75

21 Three reasons

(a) To aid in the prevention of fraud
(b) To assist in the location of errors
(c) To enable the total debtors figure to be known at any time

22 Sales ledger control account reconciliation

SALES LEDGER CONTROL ACCOUNT

Date 20X0	Details	Amount £	Date 20X0	Details	Amount £
1 August	Balance b/f	182,806	31 August	Sales returns	2,352
31 August	Sales	82,250	31 August	Discounts allowed	100
			31 August	Bank	73,648
			31 August	Balance c/d	188,956
		265,056			265,056
1 Sept	Balance b/d	188,956			

RECONCILIATION OF SALES LEDGER CONTROL ACCOUNT
WITH SUBSIDIARY (SALES) LEDGER
AT 31 AUGUST 20X0

	£
Closing balance of sales ledger control account	188,956
Total balance of accounts in subsidiary (sales) ledger	188,060
Imbalance	896

NOTE TO SUPERVISOR

There is an imbalance between the sales ledger control account and subsidiary (sales) ledger of £896. This may be for any number of reasons, but the most likely explanation is that the account of Smith Ltd has a credit balance of £448. Is this correct? If Smith Ltd should, in fact, be a debit balance, then the difference is 2 × £448, ie £896.

Chapter 5: Purchase ledger control account

23 Balance of PLCA

(a) Yes
(b) No, both the purchase ledger and the PLCA will record the same error.
(c) No

24 Another set off

(a) DEBIT   Purchases ledger control a/c   £200
     CREDIT   Sales ledger control a/c   £200

(b) DEBIT   Purchase ledger control a/c   £27
     CREDIT   Insurance expense   £27

Tutorial note. We have assumed that the day book has been posted already to the main ledger.

(c) DEBIT   Stationery   £10
     CREDIT   Purchases   £10

25 Transactions with suppliers

(a) DEBIT   Fixed assets
     CREDIT   Purchase ledger control account

(b) DEBIT   Sales returns
     CREDIT   Sales ledger control account

(c) DEBIT   Purchase ledger control account
     CREDIT   Bank

26 More differences

(a) No
(b) No
(c) Yes
(d) No

27 Purchase ledger control account reconciliation

PURCHASE LEDGER CONTROL ACCOUNT

Date 20X0	Details	Amount £	Date 20X0	Details	Amount £
31 Aug	Purchases returns	1,880	1 Aug	Balance b/f	67,200
31 Aug	Discounts received	200	31 Aug	Purchases	63,450
31 Aug	Bank	68,310			
31 Aug	Balance c/d	60,260			
		130,650			130,650
			1 Sept	Balance b/d	60,260

RECONCILIATION OF PURCHASE LEDGER CONTROL ACCOUNT
WITH SUBSIDIARY (PURCHASES) LEDGER
AT 31 AUGUST 20X0

	£
Closing balance of purchase ledger control account	60,260
Total balance of accounts in subsidiary (purchases) ledger	60,260
Imbalance	NIL

Chapter 6: Other control accounts

28 Cash control 1

PETTY CASH CONTROL

Date 20X1	Details	£	Date 20X1	Details	£
1 Aug	Balance b/f	175	31 Aug	Petty cash	125
31 Aug	Bank	150	31 Aug	Balance c/d	200
		325			325
1 Sept	Balance b/d	200			

The control account balance b/d shows that there should be cash in hand of £200.

29 Cash control 2

(a)

PETTY CASH CONTROL

Date 20X1	Details	£	Date 20X1	Details	£
1 Jun	Balance b/f	150	30 Jun	Petty cash	100
30 Jun	Bank	200	30 Jun	Balance c/d	250
		350			350
1 July	Balance b/d	250			

(b) £150. Current imprest is £150, spending in month was £100. Imprest is increased by £50 (£200 – £150), so reimbursement is £150 (£100 + £50).

30 Cash control 3

(a)

PETTY CASH CONTROL

Date 20X1	Details	£	Date 20X1	Details	£
1 April	Balance b/f	232	30 Apr	Petty cash	210
			30 Apr	Balance c/d	22
		232			232
1 May	Balance b/d	22			

(b)   PETTY CASH RECONCILIATION AT 30 APRIL 20X1

	£
Balance per petty cash control account	22
Cash in hand	2
Imbalance	20

(c)

		£
Cash in hand		2
Add: IOU	18	
Unrecorded voucher	2	
		20
Balance as petty cash control account		22

Tutorial note. As the voucher has not yet been recorded, it is added to cash in hand.

31 Non-trade debtors 1

NON-TRADE DEBTORS CONTROL ACCOUNT

Date 20X1	Details	£	Date 20X1	Details	£
1 April	Balance b/d	2,500	April	Cash book	4,000
April	Further debts	2,000	30 April	Balance c/d	500
		4,500			4,500
1 May	Balance b/d	500			

32 Non-trade debtors 2

NON-TRADE DEBTORS CONTROL ACCOUNT

Date 20X1	Details	£	Date 20X1	Details	£
1 May	Balance b/d	500	May	Cash book (b)	2,500
May	Further debts (a)	4,000	May	SLCA (c)	2,000
		4,500			4,500

Chapter 7: Correcting errors

33 Errors 1

DEBIT	VAT	£14	
CREDIT	Purchase ledger control account		£14

To account for VAT omitted from the original posting

34 Errors 2

DEBIT	Discounts allowed	£98	
CREDIT	Discounts received		£98

To correct wrong posting

35 Errors 3

DEBIT	Sales	£46	
	VAT	£8	
CREDIT	Sales ledger control account		£54

To correct credit note wrongly posted as if it were an invoice

Chapter 8: From ledger accounts to initial trial balance

36 MEL factors

TRIAL BALANCE AS AT 30 APRIL 20X1

	DR £	CR £
Sales		10,000
Purchases	5,000	
Expenses	2,000	
Capital		20,000
Sales ledger control account	2,000	
Purchase ledger control account		1,500
Cash at bank and in hand	3,000	
Fixed assets	19,500	
	31,500	31,500

37 Comart supplies

(a)   The difference is debit £2.500 and a suspense account needs to be set up for this amount.

(b)

SUSPENSE ACCOUNT

	£		£
Balance b/d	2,500	SLCA	3,000
PLCA	500		
	3,000		3,000

		£	£
DEBIT	Suspense account	500	
	Sales ledger control account	3,000	
CREDIT	Suspense account		3,000
	Purchase ledger control account		500

Entries to close suspense account

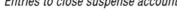

Chapter 9: Filing

38 Documents for trial balance

- Cash book
- Bank reconciliation
- Petty cash book
- Reconciliation of petty cash vouchers and cash
- Sales ledger control account reconciliation
- Purchase ledger control account reconciliation
- Non trade debtors control account reconciliation

39 Filing correspondence

File in alphabetical order of the suppliers' and customers' names.

40 Storage

MEMO

To: The owner
From: The bookkeeper
Date: 4 May 20X1
Subject: Confidentiality of ledgers

I am concerned about the confidentiality of the ledger and accounting documents which I work on, particularly the wages book, as I currently have nowhere to file these documents. When I am not in my office, including overnight, I have to leave the ledger and documents on my desk. This means that anyone in the building: employees, customers, visitors etc could, potentially, access the information contained in the documents.

I suggest that I should have a lockable filing cabinet which I can use to store the ledger and documents safely when I am not working on them.

41 Creditors' accounts

Skelton Engineers
Smithson Ltd
Snipe Associates
Sonic Partners
Souter Finance
Spartan & Co

42 Accounts personnel

- Wages book - wages clerk
- Aged debtor analysis - sales ledger clerk
- Purchase ledger accounts - purchases ledger clerk
- Bank statement - cashier
- Petty cash book - petty cashier
- Credit limits for customers - sales ledger clerk
- Standing order schedule - cashier

PART G

Full Skills based Assessments

FULL SKILLS BASED ASSESSMENT 1
T S STATIONERY

FOUNDATION STAGE – NVQ/SVQ2

Unit 3

Preparing Ledger Balances and an Initial Trial Balance

The purpose of this Full Skills Based Assessment is to give you an idea of what an AAT simulation looks like. It is not intended as a definitive guide to the tasks you may be required to perform.

The suggested time allowance for this Assessment is **three hours**. Up to 30 minutes extra time may be permitted in an AAT simulation. Breaks in assessment will be allowed in the AAT simulation, but it must normally be completed in one day.

Calculators may be used but no reference material is permitted.

DO NOT OPEN THIS PAPER UNTIL YOU ARE READY TO START
UNDER EXAM CONDITIONS

COVERAGE OF PERFORMANCE CRITERIA

All performance criteria in Unit 3 are covered by this full skills based assessment.

Element	PC Coverage
3.1	**Balance bank transactions**
	Record details from the relevant primary documentation in the cash book and ledger.
	Correctly calculate totals and balances of receipts and payments.
	Compare individual items on the bank statement and in the cash book for accuracy.
	Identify discrepancies and prepare a bank reconciliation statement.
3.2	**Prepare ledger balances and control accounts**
	Make and record authorised adjustments.
	Total relevant accounts in the main ledger.
	Reconcile control accounts with the total of the balance in the subsidiary ledger.
	Reconcile petty cash control account with cash in hand and subsidiary records.
	Identify discrepancies arising from the reconciliation of control accounts and either resolve or refer to the appropriate person.
	Ensure documentation is stored securely and in line with the organisation's confidentiality requirements.
3.3	**Draft an initial trial balance**
	Prepare the draft initial trial balance in line with the organisation's policies and procedures.
	Identify discrepancies in the balancing process.
	Identify reasons for imbalance and rectify them.
	Balance the trial balance.

Knowledge and understanding

Whilst some areas of knowledge and understanding can be inferred through performance, there will be gaps in evidence which should be plugged by other assessment methods, eg questioning.

Centres are reminded that there should be a mix of evidence across the unit, simulations cannot stand alone as evidence of competent performance, and the evidence in the portfolio should be mapped clearly to the student record.

INSTRUCTIONS

This Assessment is designed to test your ability to prepare ledger cash balances and an initial trial balance.

The situation is provided on page 234.

The tasks you are to perform are set out within the data.

You are allowed three hours to complete your work.

A high level of accuracy is required. Check your work carefully.

Correcting fluid may be used but should be used in moderation. Errors should be crossed out neatly and clearly. You should write in black ink, not pencil.

You are advised to read the whole of the Assessment before commencing, as all of the information may be of value and is not necessarily supplied in the sequence in which you might wish to deal with it.

A full suggested answer to this Assessment is provided on page 273 of this Text.

INTRODUCTION

- You are the bookkeeper for a small business supplying decorative and unusual stationery and cards called T S Stationery.

- The accounting system is a manual system with all double entry taking place in the main ledger and subsidiary ledgers kept for debtors and creditors.

- Today is 2 April 20X1 and you are trying to prepare the trial balance for the year ended 31 March 20X1.

- Before preparing the trial balance there are a number of accounting tasks for the last few days of March that must be undertaken.

Task 1

The purchases day book and purchases returns day book has not yet been posted for the last week in March. The two day books are given below, together with the relevant main ledger accounts and subsidiary ledger accounts. You are required to update the ledger accounts to reflect the entries in the day books.

PURCHASES DAY BOOK

Supplier	Gross	VAT	Net
	£	£	£
FP Paper	188	28	160
Gift Products Ltd	235	35	200
Harper Bros	141	21	120
J S Traders	282	42	240
	846	126	720

PURCHASES RETURNS DAY BOOK

Supplier	Gross	VAT	Net
	£	£	£
Gift Products Ltd	94	14	80
Harper Bros	47	7	40
	141	21	120

MAIN LEDGER ACCOUNTS

PURCHASE LEDGER CONTROL ACCOUNT

	£		£
		27 Mar Opening balance	14,325

PURCHASES ACCOUNT

	£		£
27 Mar Opening balance	166,280		

PURCHASES RETURNS ACCOUNT

	£		£
		27 Mar Opening balance	4,180

VAT ACCOUNT

	£		£
		27 Mar Opening balance	1,405

SUBSIDIARY LEDGER ACCOUNTS

F P PAPER

	£			£
		27 Mar	Opening balance	3,825

GIFT PRODUCTS LIMITED

	£			£
		27 Mar	Opening balance	4,661

HARPER BROS

	£			£
		27 Mar	Opening balance	3,702

J S TRADERS

	£			£
		27 Mar	Opening balance	2,137

Task 2

Reconcile the balance on the purchase ledger control account with the total of the four creditor balances (these are the only credit suppliers of the business).

You should now balance the purchases account, purchases returns account and VAT account.

Task 3

Journal number 336

	£	£
Bad debtors expense	400	
Sales ledger control		400

Being write off of bad debt from C Cummings

Journal number 337

	£	£
Sales ledger control	100	
Sales		100

Being undercast of sales day book

The relevant main ledger accounts are given below. You are also given all of the individual debtor accounts from the subsidiary ledger.

Enter the journal entries in the relevant main ledger and subsidiary ledger accounts and then reconcile the balance on the sales ledger control account to the total of the individual debtor accounts in the subsidiary ledger.

You can now balance the sales account and the bad debts expense account.

MAIN LEDGER

SALES LEDGER CONTROL ACCOUNT

	£		£
31 Mar Balance b/d	23,230		

SALES ACCOUNT

	£		£
		31 Mar Balance b/d	255,810

BAD DEBTS EXPENSE ACCOUNT

	£		£

SUBSIDIARY LEDGER

RETAIL ENTERPRISES

	£		£
31 Mar Balance b/d	5,114		

C CUMMINGS

	£		£
31 Mar Balance b/d	400		

PALMER LIMITED

		£		£
31 Mar	Balance b/d	6,248		

REAPERS STORES

		£		£
31 Mar	Balance b/d	5,993		

KNIGHT RETAIL

		£		£
31 Mar	Balance b/d	5,575		

Task 4

Given below is the cash receipts and payments book for the business for the month of March 20X1. You are also given the bank statement for the month.

You are required to check the cash book carefully to the bank statement and adjust the cash book for any missing entries.

CASH BOOK							
RECEIPTS				**PAYMENTS**			
Date	Detail		£	Date	Detail	Cheque no	£
1 Mar	Balance b/d		3,668	5 Mar	Harper Bros	002643	2,558
7 Mar	Palmer Ltd		2,557	12 Mar	Gift Products	002644	3,119
15 Mar	Retail Engineering		4,110	18 Mar	F P Paper	002645	2,553
20 Mar	Reapers Stores		4,782	24 Mar	J S Traders	002646	983
28 Mar	Knight Retail		3,765	31 Mar	BACS – wages		3,405

NORTHERN BANK
Royal Bank House
Trestle Square
Sandefield
SF2 3HS

Cheque account: T S Stationery Account number 10364382

SHEET 0124

		Paid out £	Paid in £	Balance £
1 Mar	Balance b/d			3,668
10 Mar	Credit		2,557	6,225
16 Mar	Cheque 002644	3,119		3,106
20 Mar	Credit		4,110	7,216
22 Mar	Cheque 002643	2,558		
	SO – District Council: rates	200		4,458
25 Mar	Credit		4,782	9,240
26 Mar	Cheque 002645	2,553		
	SO – Loan repayment	400		6,287
30 Mar	Interest		20	6,307
31 Mar	BACS	3,405		2,902

Task 5

Total and balance the adjusted cash book and complete the double entry in the ledger accounts given. You can then balance each of the ledger accounts.

RATES ACCOUNT

	£		£
31 Mar Balance b/d	2,200		

LOAN ACCOUNT

	£		£
		31 Mar Balance b/d	6,400

BANK INTEREST RECEIVABLE

	£		£
		31 Mar Balance b/d	100

Task 6

Prepare a bank reconciliation statement, in the following format.

	£
Balance per bank statement	
Add	
	_____
Less	
	_____
Balance per adjusted cash book	

Task 7

T S Stationery sublets part of its premises and has three tenants. The rent book for March is given below. The details have not yet been entered into the ledger accounts, although the payment of the rent has been entered in the cash receipts book. You are required to enter the totals in the relevant ledger accounts given and to balance the accounts.

	Rent due	Overdue rent b/f	Payment received	Outstanding rent
	£	£	£	£
M Savage	2,000	350	2,350	-
T Stiles	1,500	-	1,000	500
L Fraser	1,000	130	750	380
	4,500	480	4,100	880

NON-TRADE DEBTORS CONTROL ACCOUNT

	£		£
1 Mar Balance b/d	480		

RENT RECEIVED ACCOUNT

	£		£
		1 Mar Balance b/d	45,000

BPP
PROFESSIONAL EDUCATION

Task 8

The petty cash is run on an imprest system of £100 per month.

The petty cash vouchers in the petty cash box at 31 March were:

Voucher number	£
0264	3.67
0265	9.48
0266	6.70
0267	13.20
0268	2.36
0269	1.55
0270	10.46
0271	4.89
0272	3.69

The cash in the petty cash box was:

Note/coin	Number
£10	1
£5	4
£2	2
£1	7
50p	3
20p	4
10p	5
5p	1
2p	7
1p	1

Reconcile the petty cash vouchers and the petty cash and determine the amount that will appear in the trial balance for petty cash.

Task 9

You are now ready to prepare the initial balance at the year end, 31 March 20X1. Given below are the ledger balances at 31 March 20X1 which must be completed with the balances from the ledger accounts dealt with in earlier tasks.

You are required to prepare the initial trial balance at 31 March 20X1.

	£
Building	100,000
Motor vehicles	34,500
Office equipment	13,000
Purchases	Own figure
Purchases returns	Own figure
Capital	53,855
Sales	Own figure
Sales returns	6,800
Discounts allowed	300
Stock	16,000
Loan	Own figure
Discount received	600
Debtors (SLCA)	Own figure
Petty cash	Own figure
Creditors (PLCA)	Own figure
VAT	Own figure
Bank	Own figure
Non-trade debtors	Own figure
Rent received	Own figure
Motor expenses	4,297
Telephone	4,850
Electricity	3,630
Rates	Own figure
Miscellaneous expenses	3,900
Bad debts expense	Own figure
Bank interest receivable	Own figure

Task 10

The owner of the business is delighted that the initial trial balance does in fact balance and has said to you that he therefore assumes this means that all of the accounting entries are correct.

You are required to write a memo to the owner explaining what types of errors there may be in the accounting records that are not shown up by the trial balance, using examples of how these errors could take place in T S Stationery's books but still not cause an imbalance on the trial balance.

FULL SKILLS BASED ASSESSMENT 2
WASHBROOK & CO

FOUNDATION STAGE – NVQ/SVQ2

Unit 3

Preparing Ledger Balances and an Initial Trial Balance

The purpose of this Full Skills Based Assessment is to give you an idea of what an AAT simulation looks like. It is not intended as a definitive guide to the tasks you may be required to perform.

The suggested time allowance for this Assessment is **three hours**. Up to 30 minutes extra time may be permitted in an AAT simulation. Breaks in assessment will be allowed in the AAT simulation, but it must normally be completed in one day.

Calculators may be used but no reference material is permitted.

DO NOT OPEN THIS PAPER UNTIL YOU ARE READY TO START
UNDER EXAM CONDITIONS

 245

COVERAGE OF PERFORMANCE CRITERIA

All performance criteria in Unit 3 are covered by this full skills based assessment.

Element	PC Coverage
3.1	**Balance bank transactions**
	Record details from the relevant primary documentation in the cash book and ledger.
	Correctly calculate totals and balances of receipts and payments.
	Compare individual items on the bank statement and in the cash book for accuracy.
	Identify discrepancies and prepare a bank reconciliation statement.
3.2	**Prepare ledger balances and control accounts**
	Make and record authorised adjustments.
	Total relevant accounts in the main ledger.
	Reconcile control accounts with the total of the balance in the subsidiary ledger.
	Reconcile petty cash control account with cash in hand and subsidiary records.
	Identify discrepancies arising from the reconciliation of control accounts and either resolve or refer to the appropriate person.
	Ensure documentation is stored securely and in line with the organisation's confidentiality requirements.
3.3	**Draft an initial trial balance**
	Prepare the draft initial trial balance in line with the organisation's policies and procedures.
	Identify discrepancies in the balancing process.
	Identify reasons for imbalance and rectify them.
	Balance the trial balance.

Knowledge and understanding

Whilst some areas of knowledge and understanding can be inferred through performance, there will be gaps in evidence which should be plugged by other assessment methods, eg questioning.

Centres are reminded that there should be a mix of evidence across the unit, simulations cannot stand alone as evidence of competent performance, and the evidence in the portfolio should be mapped clearly to the student record.

INSTRUCTIONS

This Assessment is designed to test your ability to prepare ledger cash balances and an initial trial balance.

The situation is provided on page 248.

The tasks you are to perform are set out within the data.

You are allowed three hours to complete your work.

A high level of accuracy is required. Check your work carefully.

Correcting fluid may be used but should be used in moderation. Errors should be crossed out neatly and clearly. You should write in black ink, not pencil.

You are advised to read the whole of the Assessment before commencing, as all of the information may be of value and is not necessarily supplied in the sequence in which you might wish to deal with it.

A full suggested answer to this Assessment is provided on page 285 of this Text.

THE SITUATION

This simulation is concerned with Washbrook & Co, a wholesaler of computer equipment, and specifically with transactions in the months of August and September 2003. 'Today' is 12 September 2003.

Your name is Amir Pershawa and you work for Washbrook & Co as an accounts assistant. You report to the accounts supervisor, Edna Lockey.

Sales and purchases

All sales and purchases are on credit terms and are subject to VAT at the standard rate. They are recorded in a subsidiary (sales) ledger and a subsidiary (purchases) ledger respectively. A sales ledger control account and a purchases ledger control account are maintained in the main ledger.

Wages and salaries

Wages and salaries are paid monthly by direct credit transfer into the bank accounts of employees. Washbrook & Co's bank is informed of the net amounts to be paid by means of a 'Data submission form' submitted each month. These net amounts in turn are extracted from a more detailed 'Wages and salaries analysis' prepared each month by Edna Lockey.

Bank account and cash book

A bank statement is received weekly. This is checked by reference to cash book entries, credit transfer details, and a schedule of direct debits and standing orders. Any entries appearing in the bank statement, but not in the cash book, are checked as appropriate and entered in the cash book if correct.

THE TASKS TO BE PERFORMED

Task 1

A debtor (Paxton Limited) has gone into liquidation and the amount owing to Washbrook & Co (£1,150.00) must be written off as a bad debt.

- Make appropriate adjustments in the main ledger, dating the entries 31 August 2003. The main ledger accounts, written up for the month of August 2003, are displayed on pages 256 –261 of the answer booklet.

Task 2

- Total the list of creditors' balances as at 31 August 2003 on page 262 of the answer booklet, and agree the total to the balance on the purchases ledger control account on page 258 of the answer booklet at that date.

- If you note a discrepancy, explain the cause and the action required in the space provided on page 262 of the answer booklet.

Task 3

- Total the list of debtors' balances as at 31 August 2003 on page 263 of the answer booklet, and agree the total to the balance on the sales ledger control account on page 259 of the answer booklet at that date.

- If you note a discrepancy, explain the cause and the action required in the space provided on page 263 of the answer booklet.

Task 4

- Check the total cash payments in respect of wages and salaries in August 2003. To do this you should complete the reconciliation form on page 264 of the answer booklet. You will need to refer to the wages and salaries analysis for July 2003 and the bank data submission form for August 2003 on page 251 of this booklet.

Task 5

- Total all accounts in the main ledger and bring down balances as at the start of business on 1 September 2003.

Task 6

- Enter the balances at 1 September 2003 in the trial balance on page 265 of the answer booklet and total the trial balance. Enter a suspense account to make the total debits and credits balance.

Task 7

Having informed Edna Lockey of the suspense account balance you have now received the email on page 252.

- Prepare the journals referred to in the email, including appropriate narrative, using the journal vouchers on page 266 of the answer booklet.

Task 8

- Check the entries on the business bank statement for week ending 7 September (page 253). You will need to refer to the schedule of standing orders and direct debits on page 253 and to the cash book for week ending 7 September on page 267 of the answer booklet.

- Make further entries in the cash book where appropriate.

Task 9

- Total the cash book for the week ending 7 September 2003 and bring down a balance as at start of business on 8 September 2003.

Task 10

- Prepare a bank reconciliation statement as at 7 September 2003, clearly identifying all discrepancies between the cash book and the bank statement. Use the blank page 268 of the answer booklet.

Task 11

The petty cash book has been written up for the week ending 7 September 2003 on page 269 of the answer booklet. On the same page you will see a list of the notes and coins in the petty cash tin at close of business on 7 September 2003, and a reconciliation schedule.

- Total the petty cash book and bring down a balance at close of business on 7 September 2003.
- Complete the reconciliation schedule, including a note of any discrepancy.

Wages and salaries analysis

Month: July 2003

Employee name	PAYE £	Employee NIC £	Net pay £	Employer NIC £	Total £
Alan Benyon	256.02	103.56	1,349.58	166.07	1,875.23
Kaulinder Bhopal	1,471.08	170.90	3,309.69	473.04	5,424.71
Emily Dingle	265.75	91.65	1,254.40	153.63	1,765.43
Norman French	355.90	150.00	1,603.34	191.77	2,301.01
Edna Lockey	231.84	101.96	1,359.22	150.88	1,843.90
Petra Nugent	632.00	181.91	2,296.08	305.86	3,415.85
Amir Pershawa	234.45	70.01	1,167.63	129.34	1,601.43
Lillian Staples	281.06	105.63	1,381.62	165.90	1,934.21
	3,728.10	975.62	13,721.56	1,736.49	20,161.77

Midlands Bank plc

Sort code: 28-92-45

Data submission form: net salary payments

Customer name: Washbrook & Co

Account number: 21176938

Due date for payments: 28 August 2003

Total value of payments: £14,245.05

Payee	Sort code	Account no	Amount £
Alan Benyon	20-75-40	21156789	1,349.02
Kaulinder Bhopal	30-60-68	45113214	3,511.68
Emily Dingle	20-75-40	23134456	1,305.60
Norman French	33-65-01	01876543	1,660.45
Edna Lockey	30-60-55	12543210	1,390.51
Petra Nugent	30-60-68	43120089	2,401.76
Amir Pershawa	20-75-40	24123098	1,202.35
Lillian Staples	35-61-32	00876543	1,423.65

Signature of customer .... *Edna Lockey* ....   Date ...... *21 August 2003* ....

From: Edna Lockey

To: Amir Pershawa

Subject: Correcting the trial balance

Thanks for doing the initial TB at 1 September 2003. I've looked into why it doesn't balance. There are two things that need to be adjusted.

Firstly, we returned goods to a supplier to the value of £500. We correctly entered this in the subsidiary (purchases) ledger, and in the purchases ledger control account. However, in the purchases account we mistakenly entered it as a debit.

Secondly, we received a cheque for £5,000 which was correctly debited to bank account. However, no credit entry was made. The double entry should have been completed in the capital account.

Please could you draft journals dated 31 August 2003 to deal with both of these items?

Thanks

Edna

Midlands Bank plc
27 High Street, Blanktown BW3 7AP

STATEMENT
28-92-45

Account: Washbrook & Co
Account number: 21176938

Statement no: 317

Date	Details		Payments £	Receipts £	Balance £
2003					
1 Sep	Balance from previous sheet				21,025.75
1 Sep	Safeguard Insurance Co 19632471	SO	480.00		20,545.75
2 Sep	Cheques/cash received	CC		3,864.92	24,410.67
3 Sep	CHGS quarter to 25 August 2003		104.97		24,305.70
4 Sep	Cheque 300928	CC	100.00		
4 Sep	Cheques/cash received	CC		1,100.96	
4 Sep	Cheque 300924		3,794.20		
5 Sep	Cheque 300925		2,836.67		
5 Sep	Cheque 300926		5,100.69		
5 Sep	Cheque 300923		1,425.68		
5 Sep	Midlands Electricity Board 42773915	DD	520.00		11,629.42

KEY	SO Standing Order CC Cash and/or cheques DD Direct debit
	CHGS Bank charges O/D Overdrawn

Schedule of standing orders and direct debits (extract)

Payee/reference	Amount	When payable
Midlands Electricity Board 42773915	Variable	Mar, Jun, Sep, Dec
Safeguard Insurance 19632471	£480.00	Mar, Sep

WASHBROOK & CO

ANSWER BOOKLET

Unit 3

Tasks 1, 5

Main (general) ledger

Account: Administration overheads

Debit			Credit		
Date 2003	*Details*	*Amount* £	*Date* 2003	*Details*	*Amount* £
1 Aug	Balance b/f	5,633.10			
31 Aug	Purchases ledger control	1,239.86			

Account: Bad debts

Debit			Credit		
Date 2003	*Details*	*Amount* £	*Date* 2003	*Details*	*Amount* £
1 Aug	Balance b/f	792.77			

Account: Bank control

Debit			Credit		
Date 2003	*Details*	*Amount* £	*Date* 2003	*Details*	*Amount* £
1 Aug	Balance b/f	16,809.25	31 Aug	Payments in month	64,719.45
31 Aug	Receipts in month	67,510.27			

Account: Capital

Debit			Credit		
Date 2003	*Details*	*Amount* £	*Date* 2003	*Details*	*Amount* £
			1 Aug	Balance b/f	47,355.37

Account: Fixed assets

Debit			Credit		
Date 2003	*Details*	*Amount* £	*Date* 2003	*Details*	*Amount* £
1 Aug	Balance b/f	50,100.65			

Account: PAYE/NIC liability

Debit			Credit		
Date 2003	*Details*	*Amount* £	*Date* 2003	*Details*	*Amount* £
31 Aug	Bank	6,440.21	1 Aug	Balance b/f	6,440.21
			31 Aug	Wages/salaries control	6,910.43

Account: Petty cash control

Debit			Credit		
Date 2003	*Details*	*Amount* £	*Date* 2003	*Details*	*Amount* £
1 Aug	Balance b/f	148.60	31 Aug	Sundry expenses	75.24
31 Aug	Bank	100.00			

Account: Purchases

Debit			Credit		
Date 2003	*Details*	*Amount* £	*Date* 2003	*Details*	*Amount* £
1 Aug	Balance b/f	125,217.56			
31 Aug	Purchases ledger control	35,323.30			

Account: Purchases ledger control

Debit			Credit		
Date 2003	*Details*	*Amount* £	*Date* 2003	*Details*	*Amount* £
31 Aug	Bank	40,078.96	1 Aug	Balance b/f	30,115.79
			31 Aug	Expenses/VAT	44,410.00

Account: Sales

Debit			Credit		
Date 2003	*Details*	*Amount* £	*Date* 2003	*Details*	*Amount* £
			1 Aug	Balance b/f	290,550.48
			31 Aug	Sales ledger control	52,402.80

Account: Sales ledger control

Debit			Credit		
Date 2003	*Details*	*Amount* £	*Date* 2003	*Details*	*Amount* £
1 Aug	Balance b/f	57,179.30	31 Aug	Bank	62,510.27
31 Aug	Sales/VAT	61,573.29			

Account: Selling and distribution overheads

Debit			Credit		
Date 2003	*Details*	*Amount* £	*Date* 2003	*Details*	*Amount* £
1 Aug	Balance b/f	5,370.26			
31 Aug	Purchases ledger control	1,607.59			

Account: Stock

Debit			Credit		
Date 2003	*Details*	*Amount* £	*Date* 2003	*Details*	*Amount* £
1 Aug	Balance b/f	31,400.12			

Account: Sundry expenses

Debit			Credit		
Date 2003	*Details*	*Amount* £	*Date* 2003	*Details*	*Amount* £
1 Aug	Balance b/f	1,875.64			
31 Aug	Purchases ledger control	625.00			
31 Aug	Petty cash	74.25			

Account: VAT control

Debit			Credit		
Date 2003	*Details*	*Amount* £	*Date* 2003	*Details*	*Amount* £
31 Aug	Purchases ledger control	6,614.25	1 Aug	Balance b/f	4,135.66
31 Aug	Bank	3,855.23	31 Aug	Sales ledger control	9,170.49

Account: Wages/salaries control

Debit			Credit		
Date 2003	*Details*	*Amount* £	*Date* 2003	*Details*	*Amount* £
31 Aug	Bank	14,245.05	31 Aug	Wages/salaries expense	21,155.48
31 Aug	PAYE/NIC liability	6,910.43			

Account: Wages/salaries expense

Debit			Credit		
Date 2003	*Details*	*Amount* £	*Date* 2003	*Details*	*Amount* £
1 Aug	Balance b/f	84,070.26			
31 Aug	Wages/salaries control	21,155.48			

Task 2

Schedule of creditors at 31 August 2003

Name of creditor	Amount owing at 31 August 2003
	£
Bilbrook & Co	5,441.06
Muldoon Partnership	6,145.29
Pangloss Limited	7,223.49
Raveleigh Limited	8,934.01
Roses plc	2,990.21
Vansittart plc	3,712.77

Total of creditors' balances

Total per control account

Difference (if any)

Explanation of difference/action required:

....

....

....

....

....

....

Task 3

Schedule of debtors at 31 August 2003

Name of debtor	Amount owing at 31 August 2003 £
Allenby & Co	6,200.61
Charles Limited	4,459.12
Elleray plc	5,199.22
Farrell plc	3,107.42
Kingston Partners	6,487.10
Liberty Limited	5,015.59
Michaels plc	1,823.81
Norman Limited	6,167.91
Paxton Limited	1,150.00
Vinjay plc	16,631.54

Total of debtors' balances

Total per control account

Difference (if any)

Explanation of difference/action required:

....

....

....

....

....

....

Task 4

Reconciliation of wages/salaries payments in month

MONTH ....

	£
Total PAYE from previous month	
Total employees' NIC from previous month	
Total employer's NIC from previous month	_____
Subtotal = balance b/f on PAYE/NIC liability account	
Total net pay in current month (= bank payments figures in wages/salaries control)	_____
Total wages/salaries payments in month	_____

Task 6

Trial balance at 1 September 2003

Account name	Debit £	Credit £
Administration		
Bad debts		
Bank control		
Capital		
Fixed assets		
PAYE/NIC liability		
Petty cash control		
Purchases		
Purchases ledger control		
Sales		
Sales ledger control		
Selling and distribution overheads		
Stock		
Sundry expense		
VAT control		
Wages/salaries control		
Wages/salaries expense		
	_____	_____
Totals	_____	_____

Task 7

Journal

Date	Account names and narrative	Debit £	Credit £

Tasks 8, 9

Cash book

RECEIPTS						PAYMENTS			
Debtors	Other receipts	Total	Date	Details		Cheque no	Total	Creditors	Other payments
£	£	£	2003				£	£	£
		19,600.07	1 Sep	Balance b/f					
3,864.92		3,864.92	2 Sep	Charles Limited					
			2 Sep	Bilbrook & Co		300924	3,794.20	3,794.20	
			2 Sep	HM Customs & Excise		300925	2,836.67		2,836.67
1,100.96		1,100.96	3 Sep	Michaels plc					
			3 Sep	Pangloss Limited		300926	5,100.69	5,100.69	
			3 Sep	Raveleigh Limited		300927	4,207.33	4,207.33	
4,221.79		4,221.79	4 Sep	Vinjay plc					
			4 Sep	Petty cash		300928	100.00		100.00

Task 10

Task 11

PETTY CASH BOOK   **PCB 19**

Receipts £	Date 2003	Details	Voucher	Total £	VAT £	Sundry expenses £
173.36	1 Sep	Balance b/f				
	5 Sep	Postage	215	2.41		2.41
	5 Sep	Stationery	216	5.45	0.81	4.64
	5 Sep	Postage	217	2.85		2.85
	5 Sep	Tea, coffee etc	218	6.75		6.75
	5 Sep	Stationery	219	3.41	0.51	2.90
	5 Sep	Postage	220	4.05		4.05

Notes and coins in the petty cash tin, 7 September 2003

Value	Number	Total value £
£20	5	
£10	3	
£5	2	
£2		
£1	6	
50p	3	
20p	2	
10p	4	
5p	1	
2p	3	
1p	3	

Petty cash reconciliation

Date ....

£

Balance per petty cash book

Total of notes and coins _____

Discrepancy (if any) _____

Explanation of discrepancy (if any)

....

....

....

Answers to Full Skills based Assessments

ANSWERS TO FULL SKILLS BASED ASSESSMENT 1

T S STATIONERY

**DO NOT TURN THIS PAGE UNTIL YOU HAVE COMPLETED
THE FULL SKILLS BASED ASSESSMENT**

Task 1

MAIN LEDGER ACCOUNTS

PURCHASE LEDGER CONTROL ACCOUNT

		£			£
31 Mar	PRDB	141	27 Mar	Opening balance	14,325
			31 Mar	PDB	846

PURCHASES ACCOUNT

		£			£
27 Mar	Opening balance	166,280	31 Mar	Balance c/d	167,000
31 Mar	PDB	720			
		167,000			167,000
1 Apr	Balance b/d	167,000			

PURCHASES RETURNS ACCOUNT

		£			£
31 Mar	Balance c/d	4,300	27 Mar	Opening balance	4,180
			31 Mar	PRDB	120
		4,300			4,300
			1 Apr	Balance b/d	4,300

VAT ACCOUNT

		£			£
31 Mar	PDB	126	27 Mar	Opening balance	1,405
31 Mar	Balance c/d	1,300	31 Mar	PRDB	21
		1,426			1,426
			1 Apr	Balance b/d	1,300

SUBSIDIARY LEDGER ACCOUNTS

F P PAPER

	£			£
		27 Mar	Opening balance	3,825
		31 Mar	PDB	188

GIFT PRODUCTS LTD

		£			£
31 Mar	PRDB	94	27 Mar	Opening balance	4,661
			31 Mar	PDB	235

HARPER BROS

		£			£
31 Mar	PRDB	47	27 Mar	Opening balance	3,702
			31 Mar	PDB	141

J S TRADERS

		£			£
			27 Mar	Opening balance	2,137
			31 Mar	PDB	282

Task 2

Main ledger

PURCHASE LEDGER CONTROL ACCOUNT

		£			£
31 Mar	PRDB	141	27 Mar	Opening balance	14,325
31 Mar	Balance c/d	15,030	31 Mar	PDB	846
		15,171			15,171
			1 Apr	Balance b/d	15,030

Subsidiary ledger

F P PAPER

		£			£
31 Mar	Balance c/d	4,013	27 Mar	Opening balance	3,825
			31 Mar	PDB	188
		4,013			4,013
			1 Apr	Balance b/d	4,013

GIFT PRODUCTS LTD

		£			£
31 Mar	PRDB	94	27 Mar	Opening balance	4,661
31 Mar	Balance c/d	4,802	31 Mar	PDB	235
		4,896			4,896
			1 Apr	Balance b/d	4,802

HARPER BROS

		£			£
31 Mar	PRDB	47	27 Mar	Opening balance	3,702
31 Mar	Balance c/d	3,796	31 Mar	PDB	141
		3,843			3,843
			31 Mar	Balance b/d	3,796

J S TRADERS

		£			£
31 Mar	Balance c/d	2,419	27 Mar	Opening balance	2,137
			31 Mar	PDB	282
		2,419			2,419
			1 Apr	Balance b/d	2,419

**Reconciliation of purchase ledger control account balance
with total of balances in the subsidiary ledger**

	£
F P Paper	4,013
Gift Products Ltd	4,802
Harper Bros	3,796
J S Traders	2,419
Purchase ledger control account balance	15,030

Task 3

Main ledger

SALES LEDGER CONTROL ACCOUNT

		£			£
31 Mar	Balance b/d	23,230	31 Mar	Journal 336	400
31 Mar	Journal 337	100	31 Mar	Balance c/d	22,930
		23,330			23,330
1 April	Balance b/d	22,930			

SALES ACCOUNT

		£			£
31 Mar	Balance b/d	255,910	31 Mar	Balance b/d	255,810
			31 Mar	Journal 337	100
		255,910			255,910
			1 April	Balance b/d	255,910

BAD DEBTS EXPENSE ACCOUNT

		£		£
31 Mar	Journal 336	400		

Subsidiary ledger

RETAIL ENTERPRISES

		£		£
31 Mar	Balance b/d	5,114		

C CUMMINGS

		£			£
31 Mar	Balance b/d	400	31 Mar	Bad debt w/o	400

PALMER LIMITED

	£		£
31 Mar Balance b/d	6,248		

REAPER STORES

	£		£
31 Mar Balance b/d	5,993		

KNIGHT RETAIL

	£		£
31 Mar Balance b/d	5,575		

**Reconciliation of sales ledger control account balance
with the total of the balances in the subsidiary ledger for debtors**

	£
Retail enterprises	5,114
C Cummings	-
Palmer Ltd	6,248
Reapers Stores	5,993
Knight Retail	5,575
	22,930

Tasks 4, 5 and 6

CASH BOOK

RECEIPTS			PAYMENTS			
Date	Details	£	Date	Details	Cheque No	£
1 Mar	Balance b/d	3,668	5 Mar	Harper Bros	002643	2,558
7 Mar	Palmer Ltd	2,557	12 Mar	Gift Products	002644	3,119
15 Mar	Retails Engineering	4,110	18 Mar	F P Paper	002645	2,553
20 Mar	Reapers Stores	4,782	24 Mar	J S Traders	002646	983
28 Mar	Knight Retail	3,765	31 Mar	BACS - wages		3,405
			31 Mar	SO rates		200
31 Mar	Bank interest	20	31 Mar	SO - loan		400
			31 Mar	Balance c/d		5,684
		18,902				18,902
1 April	Balance b/d	5,684				

RATES ACCOUNT

		£			£
31 Mar	Balance b/dB	2,200	31 Mar	Balance c/d	2,400
31 Mar	CBP	200			
		2,400			2,400
1 Apr	Balance b/d	2,400			

LOAN ACCOUNT

		£			£
31 Mar	CPB	400	31 Mar	Balance b/d	6,400
31 Mar	Balance c/d	6,000			
		6,400			6,400
			1 April	Balance b/d	6,000

BANK INTEREST RECEIVABLE

		£			£
			31 Mar	Balance b/d	100
31 Mar	Balance c/d	120	31 Mar	CRB	20
		120			120
			1 Apr	Balance b/d	120

BANK RECONCILIATION STATEMENT AT 31 MARCH 20X1

	£
Balance per bank statement	2,902
Add outstanding lodgement (Knight Retail)	3,765
	6,667
Less outstanding cheque 002646	983
Balance per adjusted cash book	5,684

Task 7

NON-TRADE DEBTORS ACCOUNT

		£			£
1 Mar	Balance b/d	480	31 Mar	CBR	4,100
31 Mar	Rent received	4,500	31 Mar	Balance c/d	880
		4,980			4,980
1 April	Balance b/d	880			

RENT RECEIVED ACCOUNT

		£			£
31 Mar	Balance c/d	49,500	1 Mar	Balance b/d	45,000
			31 Mar	Rent due	4,500
		49,500			49,500
			1 April	Balance b/d	49,500

Task 8

Voucher total

Voucher number	£
0264	3.67
0265	9.48
0266	6.70
0267	13.20
0268	2.36
0269	1.55
0270	10.46
0271	4.89
0272	3.69
	56.00

Cash

Note/coin	Number	£
£10	1	10.00
£5	4	20.00
£2	2	4.00
£1	7	7.00
50p	3	1.50
20p	4	0.80
10p	5	0.50
5p	1	0.05
2p	7	0.14
1p	1	0.01
		44.00

Voucher total	56.00
Cash total	44.00
Imprest amount	100.00

The petty cash balance to appear in the trial balance is £44.00

Task 9

Trial balance at 31 March 20X1

	£	£
Building	100,000	
Motor vehicles	34,500	
Office equipment	13,000	
Purchases (Task 1)	167,000	
Purchases returns (Task 1)		4,300
Capital		53,855
Sales (Task 3)		255,910
Sales returns	6,800	
Discounts allowed	300	
Stock	16,000	
Loan (Task 6)		6,000
Discount received		600
Debtors (Task 3)	22,930	
Petty cash (Task 8)	44	
Creditors (Task 2)		15,030
VAT (Task 1)		1,300
Bank (Task 5)	5,684	
Non-trade debtors (Task 7)	880	
Rent received (Task 7)		49,500
Motor expenses	4,297	
Telephone	4,850	
Electricity	3,630	
Rates (Task 6)	2,400	
Miscellaneous expenses	3,900	
Bad debts expense (Task 3)	400	
Bank interest receivable (Task 6)		120
	386,615	386,615

Task 10

MEMO

To: The owner
From: The bookkeeper
Date: 2 April 20X1
Subject: Errors and the trial balance

Although the trial balance does balance at the year end this does not necessarily mean that there are no errors in the accounting records. There are some types of errors that are not revealed by extracting a trial balance as they do not cause an imbalance on the trial balance. These types of errors are:

Error of omission - this is where an entry has not been made in the accounting records at all - therefore there has been neither a debit nor a credit entry. For example, if the journal entry for the bad debt write off had not been posted to the ledger accounts this would not have affected the balancing of the trial balance.

Error of commission - here the double entry has taken place but one side of the entry has been to the correct type of account but to the wrong account. For example, suppose payment of the telephone bill had been credited in the bank account but then debited to the electricity account. Both the telephone account and the electricity account are incorrect but the trial balance still balances.

Error of principle - here one side of the double entry has been to the wrong type of account. For example if the cost of petrol, a motor expense, had been debited to the motor vehicle fixed asset account the trial balance would still balance but the fixed asset account and the expense account for the motor vehicle would be incorrect.

Reversal of entries - here a debit and matching credit entry are made to the correct accounts but to the wrong side of each account. For example if the bad debt write off was accounted for as a debit to the sales ledger control account and a credit to the bad debts expense account this would not affect the balancing of the trial balance but both the sales ledger control account and bad debts expense account balances would be incorrect.

Error of original entry - with this type of error the correct accounts are debited and credited but with the incorrect amount. For example if the payment of the telephone bill of say £1,200 was entered in both the cash book and the telephone account as £2,100 the trial balance would still balance but the bank account and telephone account balances would be incorrect.

Compensating errors - this type of error is where two errors are made which exactly cancel each other out. For example if the bank interest receivable account balance was listed in the trial balance at £100 too large and the miscellaneous expenses account balance was also listed as £100 too large then the two errors would cancel each other out and the trial balance would still balance.

ANSWERS TO FULL SKILLS BASED ASSESSMENT 2

WASHBROOK & CO

DO NOT TURN THIS PAGE UNTIL YOU HAVE COMPLETED
THE FULL SKILLS BASED ASSESSMENT

Tasks 1, 5

Main (general) ledger

Account: Administration overheads

Debit			Credit		
Date 2003	*Details*	*Amount* £	*Date* 2003	*Details*	*Amount* £
1 Aug	Balance b/f	5,633.10			
31 Aug	Purchases ledger control	1,239.86	31 Aug	Balance c/d	6,872.96
		6,872.96			6,872.96
1 Sep	Balance b/d	6,872.96			

Account: Bad debts

Debit			Credit		
Date 2003	*Details*	*Amount* £	*Date* 2003	*Details*	*Amount* £
1 Aug	Balance b/f	792.77			
31 Aug	Sales ledger control	1,150.00	31 Aug	Balance c/d	1,942.77
		1,942.77			1,942.77
1 Sep	Balance b/d	1,942.77			

Account: Bank control

Debit			Credit		
Date 2003	*Details*	*Amount* £	*Date* 2003	*Details*	*Amount* £
1 Aug	Balance b/f	16,809.25	31 Aug	Payments in month	64,719.45
31 Aug	Receipts in month	67,510.27	31 Aug	Balance c/d	19,600.07
		84,319.52			84,319.52
1 Sep	Balance b/d	19,600.07			

Account: Capital

Debit			Credit		
Date 2003	*Details*	*Amount* £	*Date* 2003	*Details*	*Amount* £
			1 Aug	Balance b/f	47,355.37
31 Aug	Balance c/d	47,355.37			
		47,355.37			47,355.37
			1 Sep	Balance b/d	47,355.37

Account: Fixed assets

Debit			Credit		
Date 2003	*Details*	*Amount* £	*Date* 2003	*Details*	*Amount* £
1 Aug	Balance b/f	50,100.65			
			31 Aug	Balance c/d	50,100.65
		50,100.65			50,100.65
1 Sep	Balance b/d	50,100.65			

Account: PAYE/NIC liability

Debit			Credit		
Date 2003	*Details*	*Amount* £	*Date* 2003	*Details*	*Amount* £
31 Aug	Bank	6,440.21	1 Aug	Balance b/f	6,440.21
31 Aug	Balance c/d	6,910.43	31 Aug	Wages/salaries control	6,910.43
		13,350.64			13,350.64
			1 Sep	Balance b/d	6,910.43

Account: Petty cash control

Debit			Credit		
Date 2003	*Details*	*Amount* £	*Date* 2003	*Details*	*Amount* £
1 Aug	Balance b/f	148.60	31 Aug	Sundry expenses	75.24
31 Aug	Bank	100.00	31 Aug	Balance c/d	173.36
		248.60			248.60
1 Sep	Balance b/d	173.36			

Account: Purchases

Debit			Credit		
Date 2003	*Details*	*Amount* £	*Date* 2003	*Details*	*Amount* £
1 Aug	Balance b/f	125,217.56			
31 Aug	Purchases ledger control	35,323.30	31 Aug	Balance c/d	160,540.86
		160,540.86			160,540.86
1 Sep	Balance b/d	160,540.86			

Account: Purchases ledger control

Debit			Credit		
Date 2003	*Details*	*Amount* £	*Date* 2003	*Details*	*Amount* £
31 Aug	Bank	40,078.96	1 Aug	Balance b/f	30,115.79
31 Aug	Balance c/d	34,446.83	31 Aug	Expenses/VAT	44,410.00
		74,525.79			74,525.79
			1 Sep	Balance b/d	34,446.83

Account: Sales

Debit			Credit		
Date 2003	*Details*	*Amount* £	*Date* 2003	*Details*	*Amount* £
			1 Aug	Balance b/f	290,550.48
31 Aug	Balance c/d	342,953.28	31 Aug	Sales ledger control	52,402.80
		342,953.28			342,953.28
			1 Sep	Balance b/d	342,953.28

Account: Sales ledger control

Debit			Credit		
Date 2003	*Details*	*Amount* £	*Date* 2003	*Details*	*Amount* £
1 Aug	Balance b/f	57,179.30	31 Aug	Bank	62,510.27
31 Aug	Sales/VAT	61,573.29	31 Aug	Bad debts	1,150.00
			31 Aug	Balance c/d	55,092.32
		118,752.59			118,752.59
1 Sep	Balance b/d	55,092.32			

Account: Selling and distribution overheads

Debit			Credit		
Date 2003	*Details*	*Amount* £	*Date* 2003	*Details*	*Amount* £
1 Aug	Balance b/f	5,370.26			
31 Aug	Purchases ledger control	1,607.59	31 Aug	Balance c/d	6,977.85
		6,977.85			6,977.85
1 Sep	Balance b/d	6,977.85			

Account: Stock

Debit			Credit		
Date 2003	*Details*	*Amount* £	*Date* 2003	*Details*	*Amount* £
1 Aug	Balance b/f	31,400.12			
			31 Aug	Balance c/d	31,400.12
		31,400.12			31,400.12
1 Sep	Balance b/d	31,400.12			

Account: Sundry expenses

Debit			Credit		
Date 2003	*Details*	*Amount* £	*Date* 2003	*Details*	*Amount* £
1 Aug	Balance b/f	1,875.64			
31 Aug	Purchases ledger control	625.00			
31 Aug	Petty cash	74.25	31 Aug	Balance c/d	2,575.88
		2,575.88			2,575.88
1 Sep	Balance b/d	2,575.88			

Account: VAT control

Debit			Credit		
Date 2003	*Details*	*Amount* £	*Date* 2003	*Details*	*Amount* £
31 Aug	Purchases ledger control	6,614.25	1 Aug	Balance b/f	4,135.66
31 Aug	Bank	3,855.23	31 Aug	Sales ledger control	9,170.49
31 Aug	Balance c/d	2,836.67			
		13,306.15			13,306.15
			1 Sep	Balance b/d	2,836.67

Account: Wages/salaries control

Debit			Credit		
Date 2003	*Details*	*Amount* £	*Date* 2003	*Details*	*Amount* £
31 Aug	Bank	14,245.05	31 Aug	Wages/salaries expense	21,155.48
31 Aug	PAYE/NIC liability	6,910.43			
		21,155.48			21,155.48

Account: Wages/salaries expense

Debit			Credit		
Date 2003	*Details*	*Amount* £	*Date* 2003	*Details*	*Amount* £
1 Aug	Balance b/f	84,070.26			
31 Aug	Wages/salaries control	21,155.48	31 Aug	Balance c/d	105,225.74
		105,225.74			105,225.74
1 Sep	Balance b/d	105,225.74			

Task 2

Schedule of creditors at 31 August 2003

Name of creditor	*Amount owing at 31 August 2003* £
Bilbrook & Co	5,441.06
Muldoon Partnership	6,145.29
Pangloss Limited	7,223.49
Raveleigh Limited	8,934.01
Roses plc	2,990.21
Vansittart plc	3,712.77
Total of creditors' balances	34,446.83
Total per control account	34,446.83
Difference (if any)	n/a

Explanation of difference/action required:
  N/A

....

....

....

....

....

....

Task 3

Schedule of debtors at 31 August 2003

Name of debtor	Amount owing at 31 August 2003 £
Allenby & Co	6,200.61
Charles Limited	4,459.12
Elleray plc	5,199.22
Farrell plc	3,107.42
Kingston Partners	6,487.10
Liberty Limited	5,015.59
Michaels plc	1,823.81
Norman Limited	6,167.91
Paxton Limited	1,150.00
Vinjay plc	16,631.54
Total of debtors' balances	56,242.32
Total per control account	55,092.32
Difference (if any)	1,150.00

Explanation of difference/action required:

The list of balances still includes that of Paxton Limited, which has correctly been written off in the control account. The balance must be written off in the subsidiary (purchases) ledger after which the reconciliation will be complete. In the meantime, the control account figure is correct.

Task 4

Reconciliation of wages/salaries payments in month

MONTH ....August 2003.......................

	£
Total PAYE from previous month	3,728.10
Total employees' NIC from previous month	975.62
Total employer's NIC from previous month	1,736.49
Subtotal = balance b/f on PAYE/NIC liability account	6,440.21
Total net pay in current month (= bank payments figures in wages/salaries control)	14,245.05
Total wages/salaries payments in month	20,685.26

Task 6

Trial balance at 1 September 2003

Account name	Debit £	Credit £
Administration	6,872.96	
Bad debts	1,942.77	
Bank control	19,600.07	
Capital		47,355.37
Fixed assets	50,100.65	
PAYE/NIC liability		6,910.43
Petty cash control	173.36	
Purchases	160,540.86	
Purchases ledger control		34,446.83
Sales		342,953.28
Sales ledger control	55,092.32	
Selling and distribution overheads	6,877.85	
Stock	31,400.12	
Sundry expense	2,575.88	
VAT control		2,836.67
Wages/salaries control		
Wages/salaries expense	105,225.74	
		6,000.00
Totals	440,502.58	440,502.58

Task 7

Journal

Date	Account names and narrative	Debit £	Credit £
	Suspense account	1,000.00	
	Purchases		1,000.00
	Being returns to suppliers incorrectly entered in purchases account		
	Suspense account	5,000.00	
	Capital		5,000.00
	Being receipt of new capital previously omitted		

Tasks 8, 9

Cash book

CB 126

Debtors	Other receipts	Total	Date	Details	Cheque no	Total	Creditors	Other payments
RECEIPTS					PAYMENTS			
£	£	£	2003			£	£	£
		19,600.07	1 Sep	Balance b/f				
3,864.92		3,864.92	2 Sep	Charles Limited				
			2 Sep	Bilbrook & Co	300924	3,794.20	3,794.20	
			2 Sep	HM Customs & Excise	300925	2,836.67		2,836.67
1,100.96		1,100.96	3 Sep	Michaels plc				
			3 Sep	Pangloss Limited	300926	5,100.69	5,100.69	
			3 Sep	Raveleigh Limited	300927	4,207.33	4,207.33	
4,221.79		4,221.79	4 Sep	Vinjay plc				
			4 Sep	Petty cash	300928	100.00		100.00
			5 Sep	Safeguard Insurance	SO	480.00		480.00
			5 Sep	Bank charges	CHGS	104.97		104.97
			5 Sep	Midlands Electricity	DD	520.00		520.00
			7 Sep	Balance c/d		11,643.88		
9,187.67		28,787.74				28,787.74	13,102.22	4,041.64
		11,643.88	8 Sep	Balance b/d				

Task 10

BANK RECONCILIATION STATEMENT AT 7 SEPTEMBER 2003

	£
Balance per bank statement	11,629.42
Outstanding lodgement	4,221.79
	15,851.21
Unpresented cheque 300927	4,207.33
Balance per cash book	11,643.88

Task 11

PETTY CASH BOOK   **PCB 19**

Receipts £	Date 2003	Details	Voucher	Total £	VAT £	Sundry expenses £
173.36	1 Sep	Balance b/f				
	5 Sep	Postage	215	2.41		2.41
	5 Sep	Stationery	216	5.45	0.81	4.64
	5 Sep	Postage	217	2.85		2.85
	5 Sep	Tea, coffee etc	218	6.75		6.75
	5 Sep	Stationery	219	3.41	0.51	2.90
	5 Sep	Postage	220	4.05		4.05
		Totals		24.92	1.31	23.61
	7 Sep	Balance c/d		148.44		
173.36				173.36	1.31	23.61

Notes and coins in the petty cash tin, 7 September 2003

Value	Number	Total value £
£20	5	100.00
£10	3	30.00
£5	2	10.00
£2		0.00
£1	6	6.00
50p	3	1.50
20p	2	0.40
10p	4	0.40
5p	1	0.05
2p	3	0.06
1p	3	0.03
		148.44

Petty cash reconciliation

Date ...7 September 2003...............

	£
Balance per petty cash book	148.44
Total of notes and coins	148.44
Discrepancy (if any)	Nil

Explanation of discrepancy (if any)

N/A..

....

....

PART H

AAT Sample Simulation

REVISED STANDARDS
FOUNDATION STAGE
NVQ/SVQ IN ACCOUNTING LEVEL 2
SPECIMEN SIMULATION

AAT

ASSOCIATION
OF ACCOUNTING
TECHNICIANS

SIMULATION—SPECIMEN

PREPARE LEDGER BALANCES AND AN INITIAL TRIAL BALANCE

DATA AND TASKS

TO BE COMPLETED BY CANDIDATE

Candidate Name

Registration Number

AAC Code

I confirm that I have received in addition to this booklet an answer booklet for preparing ledger balances and an initial trial balance and that I have access to a calculator.

Signed

Date

Note to assessor:
This booklet must remain sealed until the time of the assessments. If the assessment is being attempted by separate groups at different times, the unused booklets must be stored securely until the time of the later assessment.

Note to candidate:
This booklet must be returned to your assessor with your answer booklet. After marking, the outer sheet should be removed and placed in your portfolio.

© AAT 2003
154 Clerkenwell Road, London EC1R 5AD   Tel: +44 (0)20 7837 8600   Fax: +44 (0)20 7837 6970

COVERAGE OF PERFORMANCE CRITERIA AND RANGE STATEMENTS

The following performance criteria are covered in this simulation.

Element	PC Coverage
3.1 (a) (b) (c) (d)	**Balance bank transactions** Record details from the relevant **primary documentation** in the **cashbook and ledgers.** Correct calculate totals and balances of receipts and payments. Compare individual items on the bank statement and in the **cashbook** for accuracy. Identify discrepancies and prepare a bank reconciliation statement.
3.2 (a) (b) (c) (d) (e)	**Prepare ledger balances and control accounts** Make and **record** authorised **adjustments.** Total relevant accounts in the main ledger. Reconcile **control accounts** with the totals of the balance in the subsidiary ledger. Reconcile petty cash **control account** with the cash in hand and subsidiary records. Identify **discrepancies** arising from the reconciliation of **control accounts** and either resolve or refer to the appropriate person.
3.3 (a) (b) (c) (d)	**Draft an initial trial balance** Prepare the draft **initial trial balance** in line with the organisation's policies and procedures. Identify **discrepancies** in the balancing process. Identify reasons for imbalance and **rectify** them. Balance the trial balance.

The following performance criterion is not covered in this simulation and should be assessed separately.

3.2 (f) Ensure documentation is stored securely and in line with the organisation's confidentiality requirements.

The following range statements are not covered in this simulation and should be assessed separately.

Element	Range Statement
3.1	**Cash book and ledgers:** computerised **Bank reconciliation statement:** computerised
3.2	**Record:** computerised **Control accounts:** computerised; non-trade debtors **Discrepancies:** cash in hand not agreeing with subsidiary record and control record
3.3	**Trial balance:** computerised

2

ASSOCIATION OF ACCOUNTING TECHNICIANS

DATA AND TASKS

INSTRUCTIONS

This simulation is designed to let you show your ability to prepare ledger balances and an initial trial balance.

You should read the whole simulation before you start work, so that you are fully aware of what you will have to do.

You are allowed **three hours** to complete your work.

Write your answers in the answer booklet provided. If you need more paper for your answers, ask the person in charge.

You should write your answers in blue or black ink, **not** pencil.

You may use correcting fluid, but in moderation. You should cross out your errors neatly and clearly.

You may pull apart and rearrange your booklets if you wish to do so, but you must put them back in their original order before handing them in.

Your work must be accurate, so check your work carefully before handing it in.

You are not allowed to refer to any unauthorised material, such as books or notes, while you are working on the simulation. If you have any such material with you, you must hand it to the person in charge before you start work.

Any instances of misconduct will be reported to the AAT, and disciplinary action may be taken.

Coverage of performance criteria and range statements

It is not always possible to cover all performance criteria and range statements in a single simulation. Any performance criteria and range statements not covered must be assessed by other means by the assessor before a candidate can be considered competent.

Performance criteria and range statement coverage for this simulation is shown on page 2.

3

THE SITUATION

Your name is Kim Wendell. You are a qualified accounting technician working for Weasley Supplies. You report to the manager, Ari Pottle.

All of the company's sales and purchases are on credit terms.

The books of account are maintained in manual form.

Today's date is Monday 7 July 2003, and you will be dealing with transactions taking place in June 2003.

Ledgers

A sales ledger control account and a purchases ledger control account are maintained in the main (general) ledger. There is a subsidiary (sales) ledger for customers and a subsidiary (purchases) ledger for suppliers.

Bank account and cash book

A bank statement is received monthly. Entries on the bank statement are compared with:

*   entries in the cash book:
*   a schedule of standing orders, direct debits and credit transfers.

The cash book is updated as appropriate in the light of the bank statement and the schedule of standing orders, direct debits and credit transfers. The main items paid for by standing order, direct debit and credit transfer are:

*   business rates;
*   insurance and leasing payments;
*   staff salaries;
*   the company's credit card bill.

These items are analysed as 'Other payments' in the cash book.

4

THE TASKS TO BE COMPLETED

1. Refer to the schedule of standing orders, direct debits and credit transfers on page 7, and the bank statement for June 2003 on page 8 of this booklet.
   - Enter the appropriate details from the schedule in the cash book for June 2003 on page 2 of the answer booklet.
   - Also enter any other items on the bank statement not so far recorded in the cash book

   Note: You must complete both the total columns and the analysis columns in the cash book.

2. Total all columns of the cash book and bring down a balance as at close of business on 30 June 2003.

3. Prepare a bank reconciliation statement as at 30 June 2003, clearly identifying all discrepancies between the cash book and the bank statement. Use the blank page 3 of the answer booklet.

4. Refer to the email from Ari Pottle on page 9 of this booklet.
   - Prepare the journals referred to in the email, including appropriate narrative, using the journal vouchers on page 4 of the answer booklet.

5. • Post from the cash book (Task 2) and the journals (Task 4) to the sales ledger control account and the purchases ledger control account on page 5 of the answer booklet. (You are not required to make entries in the subsidiary ledgers in respect of these journals.)
   - Total the two control accounts and bring down balances as at close of business on 30 June 2003.

6. Refer to the list of balances on page 10 of this booklet, which have been taken from the subsidiary (purchases) ledger on 30 June 2003.
   - Total the list of balances and reconcile the total with the balance on the purchases ledger control account.
   - Suggest a reason for any discrepancy you observe.

   Present your work on the blank page 6 of the answer booklet.

7. The petty cash book has been written up for the month of June 2003; see page 7 of the answer booklet. On page 8 of the answer booklet you will see a list of the notes and coins in the petty cash tin at close of business on 30 June 2003, and a reconciliation schedule.
   - Total the petty cash book and bring down a balance at close of business on 30 June 2003.
   - Complete the reconciliation schedule, including a note of any discrepancy.

5

8 Refer to the list of ledger balances prepared by Ari Pottle as at 30 June 2003 (page 11 of this booklet).

• Enter Ari's balances, and also the control account balances computed in Tasks 2, 5 and 7, onto the trial balance on page 9 of the answer booklet. Note that the balance to be entered for cash at bank should reflect the journal entries drafted in Task 4.

• Total the trial balance, and ensure that it balances by entering a suspense account balance.

9. After informing Ari Pottle of the suspense account balance, you have now received the email on page 12 of this booklet.

• Prepare the journals referred to in the email, including appropriate narrative, using the journal vouchers on page 10 of the answer booklet.

10. Enter the journals prepared in Task 9 into the suspense account on page 10 of the answer booklet and ensure that the closing balance on this account is zero.

11. Reply to Ari's email explaining how the journals prepared in task 9 will affect the trial balance and confirming that it will now balance. Use the blank email form on page 11 of the answer booklet.

6

Schedule of standing orders, direct debits and credit transfers (extract)

Standing orders	Amount	When payable
Standing orders		
Medwith Borough Council (business rates)	£600	Monthly from April to January inclusive; no payment in February, March
Safeguard Insurance	£310	Monthly
Finance Leasing plc	£425	March, June, September, December
Direct debits		
Purchasecard plc	Variable	Monthly
Credit transfers		
Staff salaries	Variable	Monthly

7

AAT SPECIMEN SIMULATION

Northern Bank plc
27 High Street, Malliton FR5 6EW

STATEMENT
27-76-54

Account: Weasley Supplies
Account number: 22314561

Statement no: 226

Date	Details		Payments £	Receipts £	Balance £
2003					
1 June	Balance from previous sheet				5,267.88
6 June	Cash/cheques received	CC		4,776.15	10,044.03
10 June	Cheque 331174		781.03		9,263.00
13 June	Cheque 331175		1,456.91		
13 June	Cash/cheques received	CC		7,715.96	15,522.05
17 June	Safeguard Insurance 30056561	SO	310.00		15,212.05
20 June	Cash/cheques received	CC		15,901.22	31,113.27
23 June	Medwith BC 4412341125	SO	600.00		30,513.27
24 June	Cheque 331176		9,912.75		
24 June	Cash/cheques received	CC		2,816.55	23,417.07
25 June	Cheque 331177		3,901.25		19,515.82
26 June	Bank interest and charges	CHGS	107.33		
26 June	Finance Leasing plc 771233115	SO	425.00		
26 June	Salaries	CT	8,215.50		10,767.99
27 June	Purchasecard plc	DD	2,341.89		8,426.10
30 June	Cash/cheques received	CC		2,451.88	
30 June	Cheque 331179		3,126.99		7,750.99

Key   SO Standing order   CC Cash and/or cheques   CT Credit transfer
          O/D Overdrawn   D/D Direct Debit   CHGS Bank charges

8

EMAIL

From:	Ari Pottle
To:	Kim Wendell
CC:	
Subject:	**Journal entries**
Date:	7 July 2003

Message

Hi Kim

Please could you draw up two journal entries for me please?

The first concerns our cheque number 331179. This has been logged in the cash book at an amount of £3,216.99, but in fact was for £3,126.99. The wrong amount has also been posted to the purchases ledger control account.

The second concerns our customer Driftway Limited. They owe us £1,233.75, but have gone into liquidation so we have no chance of recovering the debt. Later on we may be able to recover the VAT included in this amount, but for the moment please write off the whole balance and ignore VAT.

Both of these matters should be dealt with by means of journals dated 30 June 2003.

Thanks

Ari

9

Creditors' balances at 30 June 2003

	£
Earley and Partners	3,990.65
Horsfall Limited	2,561.22
James Ross	4,016.73
Peters Limited	2,351.67
Pickard Newton (debit balance)	(90.00)
Stainton and Co	3,109.81
Other creditors	5,667.54

10

Main (general) ledger: balances at 30 June 2003

	£
Administration expenses	3,276.88
Bad debts	2.010.76
Bank	Own figure
Business rates	1,800.00
Capital	46,745.76
Fixed assets	25,219.05
Inland Revenue	4,003.51
Insurance	930.00
Leasing costs	1,275.00
Petty cash	Own figure
Purchases	64,016.83
Purchases ledger control	Own figure
Purchases returns	1,125.31
Salaries expense	35,211.81
Sales	96,558.43
Sales and distribution expenses	2,006.81
Sales ledger control	Own figure
Sales returns	1,327.44
Stock	7,270.00
VAT control (credit balance)	3,995.20

11

EMAIL

From:	Ari Pottle
To:	Kim Wendell
CC:	
Subject:	**Correcting the trial balance**
Date:	7 July 2003

Message

Hi Kim

I've looked into the discrepancy on the initial trial balance, and I've found two items that cause the problem.

First, we returned goods to a supplier to the value of £200. We correctly entered this in the subsidiary (purchases) ledger, and in the purchases ledger control account. However, in the purchases returns account we mistakenly entered it as a debit.

Second, we received a cheque for £3,000 which was correctly debited to bank account. However, no credit entry was made. The double entry should have been completed in the capital account.

Please could you draft journals dated 30 June 2003 to deal with both of these items, and then let me have a reply to this message confirming that the trial balance will now balance.

Thanks

Ari

12

REVISED STANDARDS
FOUNDATION STAGE
NVQ/SVQ IN ACCOUNTING LEVEL 2
SPECIMEN SIMULATION

AAT
ASSOCIATION
OF ACCOUNTING
TECHNICIANS

SIMULATION—SPECIMEN

PREPARE LEDGER BALANCES AND AN INITIAL TRIAL BALANCE

ANSWER BOOKLET

TO BE COMPLETED BY CANDIDATE

Candidate Name

Registration Number

AAC Code

This is my own unaided work

Signed

Date

TO BE COMPLETED BY ASSESSOR

Assessor Name

Date

Overall simulation result: Satisfactory?:   Y / N

Comments

Note to assessor:
This booklet must remain sealed until the time of the assessment.

Note to candidate:
This booklet must be returned to your assessor.

© AAT 2003

154 Clerkenwell Road, London EC1R 5AD   Tel: +44 (0)20 7837 8600   Fax: +44 (0)20 7837 6970

PROFESSIONAL EDUCATION

ANSWERS (Tasks 1 and 2)

CB 241

RECEIPTS			Date 2003	Details	PAYMENTS			
Sales ledger £	Other receipts £	Total £			Cheque number	Total £	Purchases ledger £	Other payments £
		4,486.85	1 June	Balance b/f				
4,776.15		4,776.15	5 June	Metrix plc				
			6 June	Horsfall Limited	331175	1,456.91	1,456.91	
7,715.96		7,715.96	12 June	Plympton Limited				
			16 June	Stainton and Co	331176	9,912.75	9,912.75	
			16 June	Inland Revenue	331177	3,901.25		3,901.25
15,901.22		15,901.22	19 June	Maidstone plc				
			23 June	Earley and Partners	331178	3,341.20	3,341.20	
2,816.55		2,816.55	23 June	Stenshaw Limited				
			25 June	Pickard Newton	331179	3,216.99	3,216.99	
2,451.88		2,451.88	29 June	Fitzroy Limited				
1926.34		1,926.34	30 June	Dove Ambleside				

2

ANSWERS (Task 3)

3

ANSWERS (Task 4)

JOURNAL

Date 2003	Account names and narrative	Debit £	Credit £

4

AT SPECIMEN SIMULATION: ANSWER BOOKLET

ANSWERS (Task 5)

MAIN (GENERAL) LEDGER

Account Sales control ledger account

Debit   Credit

Date 2003	Details	Amount £	Date 2003	Details	Amount £
1 June	Balance b/f	30,914.66			
30 June	Invoices in month	32,617.80			

Account Purchases control ledger account

Debit   Credit

Date 2003	Details	Amount £	Date 2003	Details	Amount £
			1 June	Balance b/f	19,334.02
			30 June	Invoices in month	20,201.45

5

ANSWERS (Task 6)

6

ANSWERS (Task 7)

PETTY CASH BOOK   PCB 52

Receipts £	Date 2003	Details	Voucher number	Total £	VAT £	Postage £	Stationery £	Other expenses £

7

ANSWERS (Task 7, continued)

Notes and coin in the petty cash tin, 30 June 2003

Value	Number	Total value £
£20	4	
£10	3	
£5	2	
£1	8	
50p	8	
20p	8	
10p	8	
5p	1	
2p	2	
1p	2	

Petty cash reconciliation

Date: _____

	£
Balance per petty cash book	
Total of notes and coin	
Discrepancy (if any)	

Explanation of discrepancy (if any)

_____

_____

_____

8

ANSWERS (Task 8)

Trial balance at 30 June 2003

	Ledger balances	
Account name	Debit £	Credit £
Administration expenses		
Bad debts		
Bank		
Business rates		
Capital		
Fixed assets		
Inland Revenue		
Insurance		
Leasing costs		
Petty cash		
Purchases		
Purchases ledger control		
Purchases returns		
Salaries expense		
Sales		
Sales and distribution expenses		
Sales ledger control		
Sales returns		
Stock		
VAT control		
Totals		

9

ANSWERS (Tasks 9 and 10)

JOURNAL

Date 2003	Account names and narrative	Debit £	Credit £

Account Suspense

	Debit			Credit	
Date 2003	Details	Amount £	Date 2003	Details	Amount £

10

ANSWERS (Task 11)

EMAIL

From:	Kim Wendell
To:	Ari Pottle
CC:	
Subject:	**Re: Correcting the trial balance**
Date:	7 July 2003

Message

11

Answers to AAT Sample Simulation

ANSWERS (Tasks 1 and 2)

CB 241

RECEIPTS Sales ledger £	Other receipts £	Total £	Date 2003	Details	Cheque number	PAYMENTS Total £	Purchases ledger £	Other payments £
		4,486.85	1 June	Balance b/f				
4,776.15		4,776.15	5 June	Metrix plc				
			6 June	Horsfall Limited	331175	1,456.91	1,456.91	
7,715.96		7,715.96	12 June	Plympton Limited				
			16 June	Stainton and Co	331176	9,912.75	9,912.75	
			16 June	Inland Revenue	331177	3,901.25		3,901.25
15,901.22		15,901.22	19 June	Maidstone plc				
			23 June	Earley and Partners	331178	3,341.20	3,341.20	
2,816.55		2,816.55	23 June	Stenshaw Limited				
			25 June	Pickard Newton	331179	3,216.99	3,216.99	
2,451.88		2,451.88	29 June	Fitzroy Limited				
1926.34		1,926.34	30 June	Dove Ambleside				
				Medwith BC	SO	600.00		600.00
				Safeguard Insurance	SO	310.00		310.00
				Finance Leasing plc	SO	425.00		425.00
				Purchasecard plc	DD	2,341.89		2,341.89
				Salaries	CT	8,215.50		8,215.50
				Bank charges	CHGS	107.33		107.33
			30 June	Balance c/d		6,246.13		
35,588.10		40,074.95				40,074.95	17,927.85	15,900.97
		6,246.13	1 July	Balance b/d				

20

ANSWERS (Task 3)

Bank reconciliation statement at 30 June 2003

		£	£
Balance per bank statement at 30 June			7,750.99
Add:	outstanding lodgement		1,926.34
			9,677.33
Deduct:	unpresented cheque 331178	3,341.20	
	discrepancy on cheque 331179	90.00	
			3,431.20
Balance per cash book at 30 June			6,246.13

Note for assessors: Some candidates may spot the discrepancy on cheque 331179 while performing Tasks 1 and 2, and may alter the cash book to reflect this. Such candidates will not have the £90.00 discrepancy as an item in their bank reconciliation for Task 3 and will not need the first journal in Task 4. This alternative approach is acceptable and should not be penalised.

21

ANSWERS (Task 4)

JOURNAL

Date 2003	Account names and narrative	Debit £	Credit £
30 June	Cash at bank	90.00	
	Purchases ledger control account		90.00
	Being correction of mistake in recording cheque 331179		
30 June	Bad debts	1,233.75	
	Sales ledger control account		1,233.75
	Being write-off of balanced owed by Driftway Limited		

22

ANSWERS (Task 5)

MAIN (GENERAL) LEDGER

Account Sales control ledger account

Debit   Credit

Date 2003	Details	Amount £	Date 2003	Details	Amount £
1 June	Balance b/f	30,914.66	30 June	Bank	35,588.10
30 June	Invoices in month	32,617.80	30 June	Journal: bad debt	1,233.75
			30 June	Balance c/d	26,710.61
		63,532.46			63,532.46
1 July	Balance b/d	26,710.61			

Account Purchases control ledger account

Debit   Credit

Date 2003	Details	Amount £	Date 2003	Details	Amount £
30 June	Bank	17,927.85	1 June	Balance b/f	19,334.02
30 June	Balance c/d	21,697.62	30 June	Invoices in month	20,201.45
			30 June	Journal: cheque misstated	90.00
		39,625.47			39,625.47
			1 July	Balance b/d	21,697.62

23

330
BPP
PROFESSIONAL EDUCATION

ANSWERS (Task 6)

Creditors reconciliation at 30 June 2003

	£
Total of balances in subsidiary (purchases) ledger	21,607.62
Balance on control account	21,697.62
Discrepancy	90.00

Explanation of discrepancy

It seems likely that the journal relating to cheque number 331179 has not yet been actioned in the subsidiary ledger. Once this is adjusted for the balance owing to Pickard Newton becomes zero, and the total balances amount to £21,697.62, agreeing with the balance on the control account.

24

ANSWERS (Task 7)

PETTY CASH BOOK								PCB 52	
Receipts £	Date 2003	Details	Voucher number	Total £	VAT £	Postage £	Stationery £	Other expenses £	
200.00	1 June	Balance b/f							
	5 June	Postage	358	4.26		4.26			
	9 June	Stationery	359	12.87	1.91		10.96		
	12 June	Tea, coffee etc	360	7.02				7.02	
	16 June	Postage	361	3.12		3.12			
	18 June	Stationery	362	13.51	2.01		11.50		
	23 June	Stationery	363	6.58	0.98		5.60		
	26 June	Stationery	364	5.73	0.85		4.88		
	27 June	Postage	365	5.90		5.90			
	30 June	Tea, coffee etc	366	6.50				6.50	
		Totals		**65.49**	**5.75**	**13.28**	**32.94**	**13.52**	
	30 June	Balance c/d		134.51					
200.00				200.00					

25

BPP
PROFESSIONAL EDUCATION

ANSWERS (Task 7, continued)

Notes and coin in the petty cash tin, 30 June 2003

Value	Number	Total value £
£20	4	80.00
£10	3	30.00
£5	2	10.00
£1	8	8.00
50p	8	4.00
20p	8	1.60
10p	8	0.80
5p	1	0.05
2p	2	0.04
1p	2	0.02
		134.51

Petty cash reconciliation

Date: 14 July 2003

	£
Balance per petty cash book	134.51
Total of notes and coin	134.51
Discrepancy (if any)	NIL

Explanation of difference (if any)

N/A

26

ANSWERS (Task 8)

Trial balance at 30 June 2003

Account name	Ledger balances	
	Debit £	Credit £
Administration expenses	3,276.88	
Bad debts	2,010.76	
Bank	6,336.13	
Business rates	1,800.00	
Capital		46,745.76
Fixed assets	25,219.05	
Inland Revenue		4,003.51
Insurance	930.00	
Leasing costs	1,275.00	
Petty cash	134.51	
Purchases	64,016.83	
Purchases ledger control		21,697.62
Purchases returns		1,125.31
Salaries expense	35,211.81	
Sales		96,558.43
Sales and distribution expenses	2,006.81	
Sales ledger control	26,710.61	
Sales returns	1,327.44	
Stock	7,270.00	
VAT control		3,995.20
		3,400.00
Totals	**177,525.83**	**177,525.83**

27

ANSWERS (Tasks 9 and 10)

JOURNAL

Date 2003	Account names and narrative	Debit £	Credit £
30 June	Suspense account	400.00	
	Purchases returns		400.00
	Being purchases returns of £200 wrongly debited to the returns account		
	Suspense account	3,000.00	
	Capital		3,000.00
	Being cash receipt previously not posted		

Account Suspense

Date 2003	Details	Amount £	Date 2003	Details	Amount £
30 June	Jnl: purchase returns	400.00	30 June	To balance TB	3,400.00
	Jnl: capital introduced	3,000.00			
		3,400.00			3,400.00

Debit   Credit

28

ANSWERS (Task 11)

EMAIL	
From:	Kim Wendell
To:	Ari Pottle
CC:	
Subject:	**Re: Correcting the trial balance**
Date:	7 July 2003

Message

Hi Ari

I've made the changes you mentioned in your email. The effects are as follows.

First, the purchases returns figure (a credit balance on the trial balance) will increase by £400.

Second, the capital figure (also a credit balance on the trial balance) will increase by £3,000.

Finally, the £3,400 credit balance on suspense account will vanish, having been replaced by the above.

The net effect is that the trial balance will balance without any suspense account.

Regards, Kim

29

SECTION D

SPECIMEN

COVERAGE OF PERFORMANCE CRITERIA AND RANGE STATEMENTS

The following performance criteria are covered in this simulation. An indication of which performance criteria are covered by the individual tasks is given in the assessment criteria table on page 33.

Element	PC Coverage
3.1	**Balance bank transactions**
(a)	Record details from the relevant **primary documentation** in the **cashbook and ledgers.**
(b)	Correct calculate totals and balances of receipts and payments.
(c)	Compare individual items on the bank statement and in the **cashbook** for accuracy.
(d)	Identify discrepancies and prepare a bank reconciliation statement.
3.2	**Prepare ledger balances and control accounts**
(a)	Make and **record** authorised **adjustments.**
(b)	Total relevant accounts in the main ledger.
(c)	Reconcile **control accounts** with the totals of the balance in the subsidiary ledger.
(d)	Reconcile petty cash **control account** with the cash in hand and subsidiary records.
(e)	Identify **discrepancies** arising from the reconciliation of **control accounts** and either resolve or refer to the appropriate person.
3.3	**Draft an initial trial balance**
(a)	Prepare the draft **initial trial balance** in line with the organisation's policies and procedures.
(b)	Identify **discrepancies** in the balancing process.
(c)	Identify reasons for imbalance and **rectify** them.
(d)	Balance the trial balance.

The following performance criterion is not covered in this simulation and should be assessed separately, for example by means of oral questioning, suitable evidence from the workplace, or cross-referencing to other units in the portfolio.

3.2 (f) Ensure documentation is stored securely and in line with the organisation's confidentiality requirements.

31

The following range statements are not covered in this simulation and should be assessed separately, for example by means of work documents or written activities.

Element	Range Statement
3.1	**Cash book and ledgers:** computerised **Bank reconciliation statement:** computerised
3.2	**Record:** computerised **Control accounts:** computerised; non-trade debtors **Discrepancies:** cash in hand not agreeing with subsidiary record and control record
3.3	**Trial balance:** computerised

32

ASSESSMENT CRITERIA

Assessors should refer to the Standards of Competence for Accounting and be guided by the performance criteria when evaluating candidates' work.

Task	Commentary	Mapping to PCs	
1	One error allowed. See also the 'note for assessors' which accompanies the solution to Task 3.	3.1	a
2	Candidates should calculate the totals and balance correctly on the basis of their own figures from Task 1.	3.1	b
3	One omission allowed.	3.1	c, d
4	The journals should be prepared accurately, including dates and narrative.	3.2	a
5	Correct balances should be calculated on each control account.	3.2	b
6	The listing should be totalled correctly, and the difference identified as compared with the control account balance.	3.2	c, e
7	The petty cash book should be totalled correctly and the closing balance agreed to the total cash on hand. One error of addition allowed.	3.2	d
8	One error may be allowed in listing the balances or in addition.	3.3	a
9	The journals should be prepared accurately, including dates and narrative.	3.3	b, c
10	One error allowed.	3.3	d
11	Candidates should explain that the journals will have the effect of rectifying the trial balance.	3.3	d

Candidates should not be penalised more than once for an error. In particular, if a candidate makes an error early on in deciding whether or not to process documentation in a particular case, they should not be penalised again so long as they carry the totals through accurately.

33

OVERALL ASSESSMENT

Candidates may be allowed to make further minor errors, provided such errors do not suggest a fundamental lack of understanding.

General

- Work should be neatly and competently presented.

- Pencil is not acceptable.

- Correcting fluid may be used but in moderation.

Discretion

In having regard to the above criteria, the assessor is entitled in marginal cases to exercise discretion in the candidate's favour. Such discretion shall only be exercised where other criteria are met to above the required standard and, in the opinion of the assessor, the assessment overall demonstrates competence and would be an acceptable standard in the workplace.

34

P A R T   I

Full Exam based
Assessment

FULL EXAM BASED ASSESSMENT
DECEMBER 2002 (AMENDED)

FOUNDATION STAGE – NVQ/SVQ2

Unit 3

Preparing Ledger Balances and an Initial Trial Balance

**DO NOT OPEN THIS PAPER UNTIL YOU ARE READY TO START
UNDER EXAM CONDITIONS**

This Central Assessment is in two sections.

You have to show competence in both sections, so attempt and aim to complete EVERY task in BOTH sections.

Section 1   Processing exercise
                                Complete all five tasks

Section 2   10 tasks and questions
                                Complete all tasks and questions

You should spend about 90 minutes on each section.

Include all essential workings within your answers, where appropriate.

Sections 1 and 2 both relate to the business described below.

Introduction

- Roger McGee is the owner of McGee Autos, a business that supplies vehicle spare parts.

- You are employed by the business as a bookkeeper.

- The business uses a manual accounting system.

- Double entry takes place in the Main (General) Ledger. Individual accounts of debtors and creditors are kept in subsidiary ledgers as memorandum accounts.

- Assume today's date is 30 November 2002 unless you are told otherwise.

SECTION 1 – PROCESSING EXERCISE

You should spend about 90 minutes on this section.

Data

Balances at the start of the day on 30 November 2002

The following balances are relevant to you at the start of the day on 30 November 2002.

	£
Credit suppliers	
B Lennon Limited	25,187
Bissell Autos	13,201
Perry and Company	15,000
Cartwright and Company	1,454
Purchases	167,600
Purchases returns	2,306
Purchase ledger control	117,293
Loan payable	10,000
Heat and light	1,500
Rent	3,000
Stationery	1,020
VAT (credit balance)	27,511

Task 1.1

Enter these opening balances into the following accounts, given on pages 348-351.

Subsidiary (Purchases) Ledger

> B Lennon Limited
> Bissell Autos
> Perry and Company
> Cartwright and Company

Main (General) Ledger
> Purchases
> Purchases returns
> Purchase ledger control
> Loan payable
> Heat and light
> Rent
> Stationery
> VAT

Data

Transactions

The following transactions all took place on 30 November 2002 and have been entered into the relevant books of prime entry as shown below. No entries have yet been made into the ledger system. The VAT rate is 17½%.

PURCHASES DAY BOOK

Date	Details	Invoice number	Total £	VAT £	Net £
2002					
30 Nov	B Lennon Limited	167	940	140	800
30 Nov	Bissell Autos	T041	11,750	1,750	10,000
30 Nov	Perry and Company	1800C	7,050	1,050	6,000
30 Nov	Cartwright and Company	15167	4,136	616	3,520
	Totals		23,876	3,556	20,320

PURCHASES RETURNS DAY BOOK

Date	Details	Credit note no	Total £	VAT £	Net £
2002					
30 Nov	Perry and Company	C02	4,230	630	3,600
30 Nov	Cartwright and Company	604C	1,140	210	1,200
	Totals		5,640	840	4,800

CASH BOOK

Date	Details	VAT £	Bank £	Date	Details	VAT £	Bank £
2002				2002			
30 Nov	Balance b/f		15,308	30 Nov	B Lennon Limited (trade creditor)		6,187
				30 Nov	Loan repayment		1,000
				30 Nov	Heat and light		850
				30 Nov	Rent		1,500
				30 Nov	Stationery	42	282
				30 Nov	Balance c/f		5,489
	Totals		15,308			42	15,308

Task 1.2

From the day books and cash books shown above, make the relevant entries into the accounts in the Subsidiary (Purchases) Ledger and Main (General) Ledger.

Task 1.3

Balance the accounts showing clearly the balances carried down at 30 November *and* brought down at 1 December.

Subsidiary (Purchases) Ledger

B LENNON LIMITED

Date	Details	Amount £	Date	Details	Amount £

BISSELL AUTOS

Date	Details	Amount £	Date	Details	Amount £

PERRY AND COMPANY

Date	Details	Amount £	Date	Details	Amount £

CARTWRIGHT AND COMPANY

Date	Details	Amount £	Date	Details	Amount £

Main (General) Ledger

PURCHASES

Date	Details	Amount £	Date	Details	Amount £

PURCHASES RETURNS

Date	Details	Amount £	Date	Details	Amount £

PURCHASE LEDGER CONTROL

Date	Details	Amount £	Date	Details	Amount £

LOAN PAYABLE

Date	Details	Amount £	Date	Details	Amount £

HEAT AND LIGHT

Date	Details	Amount £	Date	Details	Amount £

RENT

Date	Details	Amount £	Date	Details	Amount £

STATIONERY

Date	Details	Amount £	Date	Details	Amount £

VAT

Date	Details	Amount £	Date	Details	Amount £

BPP PROFESSIONAL EDUCATION

Data

Other balances to be transferred to the trial balance:

	£
Motor vehicles	44,100
Office equipment	20,360
Stock	18,700
Cash	100
Sales ledger control	208,105
Capital	25,814
Sales	350,800
Sales returns	2,000
Wages	35,612
Insurance	3,600
Rates	2,750
Telephone	1,103
Motor expenses	2,811
Hotel expenses	629
Miscellaneous expenses	5,426

Task 1.4

Transfer the balances that you calculated in Task 1.3, and the bank balance, to the trial balance on page 353.

Task 1.5

Transfer the remaining balances shown above to the trial balance, and total each column.

TRIAL BALANCE AS AT 30 NOVEMBER 2002

	Debit £	Credit £
Motor vehicles		
Office equipment		
Stock		
Bank		
Cash		
Sales ledger control		
Purchase ledger control		
VAT		
Capital		
Sales		
Sales returns		
Purchases		
Purchases returns		
Loan payable		
Wages		
Insurance		
Heat and light		
Rent		
Rates		
Telephone		
Motor expenses		
Stationery		
Hotel expenses		
Miscellaneous expenses		
Total		

SECTION 2 – TASKS AND QUESTIONS

You should spend about 90 minutes on this section.

Answer all of the following questions on pages 354 - 358.

Write your answers in the spaces provided.

Note. You do not need to adjust the accounts in Section 1 as part of any of the following tasks.

Task 2.1

The documents below has been received by McGee Autos from one of its credit customers.

BACS REMITTANCE ADVICE	
To: McGee Autos	From: Motormania Limited
Your Ref: Mc600	Our Ref: MM1091

01 December 2002	BACS Transfer	£235

Payment has been made by BACS and will be paid directly into your bank account on the date shown above.

(a)   What will be the entries needed in the Main (General) Ledger of McGee Autos to record this transaction?

Dr _____   £ _____

Cr _____   £ _____

(b)   Give TWO advantages to McGee Autos of being paid by BACS transfer.

_____

_____

Task 2.2

A purchases day book and purchases returns day book are examples of primary accounting records.

Name THREE other primary accounting records.

_____

_____

_____

_____

Task 2.3

McGee Autos has given a customer a settlement discount of £100.

What will be the accounting entries needed in McGee Autos Main (General) Ledger to record this transaction? (Ignore VAT.)

Dr _____ £ _____

Cr _____ £ _____

Task 2.4

McGee Autos operates a cash control and the petty cash book is the subsidiary record.

Give TWO examples of details that would be shown in the petty cash book, which would not be shown in the cash control account.

_____

_____

_____

Task 2.5

List THREE reasons for maintaining a Purchase Ledger Control account.

_____

_____

_____

Task 2.6

Roger McGee is considering changing from a manual to a computerised accounting system. He has been advised to make sure that each member of staff has his or her own password to access the system.

List THREE rules staff should observe to ensure security of their passwords.

_____

_____

_____

_____

Task 2.7

McGee Autos has a current account at the bank and is considering opening a deposit account.

Give TWO advantages the deposit account will offer the business.

_____

_____

_____

_____

Task 2.8

The following errors have been made in the Main (General) Ledger of McGee Autos.

(a)   £25 has been credited to the Discounts Received account instead of to the Interest Received account.

(b)   The total of the sales day book has been posted incorrectly as £51,010 instead of the correct amount of £50,101. (Ignore VAT.)

(c)   A payment of £100 to settle a hotel bill has been incorrectly credited to the Hotel Expenses account and debited to the Bank account.

Record the journal entries necessary in the Main (General) Ledger to correct the errors shown above. Date and narratives are not required.

Note. You do NOT need to adjust the accounts in Section 1.

THE JOURNAL

Date	Details	Dr £	Cr £

Task 2.9

The following is a summary of sales activities during the month of November.

	£
Balance of debtors at 1 November 2002	220,617
Goods sold on credit	99,300
Money received from credit customers	109,262
Sales returns from credit customers	2,000
Journal credit to correct an error	550

(a) Prepare a sales ledger control account from the above details. Show clearly the balance carried down at 30 November 2002, and brought down at 1 December 2002.

SALES LEDGER CONTROL

Date	Details	Amount £	Date	Details	Amount £

The following closing balances were in the Subsidiary (Sales) Ledger on 30 November.

	£
Robertson Mechanics	15,016 Debit
Parkes and Company	52,109 Debit
JJP Limited	13,200 Debit
Components Limited	42,982 Debit
OKK Parts	44,798 Debit
Stevens Limited	550 Debit
Mechanics Supplies	40,000 Debit

(b) Reconcile the balances shown above with the sales ledger control account balance you have calculated in part (a) above.

	£
Sales ledger control account balance as at 30 November 2002	
Total of subsidiary (sales) ledger accounts as at 30 November 2002	_____
Difference	_____

(c) What may have caused the difference you calculated in part (b) above?

_____

_____

_____

_____

Task 2.10

On 28 June Senator Safes received the following bank statement as at 22 November 2002.

COMMERCIAL BANK plc
The Strand, Coventry CV18 3DZ

To: McGee Autos   Account No. 30001874   22 November 2002

STATEMENT OF ACCOUNT

Date	Details	Paid out	Paid in	Balance
2002		£	£	£
3 Nov	Balance b/f			15,019 C
4 Nov	Cheque no 111609	4,000		11,019 C
6 Nov	Cheque no 111610	1,100		9,919 C
11 Nov	Cheque no 111612	1,861		8,058 C
11 Nov	Bank Giro Credit – Ray's Cabs		3,000	11,058 C
12 Nov	Direct Debit – Insurance Direct	883		10,175 C
15 Nov	Direct Debit – Dodson Limited	2,000		8,175 C
21 Nov	Direct Debit – Coventry Met	3,588		4,587 C
22 Nov	Bank charges	91		4,496 C

D = Debit   C = Credit

The cash book as at 28 November 2002 is shown below.

CASH BOOK

Date	Details	Amount	Date	Cheque	Details	Amount
2002		£	2002	No		£
1 Nov	Balance b/f	15,019	1 Nov	111609	King and Company	4,000
22 Nov	B Bragg	2,250	1 Nov	111610	Leigh Limited	1,100
23 Nov	J Sahota	1,500	6 Nov	111611	Elite Cars	6,141
			6 Nov	111612	Briggs Supplies	1,861

(a)   Check the items on the bank statement against the items in the cash book.

(b)   Update the cash book as needed.

(c)   Total the cash book and clearly show the balance carried down at 28 November and brought down at 29 November.

Note. You do not need to adjust the accounts in Section 1.

(d)   Using the information above, list THREE items which explain the difference between the balance in your *updated* cash book and the closing balance on the bank statement.

_____

_____

_____

_____

Answers to Full Exam based Assessments

ANSWERS TO FULL EXAM BASED ASSESSMENT

DECEMBER 2002 EXAM

DO NOT TURN THIS PAGE UNTIL YOU HAVE COMPLETED
THE FULL EXAM BASED ASSESSMENT

SECTION 1

Tasks 1.1, 1.2 and 1.3

Subsidiary (Purchases) Ledger

B LENNON LIMITED

Date	Details	Amount £	Date	Details	Amount £
30 Nov	Bank	6,187	30 Nov	Balance b/f	25,187
30 Nov	Balance c/d	19,940	30 Nov	Purchases	940
		26,127			26,127
			1 Dec	Balance b/d	19,940

BISSELL AUTOS

Date	Details	Amount £	Date	Details	Amount £
30 Nov	Balance c/d	24,951	30 Nov	Balance b/f	13,201
			30 Nov	Purchases	11,750
		24,951			24,951
			1 Dec	Balance b/d	24,951

PERRY AND COMPANY

Date	Details	Amount £	Date	Details	Amount £
30 Nov	Purchases returns	4,230	30 Nov	Balance b/f	15,000
30 Nov	Balance c/d	17,820	30 Nov	Purchases	7,050
		22,050			22,050
			1 Dec	Balance b/d	17,820

CARTWRIGHT AND COMPANY

Date	Details	Amount £	Date	Details	Amount £
30 Nov	Purchases returns	1,410	30 Nov	Balance b/f	1,454
30 Nov	Balance c/d	4,180	30 Nov	Purchases	4,136
		5,590			5,590
			1 Dec	Balance b/d	4,180

Main (General) Ledger

PURCHASES

Date	Details	Amount £	Date	Details	Amount £
30 Nov	Balance b/f	167,600	30 Nov	Balance c/d	187,920
30 Nov	Creditors	20,320			
		187,920			187,920
1 Dec	Balance b/d	187,920			

PURCHASES RETURNS

Date	Details	Amount £	Date	Details	Amount £
30 Nov	Balance c/d	7,106	30 Nov	Balance b/f	2,306
			30 Nov	Creditors	4,800
		7,106			7,106
			1 Dec	Balance b/d	7,106

PURCHASE LEDGER CONTROL

Date	Details	Amount £	Date	Details	Amount £
30 Nov	Purchases returns	5,640	30 Nov	Balance b/f	117,293
30 Nov	Bank	6,187	30 Nov	Purchases	23,876
30 Nov	Balance c/d	129,342			
		141,169			141,169
			1 Dec	Balance b/d	129,342

LOAN PAYABLE

Date	Details	Amount £	Date	Details	Amount £
30 Nov	Bank	1,000	30 Nov	Balance b/f	10,000
30 Nov	Balance c/d	9,000			
		10,000			10,000
			1 Dec	Balance b/d	9,000

HEAT AND LIGHT

Date	Details	Amount £	Date	Details	Amount £
30 Nov	Balance b/f	1,500	30 Nov	Balance c/d	2,350
30 Nov	Bank	850			
		2,350			2,350
1 Dec	Balance b/d	2,350			

RENT

Date	Details	Amount £	Date	Details	Amount £
30 Nov	Balance b/f	3,000	30 Nov	Balance c/d	4,500
30 Nov	Bank	1,500			
		4,500			4,500
1 Dec	Balance b/d	4,500			

STATIONERY

Date	Details	Amount £	Date	Details	Amount £
30 Nov	Balance b/f	1,020	30 Nov	Balance c/d	1,260
30 Nov	Bank	240			
		1,260			1,260
1 Dec	Balance b/d	1,260			

VAT

Date	Details	Amount £	Date	Details	Amount £
30 Nov	Purchases	3,556	30 Nov	Balance b/f	27,511
30 Nov	Bank	42	30 Nov	Purchases returns	840
30 Nov	Balance c/d	24,753			
		28,351			38,351
			1 Dec	Balance b/d	24,753

Tasks 1.4 and 1.5

TRIAL BALANCE AS AT 30 NOVEMBER 2002

	Debit £	Credit £
Motor vehicles	44,100	
Office equipment	20,360	
Stock	18,700	
Bank	5,489	
Cash	100	
Sales ledger control	208,105	
Purchase ledger control		129,342
VAT		24,753
Capital		25,814
Sales		350,800
Sales returns	2,000	
Purchases	187,920	
Purchases returns		7,106
Loan payable		9,000
Wages	35,612	
Insurance	3,600	
Heat and light	2,350	
Rent	4,500	
Rates	2,750	
Telephone	1,103	
Motor expenses	2,811	
Stationery	1,260	
Hotel expenses	629	
Miscellaneous expenses	5,426	
Total	546,815	546,815

SECTION 2

Note. These are *suggested* answers; where appropriate, other relevant answers will be accepted.

Task 2.1

(a) Dr   Bank   £235.00
     Cr   Sales ledger control   £235.00

(b) Any two from:

-   Cash available immediately as no clearance time needed
-   Less time-consuming as no visit to the bank needed to pay in the funds
-   More secure as the payment is not handled

Task 2.2

Any three from:

-   Sales day book
-   Sales returns day book
-   Journal
-   Cash book
-   Petty cash book

Task 2.3

Dr   Discounts allowed   £100.00
Cr   Sales ledger control   £100.00

Task 2.4

Any two from:

-   Petty cash voucher numbers
-   Individual transactions
-   Individual transaction dates
-   Analysis totals (optional)

Task 2.5

Any three from:

- To aid in the prevention of fraud
- To assist in the location of errors
- To enable the total creditors figure to be known at any time
- To help in the preparation of final accounts

Task 2.6

Any three from:

- Commit the password to memory
- Never write the password down
- Never tell anyone the password
- Change the password regularly
- Never use an obvious password
- Never type in the password when the keyboard is being overlooked

Task 2.7

Any two from:

- Interest earned on the balance
- Flexibility of moving funds from one account to another as required
- More confidence in the business on the part of the bank

Task 2.8

	Details	Dr £	Cr £
(a)	Discounts received	25	
	Interest received		25
(b)	Sales	909	
	Sales ledger control		909
(c)	Hotel expenses	200	
	Bank		200

Task 2.9

(a)

SALES LEDGER CONTROL

Date	Details	Amount £	Date	Details	Amount £
1 Nov	Balance b/f	220,617	30 Nov	Bank	109,262
30 Nov	Credit sales	99,300	30 Nov	Sales returns	2,000
			30 Nov	Journal	550
			30 Nov	Balance c/d	208,105
		319,917			319,917
1 Dec	Balance b/d	208,105			

(b)

	£
Sales ledger control account balance as at 30 November 2002	208,105
Total of subsidiary (sales) ledger accounts as at 30 November 2002	208,655
Difference	550

(c) The journal entry of £550 in the sales ledger control account may not have been entered in the subsidiary (sales) ledger, and could relate to the account of Stevens Limited.

Task 2.10

(a), (b) and (c)

CASH BOOK

Date 2002	Details	Amount £	Date 2002	Cheque No	Details	Amount £
1 Nov	Balance b/f	15,019	1 Nov	111609	King and Company	4,000
22 Nov	B Bragg	2,250	1 Nov	111610	Leigh Limited	1,100
23 Nov	J Sahota	1,500	6 Nov	111611	Elite Cars	6,141
			6 Nov	111612	Briggs Supplies	1,861
			12 Nov		Insurance Direct	883
			15 Nov		Dodson Limited	2,000
			21 Nov		Coventry Met	3,588
			22 Nov		Bank charges	91
			28 Nov		Balance c/d	2,105
		21,769				21,769
29 Nov	Balance b/d	2,105				

(d)
- Receipt from B Bragg not on bank statement   £2,250
- Receipt from J Sahota not on bank statement   £1,500
- Payment to Elite Cars not on bank statement   £6,141

Total   £2,391

Being difference between bank statement and cash book balances.

Note. Under the 2003 standards, you will be expected to prepare a bank reconciliation.

PART J

AAT Specimen Exam

SPECIMEN EXAM PAPER

FOUNDATION STAGE – NVQ/SVQ2

Unit 3

Preparing Ledger Balances and an Initial Trial Balance

DO NOT OPEN THIS PAPER UNTIL YOU ARE READY TO START
UNDER EXAM CONDITIONS

This Exam is in two sections.

You have to show competence in both sections, so attempt and aim to complete EVERY task in BOTH sections.

Section 1   Processing exercise
                   Complete all five tasks

Section 2   10 tasks and questions
                   Complete all tasks and questions

You should spend about 90 minutes on each section.

Include all essential workings within your answers, where appropriate.

The original paper contained two blank pages for workings.

Sections 1 and 2 both relate to the business described below.

Introduction

- Karen Davies is the owners of Senator Safes, a business that supplies fireproof safes.

- You are employed by the business as a bookkeeper.

- The business uses a manual accounting system.

- Double entry takes place in the Main (General) Ledger. Individual accounts of debtors and creditors are kept in subsidiary ledgers as memorandum accounts.

- Assume today's date is 30 June 2002 unless you are told otherwise.

SECTION 1 – PROCESSING EXERCISE

You should spend about 90 minutes on this section.

Data

Balances at the start of the day on 30 June 2002

The following balances are relevant to you at the start of the day on 30 June 2002.

	£
Credit customers	
JPD Limited	15,873
Lewis and Lane	25,109
Barker and Company	2,192
Higgins Limited	10,354
Sales	573,012
Sales returns	1,200
Sales ledger control	134,100
Loan payable	6,500
Discounts allowed	870
Rent	5,350
Motor expenses	2,760
VAT (credit balance)	15,400

Task 1.1

Enter these opening balances into the following accounts, given on pages 378 – 381.

Subsidiary (Sales) Ledger

JPD Limited
Lewis and Lane
Barker and Company
Higgins Limited

Main (General) Ledger
Sales
Sales returns
Sales ledger control
Loan payable
Discounts allowed
Rent
Motor expenses
VAT

Data

Transactions

The following transactions all took place on 30 June 2002 and have been entered into the relevant books of prime entry as shown below. No entries have yet been made into the ledger system. The VAT rate is 17½%.

SALES DAY BOOK

Date	Details	Invoice number	Total £	VAT £	Net £
2002					
30 June	JPD Limited	1216	2,350	350	2,000
30 June	Lewis and Lane	1217	9,400	1,400	8,000
30 June	Barker and Company	1218	1,880	280	1,600
30 June	Higgins Limited	1219	3,525	525	3,000
	Totals		17,155	2,555	14,600

SALES RETURNS DAY BOOK

Date	Details	Credit note no	Total £	VAT £	Net £
2002					
30 June	Barker and Company	CR30	4,230	630	3,600
30 June	Higgins Limited	CR31	1,140	210	1,200
	Totals		5,640	840	4,800

CASH BOOK

Date	Details	Discounts allowed £	Bank £	Date	Details	Discounts received £	Bank £
2002				2002			
30 June	Balance b/f		9,036	30 June	Loan repayment		500
30 June	JPD Limited	35	2,100	30 June	Rent		1,000
30 June	Higgins Limited		200	30 June	Motor expenses		180
				30 June	Balance c/f		9,656
	Totals	35	11,336				11,336

Task 1.2

From the day books and cash books shown above, make the relevant entries into the accounts in the Subsidiary (Sales) Ledger and Main (General) Ledger.

Task 1.3

Balance the accounts showing clearly the balances carried down at 30 June (closing balance).

Task 1.4

Now that you have closed the accounts for June, prepare the accounts for the coming month by clearly showing the balance bought down at 1 July (opening balance).

Subsidiary (Sales) Ledger

JPD LIMITED

Date	Details	Amount £	Date	Details	Amount £

LEWIS AND LANE

Date	Details	Amount £	Date	Details	Amount £

BARKER AND COMPANY

Date	Details	Amount £	Date	Details	Amount £

BPP
PROFESSIONAL EDUCATION

HIGGINS LIMITED

Date	Details	Amount £	Date	Details	Amount £

Main (General) Ledger

SALES

Date	Details	Amount £	Date	Details	Amount £

SALES RETURNS

Date	Details	Amount £	Date	Details	Amount £

SALES LEDGER CONTROL

Date	Details	Amount £	Date	Details	Amount £

LOAN

Date	Details	Amount £	Date	Details	Amount £

DISCOUNTS ALLOWED

Date	Details	Amount £	Date	Details	Amount £

RENT

Date	Details	Amount £	Date	Details	Amount £

MOTOR EXPENSES

Date	Details	Amount £	Date	Details	Amount £

VAT

Date	Details	Amount £	Date	Details	Amount £

Data

Other balances to be transferred to the trial balance:

	£
Motor vehicles	36,100
Office equipment	18,350
Stock	25,000
Cash	150
Purchases ledger control	32,060
Capital	9,600
Purchases	346,012
Purchases returns	3,600
Discounts received	2,000
Wages	38,249
Insurance	1,600
Rates	6,800
Telephone	1,845
Heat and light	2,100
Miscellaneous expenses	12,650

Task 1.5

Transfer the balances that you calculated in Task 1.3, and the bank balance, to the trial balance on page 383.

Task 1.6

Transfer the remaining balances shown above to the trial balance, and total each column.

TRIAL BALANCE AS AT 30 JUNE 2002

	Debit £	Credit £
Motor vehicles		
Office equipment		
Stock		
Bank		
Cash		
Sales ledger control		
Purchases ledger control		
VAT		
Capital		
Sales		
Sales returns		
Purchases		
Purchases returns		
Discounts allowed		
Loan		
Discounts received		
Wages		
Insurance		
Rent		
Rates		
Motor expenses		
Telephone		
Heat and light		
Miscellaneous expenses		
Total		

SECTION 2 – TASKS AND QUESTIONS

You should spend about 90 minutes on this section.

Answer all of the following questions on pages 384 - 390.

Write your answers in the spaces provided.

Task 2.1

The cheque below has been received today.

Northern Bank	46-30-28
1 Main Street	
Dudley Dy7 3AV	Date *31 June 2002*
PAY *Senator Safes*	£ *552.00*
Five hundred and twenty-five	
pounds only	
	BBP Limited
⑈00744 46 3028 33357800	

(a) Give THREE reasons why the cheque will not be honoured by the bank.

_____

_____

_____

(b) What is the branch sort code number on the cheque?

_____

Task 2.2

Complete the following sentences by writing in the name of the appropriate document.

(a) Senator Safes sends a _____

to each customer at the end of every month to show how much is outstanding and to request a payment.

(b) Senator Safes sends a _____

to a customer to correct an overcharge on an invoice.

(c)   Senator Safes sends a _____

to a supplier with a payment by cheque.

(d)   Senator Safes sends a _____

with goods despatched to a customer. One copy is signed by the customer and returned to Senator Safes. This copy is the proof of delivery.

Task 2.3

The following errors have been made in the accounting records of Senator Safes.

Show whether the errors cause an imbalance in the trial balance by circling the correct answer.

(a)   An entry made to the sales and VAT accounts but omitted from the debtors control account.

The trial balance will balance / The trial balance will not balance

(b)   Omission of a purchase invoice from all accounting records.

The trial balance will balance / The trial balance will not balance

(c)   VAT on an invoice incorrectly calculated.

The trial balance will balance / The trial balance will not balance

(d)   An invoice entered in the account of B Fox instead of C Fox.

The trial balance will balance / The trial balance will not balance

Task 2.4

Karen Davies insists that all accounting records and source documents are locked away whenever the office is left unattended.

Give TWO reasons why it is important to do this.

_____

_____

_____

_____

Task 2.5

A cheque was received from a customer, L Brown, for £400 plus VAT. The cheque was entered in the cash book and ledgers. The bank then dishonoured the cheque.

    (a)   What bookkeeping entries would you need to make in the Main (General) Ledger to record the dishonoured cheque?

Dr _____   £ _____

Cr _____   £ _____

    (b)   Name TWO methods of payment Senator Safes could insist on which would avoid this happening again.

_____

_____

Task 2.6

Karen Davies is thinking about using a computerised accounting system. The automatic calculation of totals and balances will save time.

Name TWO other features of a computerised accounting system that will save time.

_____

_____

_____

_____

Task 2.7

Senator Safes operates a petty cash imprest system. The imprest amount is £200.00 and is restored on the first day of each month.

At the end of the month the following amounts had been spent:

Tea and coffee   £12.00
Stationery   £21.15
Travel   £60.00
Window cleaning   £30.00

    (a)   How much cash is required to restore the imprest level?

_____

(b)   How much will be in the petty cash tin on 1 July?

_____

Task 2.8

The following errors have been made in the Main (General) Ledger of Senator Safes.

(a)   An amount of £50 was debited to the suspense account. The following two errors have now been discovered:

A figure in the sales account has been overstated by £75
A figure in the insurance account has been overstated by £25

(b)   Purchases returns have been entered in the accounting records as £706 instead of the correct amount of £607. (Ignore VAT.)

(c)   A credit customer, Leeson and Company, has ceased trading. The amount outstanding on its account of £800 plus VAT has been written off as a bad debt in the Subsidiary (Sales) Ledger only, but the net amount and VAT should also have been written off.

Record the journal entries necessary in the Main (General) Ledger to correct the errors shown above. Narratives are not required.

Note. You do NOT need to adjust the accounts in Section 1.

THE JOURNAL

Date	Details	Dr £	Cr £

Task 2.9

The following entries were recorded in the Subsidiary (Purchases) Ledger during the month of June.

	£
Balance of creditors at 1 June 2002	50,300
Goods purchased on credit	21,587
Paid creditors	13,750
Discounts received	500
Goods returned to suppliers	250

(a) Prepare a purchases ledger control account from the above details. Show clearly the balance carried down at 30 June 2002.

PURCHASES LEDGER CONTROL

Date	Details	Amount £	Date	Details	Amount £

The following balances were in the Subsidiary (Purchases) Ledger on 30 June.

	£
Wright and Company	12,000 Credit
CCY Limited	11,107 Credit
Carter and Company	9,380 Credit
Tomkins Limited	16,800 Credit
PP Properties	500 Debit
L Vakas	1,200 Credit
Ten Traders	6,400 Credit

(b) Reconcile the balances shown above with the purchases ledger control account balance you have calculated in part (a) above.

£

Purchases ledger control account balance as at 30 June 2002

Total of subsidiary (purchases) ledger accounts as at 30 June 2002 _____

Difference _____

(c) What may have caused the difference you calculated in part (b) above?

_____

_____

_____

_____

Task 2.10

On 28 June Senator Safes received the following bank statement as at 24 June 2002.

SOUTH BANK plc
High Street, Webley, W36 0KW

To: Senator Safes   Account No. 721982716   24 June 2002

STATEMENT OF ACCOUNT

Date	Details	Paid out	Paid in	Balance
2002		£	£	£
3 June	Balance b/f			7,000 C
5 June	Cheque no 326705	300		6,700 C
5 June	Cheque no 326710	6,900		200 D
5 June	Cheque no 326711	300		500 D
10 June	Bank Giro Credit – C Maguire		9,100	8,600 C
11 June	Cheque no 326713	76		8,524 C
14 June	Direct Debit – Bamber Limited	1,300		7,224 C
20 June	Direct Debit – Webley MBC	100		7,124 C
24 June	Bank charges	52		7,072 C

D = Debit   C = Credit

The cash book as at 28 June 2002 is shown below.

CASH BOOK

Date	Details	Amount	Date	Cheque	Details	Amount
2002		£	2002	No		£
1 June	Balance b/f	6,700	1 June	326710	B Groom Limited	6,900
26 June	P Kramer	3,100	1 June	326711	KKD Limited	300
26 June	L Jones	82	6 June	326712	F Bolton	250
			7 June	326713	Leigh & Company	76

(a) Check the items on the bank statement against the items in the cash book.

(b) Update the cash book as needed.

(c) Total the cash book and clearly show the balance carried down.

Note. You do not need to adjust the accounts in Section 1.

(d) Using the information above, prepare a bank reconciliation statement as at 28 June. The bank reconciliation statement should start with the balance as per the bank statement and reconcile to the balance as per the cash book.

BANK RECONCILIATION STATEMENT AS AT 28 JUNE 2002

£ £

Answers to
AAT Specimen Exam

SECTION 1

Tasks 1.1, 1.2, 1.3 and 1.4

Subsidiary (Sales) Ledger

JPD LIMITED

Date	Details	Amount £	Date	Details	Amount £
30 June	Balance b/f	15,873	30 June	Bank	2,100
30 June	Sales	2,350	30 June	Discounts received	35
			30 June	Balance c/d	16,088
		18,223			18,223
1 July	Balance b/d	16,088			

LEWIS AND LANE

Date	Details	Amount £	Date	Details	Amount £
30 June	Balance b/f	25,109	30 June	Balance c/d	34,509
30 June	Sales	9,400			
		34,509			34,509
1 July	Balance b/d	34,509			

BARKER AND COMPANY

Date	Details	Amount £	Date	Details	Amount £
30 June	Balance b/f	2,192	30 June	Sales returns	4,230
30 June	Sales	1,880			
30 June	Balance c/d	158			
		4,230			4,230
			1 July	Balance c/d	158

HIGGINS LIMITED

Date	Details	Amount £	Date	Details	Amount £
30 June	Balance b/f	10,354	30 June	Sales returns	1,410
30 June	Sales	3,525	30 June	Bank	200
			30 June	Balance c/d	12,269
		13,879			13,879
1 July	Balance b/d	12,269			

Main (General) Ledger

SALES

Date	Details	Amount £	Date	Details	Amount £
30 June	Balance c/d	587,612	30 June	Balance b/f	573,012
			30 June	Debtors	14,600
		587,612			587,612
			1 July	Balance b/d	587,612

SALES RETURNS

Date	Details	Amount £	Date	Details	Amount £
30 June	Balance b/f	1,200	30 June	Balance c/d	6,000
30 June	Debtors	4,800			
		6,000			6,000
1 July	Balance b/d	6,000			

SALES LEDGER CONTROL

Date	Details	Amount £	Date	Details	Amount £
30 June	Balance b/f	134,100	30 June	Sales returns	5,640
30 June	Sales	17,155	30 June	Bank	2,300
			30 June	Discounts allowed	35
			30 June	Balance c/d	143,280
		151,255			151,255
1 July	Balance b/d	143,280			

LOAN

Date	Details	Amount £	Date	Details	Amount £
30 June	Bank	500	30 June	Balance b/f	6,500
30 June	Balance c/d	6,000			
		6,500			6,500
			1 July	Balance b/d	6,000

DISCOUNTS ALLOWED

Date	Details	Amount £	Date	Details	Amount £
30 June	Balance b/f	870	30 June	Balance c/d	905
30 June	Debtors	35			
		905			905
1 July	Balance b/d	905			

RENT

Date	Details	Amount £	Date	Details	Amount £
30 June	Balance b/f	5,350	30 June	Balance c/d	6,350
30 June	Bank	1,000			
		6,350			6,350
1 July	Balance b/d	6,350			

MOTOR EXPENSES

Date	Details	Amount £	Date	Details	Amount £
30 June	Balance b/f	2,760	30 June	Balance c/d	2,940
30 June	Bank	180			
		2,940			2,940
1 July	Balance b/d	2,940			

VAT

Date	Details	Amount £	Date	Details	Amount £
30 June	Sales returns	840	30 June	Balance b/f	15,400
30 June	Balance c/d	17,115	30 June	Sales	2,555
		17,955			17,955
			1 July	Balance b/d	17,115

Tasks 1.5 and 1.6

TRIAL BALANCE AS AT 30 JUNE 2002

	Debit £	Credit £
Motor vehicles	36,100	
Office equipment	18,350	
Stock	25,000	
Bank	9,656	
Cash	150	
Sales ledger control	143,280	
Purchase ledger control		32,060
VAT		17,115
Capital		9,600
Sales		587,612
Sales returns	6,000	
Purchases	346,012	
Purchases returns		3,600
Discounts allowed	905	
Loan		6,000
Discounts received		2,000
Wages	38,249	
Insurance	1,600	
Rent	6,350	
Rates	6,800	
Motor expenses	2,940	
Telephone	1,845	
Heat and light	2,100	
Miscellaneous expenses	12,650	
Total	657,987	657,987

SECTION 2

Task 2.1

(a)   Incorrect date
      Words and figures do not match
      No signature

(b)   46-30-28.

Task 2.2

(a)   Statement
(b)   Credit note
(c)   Remittance advice
(d)   Delivery note

Task 2.3

(a)   The trial balance will not balance
(b)   The trial balance will balance
(c)   The trial balance will balance
(d)   The trial balance will balance

Task 2.4

Any two from:

- To prevent confidential information being leaked.
- To prevent the loss or damage of important information
- To prevent important information being tampered with
- To reduce the risk of fraud

Task 2.5

(a)   Dr   Sales ledger control account   £470
      Cr   Bank   £470

(b)   Bankers draft
      Cash on delivery

Task 2.6

Any two from:

- Data will only need to be input once and the computer will complete the necessary double entry automatically.

- The computer produce reports automatically.

- Up-to-date balances will be immediately available.

Task 2.7

(a) £123.15 (the amount that was spent)
(b) £200.00 (the imprest amount)

Task 2.8

	Dr £	Cr £
Sales	75	
Insurance		25
Suspense		50
Purchases returns	99	
Purchases ledger control account		99
Bad debts	800	
VAT	140	
Sales ledger control account		940

Task 2.9

(a)

PURCHASES LEDGER CONTROL

Date	Details	Amount £	Date	Details	Amount £
30 June	Bank	13,750	1 June	Balance b/f	50,300
30 June	Discounts received	500	30 June	Purchases	21,587
30 June	Purchases returns	250			
30 June	Balance c/d	57,387			
		71,887			71,887
			1 July	Balance b/d	57,387

(b)

	£
Purchases ledger control account balance as at 30 June 2002	57,387
Total of subsidiary (purchases) ledger accounts as at 30 June 2002	56,387
Difference	1,000

(c) There may have been a posting error and the debit balance of £500 for PP Properties may in fact be a credit balance.

Task 2.10

(a), (b) and (c)

CASH BOOK

Date 2002	Details	Amount £	Date 2002	Cheque No	Details	Amount £
1 June	Balance b/f	6,700	1 June	326710	B Groom Limited	6,900
26 June	P Kramer	3,100	1 June	326711	KKD Limited	300
26 June	L Jones	82	6 June	326712	F Bolton	250
10 June	C McGuire	9,100	7 June	326713	Leigh & Company	76
			14 June		Bamber Limited	1,300
			20 June		Webley MBC	100
			24 June		Bank charges	52
			28 June		Balance c/d	10,004
		18,982				18,982
29 June	Balance b/d	10,004				

(d)   BANK RECONCILIATION STATEMENT AS AT 28 JUNE 2002

	£	£
Balance as per bank statement		7,072
Add lodgements not shown on statement		
P Kramer	3,100	
L Jones	82	
		3,182
Less unpresented cheque F Bolton		250
Balance as per cash book		10,004

P A R T K

Lecturers' Resource Pack
Activities

Note to Students

The answers to these activities and assessments are provided to your lecturers, who will distribute them in class.

If you are not on a classroom based course, a copy of the answers can be obtained from Customer Services on 020 8740 2211 or e-mail publishing @bpp.com.

Note to Lecturers

The answers to these activities and assessments are included in the Lecturers' Resource Pack, provided free to colleges.

If your college has not received the Lecturers' Resource Pack, please contact Customer Services on 020 8740 2211 or e-mail publishing @bpp.com.

BPP
PROFESSIONAL EDUCATION

Lecturers'
Practice Activities

Chapter 1: Revision of basic bookkeeping

1 Revenue

If revenue expenditure is treated as capital expenditure, then:

(a) the total of the expenses for the period will be:

Too high/Too low/Unaffected

(b) the value of the fixed assets will be:

Too high/Too how/Unaffected

2 Classify

Classify the following ledger accounts according to whether they represent asset, liability, expense or revenue.

(a) Stock

Asset / Liability / Expense / Revenue

(b) Rent received

Asset / Liability / Expense / Revenue

(c) Heat, light and water

Asset / Liability / Expense / Revenue

(d) Bank overdraft

Asset / Liability / Expense / Revenue

3 MEL

MEL Motor Factors Ltd sends a cheque to a supplier. What is the appropriate document to send with the cheque?

Chapter 2: Recording, summarising and posting transactions

4 Primary records

The sales and purchases day books are primary records used for listing data taken from source documents. Double entry is carried out by transferring relevant totals from the day books into the main ledger.

True / False

5 Ledger accounts

The sales ledger and purchases ledger are part of the double entry system.

True / False

Chapter 3: Bank reconciliations

6 Debit or credit

The following bank statement was received from the company's bankers on 2 June 20X3.

<table>
<tr><td colspan="5" align="center">**Midwest Bank plc**</td></tr>
<tr><td colspan="5" align="center">Future Electrical Ltd</td></tr>
<tr><td colspan="5" align="center">Statement of Account</td></tr>
<tr><td colspan="2">Account No 60413658</td><td colspan="3">Statement Date: 1 June 20X3</td></tr>
<tr><td>Date</td><td>Details</td><td>Debit</td><td>Credit</td><td>Balance</td></tr>
<tr><td></td><td></td><td>£</td><td>£</td><td>£</td></tr>
<tr><td>1 June</td><td>Balance forward</td><td></td><td></td><td>1,791</td></tr>
<tr><td>1 June</td><td>Dividend</td><td></td><td>104</td><td>1,895</td></tr>
<tr><td>1 June</td><td>Counter credit</td><td></td><td>7,084</td><td>8,979</td></tr>
<tr><td>1 June</td><td>GR Insurance DD</td><td>89</td><td></td><td>8,890</td></tr>
<tr><td>1 June</td><td>000415</td><td>300</td><td></td><td>8,590</td></tr>
</table>

In updating the cash book balance of £4,892:

(a)   Which item or items should now be debited to the cash book?

£104/£7,084/£89/£300

(b)   Which items or items should now be credited to the cash book?

£104/£7,084/£89/£300

7 Fill in

MMS Textiles Ltd banks at the Moxley branch of the Norwest Bank, sort code no 36-24-41, and its account number is 479836806.

Fill in the paying-in slip and counterfoil given below to bank the cash takings on 1 December which are as follows.

Four   £50 notes
Twenty-three   £20 notes
Thirty-two   £10 notes
Seven   £5 notes
Eight   50 pence coins
Twelve   10 pence coins

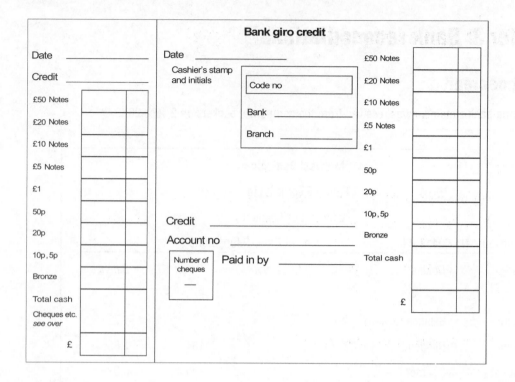

8 Not accepted

| Midwest Bank Plc | 101-103 Lower High Street | 20-14-37 |

Midwest Bank Plc
101-103 Lower High Street
West Bromwich B72 3AZ

20-14-37

28 November 20 **X6**

PAY   *Centro Steelstock Limited*

One thousand four hundred and ten pounds

£ 1,401.00

MTL Limited

A/C PAYEE

002719   201437 85930617

Give *two* reasons why the above cheque, received from a debtor, would not be accepted for payment if it was presented to Midwest Bank plc.

(a) ....

(b) ....

Chapter 4: Sales ledger control account

9 Reasons

Give two reasons for maintaining the sales ledger control account.

10 Contra

What double entry would you make in the main ledger in respect of the following.

(a)   A set off of £20 is to be made between Tompkinson & Co's accounts in the sales ledger and in the purchases ledger.

Debit   Amount   Credit   Amount

(b)   The account of D L Mason who owes £1,214 is to be written off as a bad debt.

Debit   Amount   Credit   Amount

Chapter 5: Purchases ledger control account

11 One reason

Give one reason for maintaining a purchase ledger control account.

Chapter 6: Other control accounts

12 Imprest

The company operates its petty cash using the imprest system. The imprest amount is £250.00. At the end of a particular period the five analysis columns were totalled to give the following amounts.

Column 1	£26.19
Column 2	£45.27
Column 3	£6.94
Column 4	£12.81
Column 5	£14.38

How much cash would be required to restore the imprest amount for the following period?

£........................

Chapter 7: The correction of errors

13 Correction

Journals are used to correct an error which breaks the rules of double entry.

True / False

Chapter 8: From ledger accounts to initial trial balance

14 Suspense

(a)   A trial balance has debits totalling £50,000 and credits totalling £45,000. Set up a suspense account so that the final balance balances.

(b)   You discover that the cash balance is £5,000 to high in the list of balance. Check the suspense account.

Chapter 9: Filing

15 Codes

The cheque numbers in a cheque book are an example of:

A sequential code / a hierarchical code

16 Methods

List two classification methods for filing documents and files.

(a) ....

(b) ....

17 Documents

Suggest one classification method of filing each of the following documents. Your answer should suggest a different classification method for each document.

(a) General correspondence
(b) Invoices
(c) Insurance policies

Lecturers' Skills based Assessments

FULL SKILLS BASED ASSESSMENT
BRIGSIDE

FOUNDATION STAGE – NVQ/SVQ2

Unit 3

Preparing Ledger Balances and an Initial Trial Balance

The purpose of this Full Skills Based Assessment is to give you an idea of what an AAT simulation looks like. It is not intended as a definitive guide to the tasks you may be required to perform.

The suggested time allowance for this Assessment is **three hours**. Up to 30 minutes extra time may be permitted in an AAT simulation. Breaks in assessment will be allowed in the AAT simulation, but it must normally be completed in one day.

Calculators may be used but no reference material is permitted.

DO NOT OPEN THIS PAPER UNTIL YOU ARE READY TO START
UNDER TIMED CONDITIONS

INSTRUCTIONS

This simulation is designed to test your ability to prepare ledger balances and an initial trial balance.

The situation is provided on page 419. The tasks to be performed are set out on pages 419 and 420.

The simulation also contains a large volume of data which you may need in order to complete the tasks.

You are advised to read the whole of the simulation before commencing as all of the information may be of value and is not necessarily supplied in the sequence in which you might wish to deal with it.

Your answers should be set out in the answer booklet provided. If you require additional answer pages, ask the person in charge.

You may take apart and rearrange this booklet but it must be put back in its original order before collection.

You are allowed **three hours** to complete your work.

A high level of accuracy is required. Check your work carefully before handing it in.

Correcting fluid may be used but it should be used in moderation. Errors should be crossed out neatly and clearly. You should write in black ink, not pencil.

THE SITUATION

Your name is Lesley Davis. You work as an accounts assistant for Brigside Fashions, a wholesaler of men's fashions. You report to the firm's accountant, Harvinder Patel.

All purchases and sales are on credit terms, and are subject to VAT at the standard rate of 17.5%.

Brigside makes up its accounts to 30 June each year.

Ledgers

The business's main (general) ledger is maintained in manual form. A debtors control account and a creditors control account are maintained in the main (general) ledger. There is a subsidiary (sales) ledger for debtors and a subsidiary (purchases) ledger for creditors. Like the main (general) ledger, both of the subsidiary ledgers are maintained in manual form.

Salaries

Salaries are paid monthly by BACS (credit transfer from the business bank account to the bank accounts of employees).

Bank account and cash book

One of your regular duties is to enter amounts in the cash book from a schedule of credit transfers and standing orders. You also compare entries in the cash book each month with entries on the business bank statement and advise Harvinder Patel of any discrepancies. However, while waiting for advice on how to handle such discrepancies, the procedure is to make entries in the cash book on the assumption that the bank statement is correct.

THE TASKS TO BE PERFORMED

1. Refer to page 420 for a list of ledger account balances at 30 June 2002 prepared for you by Harvinder Patel. Enter these on the proforma trial balance on page 428 of the answer booklet. Total the trial balance. In doing so, you should notice a discrepancy; this will be referred to in task 2.

2. Write a memo to Harvinder Patel, highlighting the discrepancy in the trial balance and suggesting a possible reason for it. Use the blank memo form on page 429 of the answer booklet and date your memo 8 July 2002.

3. Refer to page 421 where you will find two authorised journal entries that have not yet been entered in the main (general) ledger. Make the appropriate entries in the ledger accounts on page 430 of the answer booklet.

4. Refer to page 421 for a summary of the activity relating to sales and debtors during July 2002 and a list of debtor balances outstanding at that date.

    Write up the sales ledger control account on page 430 of the answer booklet and bring down a balance as at close of business on 31 July 2002. (You are not required to make any entries in the other ledger accounts on pages 430 - 431.)

5. Reconcile the balance on the sales ledger control account at 31 July 2002 (task 4) with the total of the list of debtor balances on page 421. Set out your reconciliation on page 432 of the answer booklet, including a suggested reason for any discrepancy you discover.

6. Refer to page 422 for a summary of the activity relating to purchases and creditors during July 2002 and a list of creditor balances outstanding at that date.

Write up the purchase ledger control account on page 432 of the answer booklet and bring down a balance as at close of business on 31 July 2002. Reconcile this balance to the total of the list of creditor balances on page 422, setting out your reconciliation on page 433 of the answer booklet.

7. Refer to page 422 for a summary of the salaries paid for the month of July 2002. Post the relevant amounts from this summary to the salaries control account on page 433 of the answer booklet, and total the account.

8. On page 423 you will find Brigside's bank statement for the month of July 2002, and an extract from Brigside's list of approved standing orders and credit transfers.

    Compare this information with Brigside's cash book for July 2002 on page 433 of the answer booklet and make any necessary additional entries in the cash book. Total the cash book and bring down a balance as at close of business on 31 July 2002.

9. Write a memo to Harvinder Patel, noting any discrepancy or discrepancies you observed in completing task 8. Use the blank memo form on page 434 of the answer booklet and date your memo 7 August 2002.

10. Using the list of ledger balances at 31 July 2002 on page 424, and the balances you calculated in tasks 4, 6 and 8, complete the trial balance at 31 July 2002, using the proforma on page 435 of the answer booklet.

Main (general) ledger: balances at 30 June 2002

	£
Advertising	15,575.93
Bad debts	2,447.08
Capital	187,017.44
Commission paid to sales staff	3,613.54
Cost of goods sold	261,917.25
Purchase ledger control	32,173.99
Sales ledger control	74,344.97
Discount allowed	2,374.19
Discount received	1,108.56
Inland Revenue	3,905.61
Insurance	2,312.66
Motor vehicles	34,721.90
Plant and equipment	153,009.74
Rent	14,110.00
Salaries expense	143,284.12
Sales	528,646.16
Stock	32,908.56
VAT control (credit balance)	12,487.36

JOURNAL		Debit	Credit
		£	£
31/7/02	Bad debts written off	242.00	
	VAT	42.35	
	Sales ledger control account		284.35
	Being write off of debt owed by Branson		
31/7/02	Sales	100.00	
	Sales ledger control account		100.00
	Being correction of miscast in sales day book		

SALES LEDGER CONTROL ACCOUNT

Summary of activity in July 2002

	£
Sales for month*	46,291.50
VAT on sales	8,101.01
Sales returns for month	1,124.50
VAT on sales returns	196.78
Payments from debtors	53,936.89
Journal entries	See task 3

* This is the figure from the sales day book before the adjustment mentioned in task 3.

BALANCES AT 31 JULY 2002 IN SUBSIDIARY (SALES) LEDGER

	£
Adams	12,802.11
Branson	284.35
Doberman	5,671.58
James	6,124.90
Lombard	3,124.76
Peters	6,318.00
Simons	2,271.07
Williams	8,014.99
Other debtors	28,767.55
Total	73,379.31

PURCHASE LEDGER CONTROL ACCOUNT

Summary of activity in July 2002

	£
Opening balance at 1 July 2002	32,173.99
Purchases for month	24,617.32
VAT on purchases	4,308.03
Purchase returns for month	924.60
VAT on purchaser returns	161.80
Payments to suppliers	30,023.55

BALANCES AT 31 JULY 2002 IN SUBSIDIARY (PURCHASES) LEDGER

	£
Baker	2,890.34
Davis	3,991.56
Jenkins	6,223.10
Oliver	4,512.99
Upton	3,312.51
Vansittart	2,095.44
Other creditors	6,963.45
Total	29,989.39

SALARIES ANALYSIS

Month: July 2002

Employee number	PAYE £	Employee NIC £	Net pay £	Employer NIC £	Total £
0001	241.51	141.60	1,145.33	181.88	1,710.32
0002	233.78	146.60	1,234.88	152.34	1,767.60
0003	190.65	121.80	962.80	182.00	1,457.25
0004	299.60	211.40	1,542.17	451.08	2,504.25
0005	203.18	132.80	1,090.71	122.98	1,549.67
0006	90.45	87.00	651.28	221.56	1,050.29
0007	112.67	102.00	882.10	160.86	1,257.63
0008	118.01	125.60	931.76	300.12	1,475.49
0009	31.70	23.20	393.12	63.60	511.62
	1,521.55	1,092.00	8,834.15	1,836.42	13,284.12

Northshires Bank plc

27 High Street, Blankton BK4 2ER

STATEMENT
22-33-65

Account: Brigside Fashion
Account number: 21596372

Statement no: 216

Date	Details		Payments £	Receipts £	Balance £
2002					
01-Jul	Balance from previous sheet				24,719.18
03-Jul	Cash/cheques received	CC		12,942.60	37,661.78
09-Jul	Cheque 229417		8,476.90		29,184.88
10-Jul	Cash/cheques received	CC		13,010.45	42,195.33
11-Jul	Vanguard Insurance 22761432	SO	500.00		41,695.33
15-Jul	Cash/cheques received	CC		8,674.29	50,369.62
22-Jul	Cheque 229418		7,369.25		
22-Jul	Cash/cheques received	CC		10,246.20	
22-Jul	Cheque 229419		3,905.61		49,340.96
24-Jul	Western Borough Council	SO	254.00		
24-Jul	Salaries	BACS	8,834.15		
24-Jul	Cash/cheques received	CC		9,063.55	49,316.16
29-Jul	Cheque 229421		3,960.07		45,356.09

Key	SO Standing order	CC Cash and/or cheques	CHGS Bank charges
	O/D Overdrawn	BACS Bankers automated clearing service	

SCHEDULE OF CREDIT TRANSFERS AND STANDING ORDERS (extract)

Credit transfers		
Payee	Amount	When payable
Brigside employees	Per salaries analysis	Monthly
Standing orders		
Payee	Amount	When payable
Western Borough Council	£254.00	Monthly
Vanguard Insurance	£500.00	March, September

MAIN (GENERAL) LEDGER: BALANCES AT 31 JULY 2002

	£
Bad debts	242.00
Capital	271,137.39
Cost of goods sold	23,692.72
Inland Revenue	4,449.97
Insurance	500.00
Motor vehicles	34,721.90
Plant and equipment	153,009.74
Rent	254.00
Salaries expense	13,284.12
Sales	45,067.00
Stock	32,908.56
VAT control (credit balance)	3,986.10

COVERAGE OF PERFORMANCE CRITERIA

The following performance criteria are covered in this simulation in the tasks noted.

Element	PC Coverage	Task(s)
3.1	**Balance bank transactions**	
i.	Details from the relevant primary documentation are recorded in the cash book	8
ii.	Totals and balances of receipts and payments are correctly calculated	8
iii.	Individual items on the bank statement and in the cash book are compared for accuracy	8
iv.	Discrepancies are identified and referred to the appropriate person	9
3.2	**Prepare ledger balances and control accounts**	
i.	Relevant accounts are totalled	4, 6, 8
ii.	Control accounts are reconciled with totals of the balance in the subsidiary ledger, where appropriate	5, 6, 7, 10
iii.	Discrepancies arising from the reconciliation of control accounts are either resolved or referred to the appropriate person	3
iv.	Documentation is stored securely and in line with the organisation's confidentiality requirements	5
v.	Draft an initial trial balance	*
vi.	Information required for the initial trial balance is identified and obtained from the relevant sources	
vii.	Relevant people are asked for advice when the necessary information is not available	
viii.	The draft initial trial balance is prepared in line with the organisation's policies and procedures	
ix.	Discrepancies are identified in the balancing process and referred to the appropriate person	
3.3	**Draft an initial trial balance**	
i.	Information required for the initial trial balance is identified and obtained from the relevant sources	1, 11
ii.	Relevant people are asked for advice when the necessary information is not available	2
iii.	The draft initial trial balance is prepared in line with the organisation's policies and procedures	1, 11
iv.	Discrepancies are identified in the balancing process and referred to the appropriate person	10

BRIGSIDE

ANSWER BOOKLET

Task 1

TRIAL BALANCE AT 30 JUNE 2002

Account name	Debit £	Credit £
Advertising		
Bad debts		
Bank control		
Capital		
Commission paid to sales staff		
Cost of goods sold		
Purchase ledger control		
Sales ledger control		
Discount allowed		
Discount received		
Inland Revenue		
Insurance		
Motor vehicles		
Plant and equipment		
Rent		
Salaries expense		
Sales		
Stock		
VAT control		
Totals		

Task 2

MEMO
To:
From:
Date:
Subject:

Tasks 3 & 4

MAIN LEDGER

Account   Bad debts

Debit   Credit

Date 2002	Details	Amount £	Date 2002	Details	Amount £

Account   Sales ledger control account

Debit   Credit

Date 2002	Details	Amount £	Date 2002	Details	Amount £

Account VAT

Debit			Credit		
Date 2002	Details	Amount £	Date 2002	Details	Amount £

Account Sales

Debit			Credit		
Date 2002	Details	Amount £	Date 2002	Details	Amount £

Task 5

SALES LEDGER CONTROL ACCOUNT: RECONCILIATION AT 31 JULY 2002

£

Balance on sales ledger control account at 31 July 2002
Total of balances in subsidiary (sales) ledger
Imbalance (if any)

Explanation of imbalance

_____

_____

_____

_____

_____

_____

_____

Task 6

Account   Purchase ledger control account
Debit   Credit

Date 2002	Details	Amount £	Date 2002	Details	Amount £

PURCHASE LEDGER CONTROL ACCOUNT: RECONCILIATION AT 31 JULY 2002

£

Balance on purchase ledger control account at 31 July 2002
Total of balances in subsidiary (purchase) ledger
Imbalance (if any)

Task 7

Account Salaries control account

Debit Credit

Date 2002	Details	Amount £	Date 2002	Details	Amount £

Task 8

CB 178

RECEIPTS						PAYMENTS			
Sales ledger £	Other receipts £	Total £	Date 2002	Details	Cheque no	Total £	Purchases ledger £	Other payments £
		24,719.18	01-Jul	Balance b/f				
12,942.60		12,942.60	03-Jul	Debtors				
			03-Jul	Jenkins	229417	8,476.90	8,476.90	
13,010.45		13,010.45	10-Jul	Debtors				
8,674.29		8,674.29	12-Jul	Debtors				
			15-Jul	Oliver	229418	7,369.25	7,369.25	
			16-Jul	Inland Revenue	229419	3,905.61		3,905.61
10,246.20		10,246.20	19-Jul	Debtors				
			22-Jul	Vansittart	229420	10,217.33	10,217.33	
			22-Jul	Davis	229421	3,960.07	3,960.07	
9,063.35		9,063.35	24-Jul	Debtors				
			25-Jul	HM Customs & Excise	229422	12,216.91		12,216.91

Task 9

MEMO	
To:	
From:	
Date:	
Subject:	

Task 10

Trial balance at 31 July 2002

Account name	Debit £	Credit £
Advertising		
Bad debts		
Bank control		
Capital		
Commission paid to sales staff		
Cost of goods sold		
Creditors control		
Debtors control		
Discount allowed		
Discount received		
Inland Revenue		
Insurance		
Motor vehicles		
Plant and equipment		
Rent		
Salaries expense		
Sales		
Stock		
VAT control		
Totals		

Lecturers' Full Exam based Assessment

DECEMBER 2001 CENTRAL ASSESSMENT
(Amended for new standards)

FOUNDATION STAGE – NVQ/SVQ2

Unit 3

Preparing Ledger Balances and an Initial Trial Balance

DO NOT OPEN THIS PAPER UNTIL YOU ARE READY TO START
UNDER TIMED CONDITIONS

INSTRUCTIONS

You are reminded that competence must be achieved in each section. You should therefore attempt and aim to complete EVERY task in BOTH sections. All essential workings should be included within your answers where appropriate

You are advised to spend 90 minutes on Section 1 and 90 minutes on Section 2.

INTRODUCTION

- John Berry is the owner of Berry Sports, a business that supplies sportswear.

- You are employed by the business as a book-keeper.

- The business operates a manual accounting system.

- Double entry takes place in the main (general) ledger. Individual accounts of debtors and creditors are kept in subsidiary ledgers as memorandum accounts.

- Assume today's date is 30 November 2001 unless otherwise instructed.

SECTION 1: PROCESSING EXERCISE
(Suggested time allocation: 90 minutes)

COMPLETE ALL TASKS

DATA

Balances at the start of the day on 30 November 2001

The following balances are relevant to you at the start of the day on 30 November 2001.

	£
Credit customers	
Jay and Company	24,000
Central Gym	15,671
BBT Limited	24,156
Leisure Unlimited	12,387
Sales	609,102
Sales returns	2,100
Sales ledger control	156,922
Loan payable	5,000
Discounts allowed	500
Rent payable	10,693
Heat and light	2,765
VAT (credit balance)	17,585

Task 1.1

Enter these opening balances into the following accounts given on pages 443 to 446.

Subsidiary (sales) ledger

> Jay and Company
> Central Gym
> BBT Limited
> Leisure Unlimited

Main (general) ledger

> Sales
> Sales returns
> Sales ledger control
> Loan payable
> Discounts allowed
> Rent payable
> Heat and light
> VAT

DATA

Transactions

The following transactions all took place on 30 November 2001 and have been entered into the relevant books of prime entry as shown below. No entries have yet been made into the ledger system. The VAT rate is 17½%.

Sales day book

Date		Invoice	Total	VAT	Net
2001		No	£	£	£
30 Nov	Jay and Company	2010	3,525	525	3,000
30 Nov	Central Gym	2011	8,225	1,225	7,000
30 Nov	BBT Limited	2012	1,175	175	1,000
30 Nov	Leisure Unlimited	2013	9,635	1,435	8,200
	Totals		22,560	3,360	19,200

Sales returns day book

Date		Credit Note	Total	VAT	Net
2001		No	£	£	£
30 Nov	BBT Limited	CR220	470	70	400
30 Nov	Leisure Unlimited	CR221	2,350	350	2,000
	Totals		2,820	420	2,400

Cash book

Date 2001	Details	Discount Allowed £	Bank £	Date 2001	Details	Discount received £	Bank £
30 Nov	Balance b/f		1,650	30 Nov	Loan repayment		600
30 Nov	Jay and Co	50	4,000	30 Nov	Rent		1,300
				30 Nov	Heat & light		350
				30 Nov	Balance c/f		3,400
	Totals	50	5,650				5,650

Task 1.2

From the day books and cash book shown above, make the relevant entries in the accounts in the subsidiary (sales) ledger and main (general) ledger.

Task 1.3

Balance the accounts showing clearly the balances carried down at 30 November and brought down at 1 December.

SUBSIDIARY (SALES) LEDGER

Jay and Company

Date	Details	Amount £	Date	Details	Amount £

Central Gym

Date	Details	Amount £	Date	Details	Amount £

BBT Limited

Date	Details	Amount £	Date	Details	Amount £

Leisure Unlimited

Date	Details	Amount £	Date	Details	Amount £

MAIN (GENERAL) LEDGER

Sales

Date	Details	Amount £	Date	Details	Amount £

Sales returns

Date	Details	Amount £	Date	Details	Amount £

Sales ledger control

Date	Details	Amount £	Date	Details	Amount £

Loan payable

Date	Details	Amount £	Date	Details	Amount £

Discounts allowed

Date	Details	Amount £	Date	Details	Amount £

Rent payable

Date	Details	Amount £	Date	Details	Amount £

Heat and light

Date	Details	Amount £	Date	Details	Amount £

VAT

Date	Details	Amount £	Date	Details	Amount £

DATA

Other balances to be transferred to the trial balance

	£
Motor vehicles	35,800
Office equipment	16,750
Stock	10,957
Cash	900
Purchase ledger control	50,226
Capital	5,541
Purchases	395,189
Purchases returns	1,820
Discounts received	1,200
Wages	46,000
Insurance	3,000
Rates	2,550
Telephone	1,298
Motor expenses	2,400
Miscellaneous expenses	1,000

Task 1.4

Transfer the balances calculated in task 1.3, and the bank balance, to the trial balance below.

Task 1.5

Transfer the remaining balances shown above to the trial balance, and total each column.

Trial balance as at 30 November 2001

	Debit £	Credit £
Motor vehicles	....	....
Office equipment	....	....
Stock	....	....
Bank	....	....
Cash	....	....
Sales ledger control	....	....
Purchase ledger control	....	....
VAT	....	....
Capital	....	....
Sales	....	....
Sales returns	....	....
Purchases	....	....
Purchases returns	....	....
Discounts allowed	....	....
Loan payable	....	....
Discounts received	....	....
Wages	....	....
Insurance	....	....
Rent payable	....	....
Rates	....	....
Heat and light	....	....
Telephone	....	....
Motor expenses	....	....
Miscellaneous expenses	....	....
Total	....	....

SECTION 2: TASKS AND QUESTIONS
(Suggested time allocation: 90 mins)

Note. Accounts in the subsidiary (sales) ledger and main (general) ledger do NOT need to be adjusted as a result of the work you do in this section.

Task 2.1

The following three credit card sale transactions have taken place today at Berry Sports.

Credit card transaction number 1	£830.00
Credit card transaction number 2	£600.00
Credit card transaction number 3	£75.00

Complete the bank summary voucher shown below in respect of these transactions.

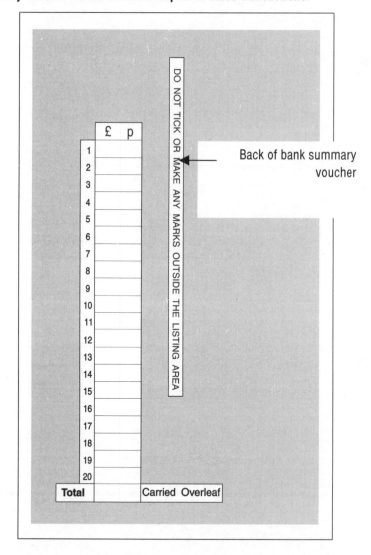

	ITEMS	AMOUNT	
SALES VOUCHERS (LISTED OVERLEAF)			
LESS REFUND VOUCHERS			
DATE	TOTAL £		

SUMMARY - RETAILER'S COPY

**BANKING
SUMMARY**

RETAILER'S SIGNATURE

Front of bank summary voucher

Task 2.2

Berry Sports is planning to buy new office furniture and has agreed to pay the supplier by twelve monthly payments of £100.

Which method of payment offered by banks would be the most appropriate?

Task 2.3

The subsidiary (sales) ledger shows the amounts owed by individual debtors; the sales ledger control account shows the total amount owed by debtors.

Give TWO reasons for maintaining a sales ledger control account.

449

Task 2.4

Berry Sports keeps a petty cash control account in the main (general) ledger and the petty cash book is the subsidiary account. In November £56 was spent from petty cash and at the end of the month £100 was put into the petty cash box from the bank.

(a)   Enter these transactions into the petty cash control account below, showing clearly the balance carried down.

Petty cash control

Date 2001	Details	Amount £	Date 2001	Details	Amount £
01 Nov	Balance b/f	100			

(b)   Name ONE other check you would carry out to ensure the petty cash book is correct.

_____

Task 2.5

John Berry is considering computerising the accounting system.

Name ONE advantage to Berry Sports of a computerised accounting system.

_____

_____

Task 2.6

Berry Sports incurs costs which would be described as revenue expenditure such as wages, rent, rates, electricity.

Give TWO examples of costs which would be described as capital expenditure.

_____

_____

Task 2.7

The following wages summary relates to the month of November 2001.

Wages summary

	£
Gross wages	4,400
Net wages	3,100
Employer's NIC	500
Employees' NIC	440
Trade Union fees	60
PAYE	800

Make the relevant entries to the wages control account and then total it.

Wages control account

Date 2001	Details	Amount £	Date 2001	Details	Amount £

Task 2.8

The following errors have been made in the accounting records of Berry Sports.

(a) £110 has been debited to the rent account instead of the rates account.

(b) Purchases returns valued at £300 have been debited to the purchases returns account and credited to the creditors control account.

(c) £2,000 has been debited to the insurance account and credited to the bank account instead of the correct amount of £200.

Record the journal entries necessary in the main (general) ledger to correct the above. Narratives are not required.

THE JOURNAL

Date	Details	Dr £	Cr £

Task 2.9

The purchase ledger control account has a credit balance of £50,226 as at 30 November 2001.

Confirm the accuracy of this figure by completing the document below using the following information:

	£
Balance of creditors control account as at 1 November 2001	49,167
Purchases invoices received in November	7,219
Purchases credit notes received in November	600
Payments made in November	5,200
Discounts received in November	360

PURCHASE LEDGER CONTROL ACCOUNT CHECK AS AT 30 NOVEMBER 2001		
	£	£
Balance as at 1 November 2001		....
Purchases invoices received	....	
Purchases credit notes received	....	
Payments made to creditors	....	
Discounts received	....	
		....
Balance as at 30 November 2001		....

Task 2.10

On 2 December Berry Sports received the bank statement as at 30 November 2001.

(a) Check the items on the bank statement against the items in the cash book.

(b) Update the cash book as needed.

(c)   Total the cash book and clearly show the balance carried down.

MIDWAY BANK PLC

To: Berry Sports   Account No. 45619822   30 November 2001

STATEMENT OF ACCOUNT

Date	Details	Paid out £	Paid in £	Balance £
2001				
1 Nov	Balance b/f			9,000C
5 Nov	Cheque no 625109	6,300		2,700C
5 Nov	Credit		10,000	12,700C
8 Nov	Bank Giro Credit: B Green		3,500	16,200C
11 Nov	Cheque no 625110	1,100		15,100C
15 Nov	Direct Debit: LBO Limited	1,300		13,800C
20 Nov	Bank charges	29		13,771C
25 Nov	Direct Debit: HB Services	1,800		11,971C

D = Debit C = Credit

Cash book

Date 2001	Details	Bank £	Date	Cheque No	Details	Bank £
1 Nov	Balance b/f	9,000	1 Nov	625109	R B Lawley	6,300
5 Nov	L Burger	10,000	5 Nov	625110	B&B Limited	1,100
22 Nov	D Smith	1,396	22 Nov	625111	M Parkes	300
			22 Nov	625112	Richards Limited	9,667

(d)   Using the data above list THREE differences to explain why the balance in your updated cash book does not match the closing balance on the bank statement.

_____

_____

_____

_____

_____

See overleaf for information on other
BPP products and how to order

AAT Order

To BPP Professional Education, Aldine Place, London W12 8AW
Tel: 020 8740 2211. Fax: 020 8740 1184
E-mail: Publishing@bpp.com Web:www.bpp.com

Mr/Mrs/Ms (Full name)

Daytime delivery address

Postcode

E-mail

Daytime Tel

	5/03 Texts	5/03 Kits	Special offer	8/03 Passcards	Tapes
FOUNDATION (£14.95 except as indicated)					
Units 1 & 2 Receipts and Payments	☐	☐	Foundation Sage Bookeeping and Excel Spreadsheets CD-ROM free if ordering all Foundation Text and Kits, including Units 21 and 22/23 ☐	Foundation ☐ £6.95	☐ £10.00
Unit 3 Ledger Balances and Initial Trial Balance	☐	☐			
Unit 4 Supplying Information for Mgmt Control	☐				
Unit 21 Working with Computers (£9.95) (6/03)	☐				
Unit 22/23 Healthy Workplace/Personal Effectiveness (£9.95)	☐				
Sage and Excel for Foundation (CD-ROM £9.95)	☐				
INTERMEDIATE (£9.95 except as indicated)					
Unit 5 Financial Records and Accounts	☐	☐		☐ £5.95	☐ £10.00
Unit 6/7 Costs and Reports (Combined Text £14.95)	☐				
Unit 6 Costs and Revenues		☐		☐ £5.95	☐ £10.00
Unit 7 Reports and Returns		☐		☐ £5.95	
TECHNICIAN (£9.95 except as indicated)					
Unit 8/9 Managing Performance and Controlling Resources	☐	☐	Spreadsheets for Technicians CD-ROM free if take Unit 8/9 Text and Kit ☐	☐ £5.95	☐ £10.00
Spreadsheets for Technician (CD-ROM)	☐				
Unit 10 Core Managing Systems and People (£14.95)	☐	☐		☐ £5.95	☐ £10.00
Unit 11 Option Financial Statements (A/c Practice)	☐	☐		☐ £5.95	
Unit 12 Option Financial Statements (Central Govnmt)	☐	☐		☐ £5.95	
Unit 15 Option Cash Management and Credit Control	☐	☐		☐ £5.95	
Unit 17 Option Implementing Audit Procedures	☐	☐		☐ £5.95	
Unit 18 Option Business Tax (FA03)(8/03 Text & Kit)	☐	☐		☐ £5.95	
Unit 19 Option Personal Tax (FA 03)(8/03 Text & Kit)	☐	☐		☐ £5.95	
TECHNICIAN 2002 (£9.95)					
Unit 18 Option Business Tax FA02 (8/02 Text & Kit)	☐	☐			
Unit 19 Option Personal Tax FA02 (8/02 Text & Kit)	☐	☐			
SUBTOTAL	£	£	£	£	£

TOTAL FOR PRODUCTS
£ ☐

POSTAGE & PACKING

Texts/Kits	First	Each extra	
UK	£3.00	£3.00	£ ☐
Europe*	£6.00	£4.00	£ ☐
Rest of world	£20.00	£10.00	£ ☐
Passcards			
UK	£2.00	£1.00	£ ☐
Europe*	£3.00	£2.00	£ ☐
Rest of world	£8.00	£8.00	£ ☐
Tapes			
UK	£2.00	£1.00	£ ☐
Europe*	£3.00	£2.00	£ ☐
Rest of world	£8.00	£8.00	£ ☐

TOTAL FOR POSTAGE & PACKING £ ☐
(Max £12 Texts/Kits/Passcards - deliveries in UK)

Grand Total (Cheques to *BPP Professional Education*)

I enclose a cheque for (incl. Postage) £ ☐

Or charge to Access/Visa/Switch

Card Number ☐☐☐☐

Expiry date ☐☐ Start Date ☐☐

Issue Number (Switch Only) ☐☐

Signature

We aim to deliver to all UK addresses inside 5 working days; a signature will be required. Orders to all UK addresses should be delivered within 6 working days. All other orders to overseas addresses should be delivered within 8 working days. * Europe includes the Republic of Ireland and the Channel Islands.

Review Form & Free Prize Draw – Unit 3 Ledger Balances and Initial Trial Balance (5/03)

All original review forms from the entire BPP range, completed with genuine comments, will be entered into one of two draws on 31 January 2004 and 31 July 2004. The names on the first four forms picked out on each occasion will be sent a cheque for £50.

Name: _____   Address: _____

_____

_____

How have you used this Interactive Text?
(Tick one box only)

☐ Home study (book only)

☐ On a course: college _____

☐ With 'correspondence' package

☐ Other _____

Why did you decide to purchase this Interactive Text? *(Tick one box only)*

☐ Have used BPP Texts in the past

☐ Recommendation by friend/colleague

☐ Recommendation by a lecturer at college

☐ Saw advertising

☐ Other _____

During the past six months do you recall seeing/receiving any of the following?
(Tick as many boxes as are relevant)

☐ Our advertisement in *Accounting Technician* magazine

☐ Our advertisement in *Pass*

☐ Our brochure with a letter through the post

Which (if any) aspects of our advertising do you find useful?
(Tick as many boxes as are relevant)

☐ Prices and publication dates of new editions

☐ Information on Interactive Text content

☐ Facility to order books off-the-page

☐ None of the above

Your ratings, comments and suggestions would be appreciated on the following areas

	Very useful	Useful	Not useful
Introduction	☐	☐	☐
Chapter contents lists	☐	☐	☐
Activities and answers	☐	☐	☐
Key learning points	☐	☐	☐
Quick quizzes and answers	☐	☐	☐
Practice activities	☐	☐	☐
Full skills based assessments	☐	☐	☐
Full exam based assessments	☐	☐	☐
Sample simulation	☐	☐	☐
Specimen exam	☐	☐	☐
Lecturers' Resource Section	☐	☐	☐

Review Form & Free Prize Draw (continued)

	Excellent	Good	Adequate	Poor
Overall opinion of this Text	☐	☐	☐	☐

Do you intend to continue using BPP Interactive Texts/Assessment Kits?   ☐ Yes   ☐ No

The BPP author of this edition can be e-mailed at: janiceross@bpp.com

Please return this form to: Janice Ross, BPP Professional Education, FREEPOST, London, W12 8BR

Please note any further comments and suggestions/errors below

Free Prize Draw Rules

1 Closing date for 31 January 2004 draw is 31 December 2003. Closing date for 31 July 2004 draw is 30 June 2004.

2 Restricted to entries with UK and Eire addresses only. BPP employees, their families and business associates are excluded.

3 No purchase necessary. Entry forms are available upon request from BPP Professional Education. No more than one entry per title, per person. Draw restricted to persons aged 16 and over.

4 Winners will be notified by post and receive their cheques not later than 6 weeks after the relevant draw date.

5 The decision of the promoter in all matters is final and binding. No correspondence will be entered into.